Library of
Davidson College

Surviving Without Governing

Surviving Without Governing

THE ITALIAN PARTIES IN PARLIAMENT

Giuseppe Di Palma

Published under the auspices of the
Institute of International Studies
University of California (Berkeley)

UNIVERSITY OF CALIFORNIA PRESS

Berkeley   Los Angeles   London

University of California Press
Berkeley and Los Angeles, California

University of California Press, Ltd.
London, England

Copyright © 1977 by
The Regents of the University of California

ISBN 0-520-03195-4
Library of Congress Catalog Card Number: 75-46035
Printed in the United States of America

A mio padre

7

Contents

	ACKNOWLEDGMENTS	ix
	PREMISE	xi
I.	THE PERFORMANCE OF THE SYSTEM: A Theoretical View	1
II.	LEGISLATIVE BEHAVIOR: Effective or Ineffective?	40
III.	THE UNCERTAIN COMPROMISE: Parliament's Decisional Rules	95
IV.	POLITICIANS IN PARLIAMENT: The Political Culture of Italian Legislators	132
V.	PARLIAMENTARY PROCEDURES AND LEGISLATIVE OUTPUTS	185
VI.	GOVERNMENT AND PARTY SYSTEM: A "Sartorian" View	219
VII.	CENTRISM, ITS USES AND ITS PRESENT CRISIS: Which Way Italy?	254
	APPENDIX: Classifying Legislative Proposals	287
	INDEX	295

A Glossary of
Italian Political Parties

    DC Democrazia Cristiana
  MSI Movimento Sociale Italiano
  PCI Partito Comunista Italiano
  PLI Partito Liberale Italiano
 PNM Partito Nazionale Monarchico
  PRI Partito Repubblicano Italiano
 PSDI Partito Socialista Democratico Italiano
  PSI Partito Socialista Italiano
PSIUP Partito Socialista Italiano di Unità Proletaria

Acknowledgments

The brevity of these acknowledgments has a reason. So many individuals and organizations have helped that I have opted for a highly selective list. Because money and logistics are essential to sound scholarship, I would first like to thank the Institute of International Studies (Berkeley) for financial and clerical assistance and Professor Alberto Spreafico, for hosting me at the *Comitato per le Scienze Politiche e Sociali* in Rome. Equally invaluable has been the cooperation of Professor Vittorio Mortara and Professor Franco Cazzola—they amply discussed with me their research on the Italian Parliament and made available their data. Surviving in Rome and in the corridors of Parliament was made easier by many. Dr. Antonio Maccanico, Secretary General of the Chamber of Deputies, opened doors for me and taught me a few things about the ways of parliamentary politics. Dr. Aiassa, of the Christian Democratic parliamentary group, the entire staff of the Communist group, and the Honorable Raffaele Di Primio, of the Socialist group, gave generous assistance in the organization of the interviews. The Honorable Di Primio was especially kind and took personal interest in the intellectual aspects of the research. Professor Ignazio Ughi and his students at the *Istituto di Sociologia Luigi Sturzo* provided assistance in the various phases of the research, and so did Dr. Sergio Lieto of the Sergio Lieto & Associates. Francine and Vittoria Di Palma, my wife and daughter respectively, held everything together by just being there and liking it.

Back in Berkeley, two years and a few hundred pages later, the finished manuscript, expertly prepared by Bojana Ristich, has greatly benefited, I hope, from the friendly readings of several colleagues. On the American side I would like in particular to mention Robert Putnam, Aaron Wildavsky, Ernst Haas and

Nelson Polsby. On the Italian side I should mention Giovanni Sartori and Gianfranco Pasquino. To Joseph LaPalombara, who straddles the two cultures with greater zest than anybody else, I owe special thanks. Both in Rome, where we spent a year together, and back in the United States, he has been prodigal of counsel and friendship as only a son of the generous *Terra d'Abruzzo* can be.

The reader should heed the cautionary note that I am ultimately accountable for this book, its defects and virtues. *Qui si parrà la mia nobilitate.*

Berkeley, March 1976   G. D. P.

Premise

In July 1973, as I started drafting this book, the Honorable Mariano Rumor, a prominent leader of Italy's Christian Democratic party, formed the country's thirty-first government since the war. The government's program was simple and unprecedented: to break the spiral of executive instability, to last until the parliamentary elections four years later. In March of 1976, as this book goes to press, Italy is ruled by yet another government (the country's thirty-fourth), headed by yet another Catholic leader. In the space of two and one half years, the clear defeat of the Christian Democratic party in the divorce referendum of May 1974 and the spectacular and unexpected success of the Communist party in the local elections of last June—one-third of the votes, almost as many as the Christian Democratic party—have for the first time seriously challenged Christian Democracy's unbroken rule. In the space of two and one half years, the country has but strengthened its reputation as Europe's "grande malade." The symptoms are there for all to see, and they are more onimous than ever. They spell social unrest, economic collapse, political and administrative ineffectiveness.

Beginning in 1969, Italy has known the most prolonged and sustained period of social conflict, turmoil, and even violence in its postwar history. While in other Western countries the beginning of the seventies has witnessed some social retrenchment, in Italy unrest has continued and even intensified. Labor disputes and strikes have become the order of the day, and have placed the country first among European Economic Community countries in terms of lost working days.[1] The reasons go beyond the

---

1. Data from the European Economic Community show that Italy accounts for the following percentages of working hours lost in all countries of the Community: 78.3 percent in 1969, 54.0 percent in 1970, 35.0 percent in 1971, 38.0 percent in 1972, 54.2 percent in 1973, 45.0 percent in 1974.

swift upsurge in the power of established labor organizations in the last seven years. As unions have expanded their scope of action and strengthened their bargaining power, they have also been faced with serious problems of organization, discipline, and containment. Among the countless strikers are not only factory workers but doctors, nurses, garbage collectors, civil servants, teachers, university professors, court clerks, pilots and airport employees, bus conductors, social workers, building-trade workers, gas station attendants, city employees, store clerks, concierges, gravediggers, museum personnel, hotel employees, railroad workers. At times strikes and disputes have been organized and channeled by unions; at times they have run contrary to union control and have been exploited to challenge responsible union leadership, to spread dissension in union ranks and tension in the country, and to impose the unprincipled economic demands of narrow service categories.

While labor has been active, students have not been dormant. Here again Italy has remained the only Western country where the student agitations of the sixties have become a permanent and routinized phenomenon. Further, the universities have not been the only places where sit-ins, occupations of buildings, confrontations between student factions and between students and the authorities, have spelled out permanent agitation. High schools, at least in the large cities, have often been in the forefront.

Needless to say, labor and student disputes have offered—often unwittingly—invaluable arenas of confrontation for extremist groups and "groupuscules" of the extraparliamentary variety. And with the groupuscules have often come violence and blood, at times unanticipated and overreactive, at times—more ominously—planned or provoked artfully to sow tensions and fear. Such violence has very often spread well beyond the geographical confines of school and factory grounds. It has spilled onto the streets of Italian cities. It has taken its toll in deaths and injuries among workers, students, policemen, among innocent bystanders, shoppers, and travelers. Public offices, banks, and trains have been bombed; so have peaceful rallies, union and political party headquarters, as well as the houses of political opponents. And when local political and social conditions have favored it, entire cities—as different as Milan in the industrial North and Reggio Calabria in the core of the impoverished South—have been engulfed by violence and brought to a standstill for months at a time. In such a climate, the murder of public officials and defenseless political opponents—often no more than young activists—becomes an accepted practice.

Where such violence ceases to be political and becomes common criminality is anybody's guess. Morally the distinction is not always worth drawing, and organizationally it is a known fact that the ransom kidnappings and bank robberies, reported almost every day in the Italian press, serve in many cases to replenish the coffers of a number of terrorist organizations. Thus the continual calls for law and order and for a determined fight against political terrorism and common criminality, coming from all parties, is no sham. It may be self-serving and one-sided—as it often fails to recognize that most violence, especially in its bloodier aspects of mass terrorism, comes from the extreme right—but it reveals a clear and imminent danger. Violence has not brought down the system yet, but is is fast eroding it, the more so as violence occurs in a climate of economic and politico-institutional crisis.

Economically, Italy presents a most explosive mix of soaring inflation and economic recession unprecedented in the postwar period. Among the significant factors of inflation is the sudden and dramatic increase in the cost of labor that followed, at the end of the sixties, the rapid expansion in economic output and productivity in the late fifties and early sixties. The ensuing fall of profits and the recession are supported by the failure of the economy first to anticipate and then to counteract rising labor costs by modernizing and rationalizing, by eliminating the waste and hidden costs of traditional productive structures, by streamlining systems of marketing and distribution, by isolating essentially parasitic and unproductive economic forces, and in sum by creating a social infrastructure capable of supporting sustained economic expansion. In other words, though the Italian economy has grown fast, it has grown haphazardly, without coordination, without planning its future capacities, and by containing labor.

Today's inflation and recession are largely the product of such improvident behavior. While salaries and wages increase, skyrocketing inflation undoes the gains. Plants work at much less than their productive capacity, not only because of strikes but also because of lack of a market and lack of business confidence. Inappropriate lending policies, high operational costs, indebtedness, lack of confidence, have substantially cut industrial investments and self-financing. The fear of collapse and the lack of resources to stem it are very real for many firms. Beyond this is the fear that, because of its economic and social crisis, Italy is failing to keep up with its partners in the European Economic Community. Many economic operators, technocrats, and politicians are indeed beginning to ask themselves whether, a few years from now, Italy will still be a legitimate member of an expanding Continental Europe or part of a more depressed Mediterranean area. To complicate matters, the answer hinges not only on how the country will deal with the present economic problems but also on whether it will eventually cope with its oldest, most serious, and still unresolved social and economic problem—the problem of the underdeveloped South. Here, little satisfactory progress has been made; here, too, is a crucial test of Italy's partnership in Europe; here, the next few years will be decisive.

The remedies to economic stagnation and crisis go well beyond the business cycle and require the active involvement of government and politics. But politics in Italy gives no fewer reasons for concern than society and economy, and the record of the past does not speak well for the future. Despite thirty years of unbroken Christian Democratic hegemony, Italian governments have compiled an embarrassing and sorrowful record of postponements and omissions. Not even the much heralded entry of the Socialist party in the government coalitions, in the now distant 1963, altered the trend. In point of fact, the event has best served to reveal the inability of Italian governments to respond to the expectations of a rapidly changing country. The Center-Left—that is, the coalition of Christian Democrats and Socialists, together with the minor Social Democratic and Republican parties—has governed Italy almost uninterruptedly for twelve years. Its program of "structural reforms" was meant to combine emphasis on welfare, social justice, and the elimination of traditional privilege with an effort to rationalize the economy through planning, modernization of the social and economic infrastructures, and support for the advanced sectors of the economy. But, as cabinets followed cabinets (fourteen between December

1963 and today), government programs went sour; major legislation was never enacted or backfired; social and economic malaise mounted. The Socialist party, a party of long-standing Marxist traditions, closely allied until the fifties with the Communist party, failed to obtain electoral reward for its change of strategy and became increasingly restive in its new government role. Meanwhile, the Communist party steadily if slowly continued to gain votes through the decade, threatening to reach the 30 percent mark, and the neofascist *Movimento Sociale Italiano* made electoral payday of the expanding social malaise. Today, after a brief and unsuccessful return to more moderate coalitions in 1972-73, after the personal defeat of the Christian Democrats in the divorce referendum, after the Communists have already passed the 30 percent mark, the survival of the Center-Left, once considered an irreversible formula, is more than ever in doubt. The present Italian governments can no more cure themselves than they can the social and economic malaise of the country. What lies ahead?

This book cannot possibly predict within any specified degree of accuracy how the question will be answered. Further, when it comes to the future of a whole country, any prediction may seem, if unfulfilled, sorrowfully disappointing. But the book can define and scrutinize the performance of the Italian political system since the war, and can examine its wider repercussions on Italian society. In particular, the book focuses on the operation of what is still a crucial structure for the articulation of issues and for their authoritative management—the Italian Parliament. It is a study of Parliament's legislative performance and of the way in which performance is hampered by an unresolved question: the question of who governs, the question of how majority and opposition should relate to each other. But before defining the goals, concepts, and procedures of the research, it may be well to take a step back. Having described the syndrome of social, economic, and political crisis in today's Italy, it may be worth discussing its causes. Is there an order within the syndrome and, if so, what are the imputed relations? As we proceed, the political focus of our research will be justified.

One final cautionary note. The syndrome presented above may appear to some excessively pessimistic and possibly off the mark. After all, Italy has successfully and swiftly reconstructed after the ravages of the war. After all, Italy has grown faster than most of its European partners and, from being an essentially agricultural society, it has become in a few years the seventh industrial power in the world. After all, the signs of prosperity and modernity are there for all to see. After all, the country has shown a significant civic growth, especially during the current years of turmoil. The introduction of divorce, the reform of the family, penal, and military codes, the imminent liberalization of abortion and drug laws, the democratization of school structures to permit parent and student participation, the spreading of grass-root neighborhood committees largely independent of parties, the greater awareness of issues that affect people's life, the greater readiness to experiment with new forms of participation, are but some examples of the rapid secularization of Italian society and of its accomplishments in matters of civil liberties and civic involvement. After all, it may finally be said, Italy has a reputation for getting itself disentangled from situations deemed hopeless by others, and the restraint and awareness with which many parties are behaving, signally the Communist party, may speak to the point.

My answer to these assorted doubts is that establishing the nature and implications of the syndrome and, finally, its correctives, is the purpose of the book. One should, however, bear in mind two things. First, many crises that often usher in collapse are indeed crises of growth. There is little doubt, for instance, that Weimar showed many symptoms of expansion and of promising cultural growth just before its crisis and demise. Second, most Italians, politicians and citizens alike, believe in the syndrome of malaise. And what one believes to be real may be real in its consequences; witness W. I. Thomas or Luigi Pirandello, depending on one's reference point.

I

The Performance of the System: A Theoretical View

THE SYNDROME AS A PHENOMENON OF WESTERN DEMOCRACIES

A number of alternative or complementary explanations have been offered for the syndrome of Italian malaise presented in the premise. One thesis at least implicit in much commentary on the events of the last years is that Italy shares in the same malaise that in the past decade has pervaded practically all highly industrial democracies. First, when it comes to social and political unrest, nowadays one cannot ignore the power of demonstration effects across countries. Because a student sit-in took place today in Berkeley, it may take place tomorrow in Pisa; because a politician was kidnapped today in Bonn, another may be kidnapped tomorrow in Rome. Second, growing economic interdependence and the destabilization of international economic equilibria are at the roots of many of the economic problems of much of the Western world. It is international economic stagnation that accounts for the serious decline in Italian exports, investments, and profits. It is the oil crisis that accounts for half of Italy's balance-of-payments deficit. Italy in sum is not alone in suffering from the consequences of a worldwide economic crisis. Third, rapid economic transformation coupled with and most probably causing a redefinition and re-ordering of social priorities and issues is exercising everywhere unexpected strains on social, economic, and political institutions. Herein, in Italy, and everywhere else, lies the cause of much turmoil and political ineffectiveness. Herein lies the syndrome.

This thesis recommends itself in many ways, but it does not bar, indeed it already implies, another course. For, if the syndrome is common to many countries, it also stands to reason that its origins, as well as its evolution and cure, also depend on local social and political circumstances. It may be true that the driving vectors shared by all Western democracies are the vectors of "post-industrialism." But they operate in countries at different stages of economic development, with different economic and social structures, and different political institutions and cultures as well. And, if the syndrome expresses a clash between old and new, it stands to reason that its origins and nature vary according to what exactly is old in each country. It also stands to reason that its evolution and outcome will be determined by the local ability of social, economic, and political structures to respond, accommodate, and anticipate.

THE SYNDROME AND ITALIAN SOCIETY

Our investigation of the syndrome must therefore begin by searching within Italy. Here a first set of explanations of the syndrome becomes relevant, all of them centered around the way in which the "economic miracle" took place in the country between the end of the fifties and the beginning of the sixties. They emphasize the fact that the miracle took place: (1) while extensive areas of underdevelopment and traditional privilege survived; (2) by relying initially on labor containment; (3) and without a needed modernization in the infrastructure of social services. These features are responsible for the fact that Italy is, with England, the industrial country most grievously affected by the present international crisis, and they augur poorly for the future.

First, the miracle has occurred in the North, in the urban areas, in the industrial sectors, and much less in the South, in the countryside, in agriculture. Hence the gap between poles has increased; witness the millions of able-bodied peasants and Southerners who have flocked in recent years to the cities and the North, depopulating the countryside and leaving behind the old and marginals. To give just some figures, according to the last national census the population actively occupied in agriculture has decreased from 42.6 percent in 1951 to 29.1 percent in 1961 and to 17.3 percent in 1971. This means that of one hundred persons actively employed in agriculture in 1961, forty-three have left. It may be argued by some that the existence of poles of development is natural and beneficial for economic growth, but the point is that it is not beneficial in the syndrome. For one thing, the widening of the gap and the survival of extensive areas of underdevelopment within an expanding society signify the growing of tensions between development and underdevelopment. Tensions manifest themselves in local populistic uprisings against the center—as have occurred in some Southern cities—in the growth of right-wing appeals in retarded areas, and in increasing pressures by traditional interests to preserve their privileges in the face of change. For another thing, conflict due to traditional economic inequality survives in the areas of underdevelopment. On both counts, the country is overloaded with the accumulation of old and new conflicts.

The second feature of the economic miracle reveals that the syndrome it triggers is not just a natural tension between old and new. Indeed, the success of the miracle owes much to traditional policies of labor containment and to the entrepreneurship of small labor-intensive industries. It is the failure of these strategies at the end of the sixties, compounded by the international crisis, that also accounts for the present economic and social predicament. In short, the miracle relied on an oversupply of cheap labor, poorly protected by weak labor organizations.[1] Hence productivity increased and expansion took place till the early sixties not so much by technological innovation and industrial restructuring as by the exploitation and rationalization of labor resources. The process especially assisted small and medium labor-intensive industries, heavily favored by an expanding foreign demand for semidurable and mass-consumption goods. These industries played a crucial role in sustaining the miracle. While employment expanded, new workers were almost totally absorbed by small and medium industries—which still remain the backbone of the industrial system—or they replaced women as well as older workers. While productivity increased drastically, labor costs remained essentially the same.

But these improvident policies of labor containment and their short-range industrial effects came to an end abruptly with the

1. Michele Salvati, "L'Origine della Crisi in Corso," *Quaderni Piacentini*, Vol. II, No. 46 (March 1972), pp. 2-30; Romano Prodi, *Sistema Industriale e Sviluppo Economico* (Bologna: Il Mulino, 1973), pp. 11-43.

increasing social and economic militancy of the unions and with the strengthening of their bargaining power, two developments which are here to stay. The fall in industrial profits and investments and the ensuing slump stem originally from the tremendous increase in labor costs, which makes Italian firms no longer competitive with firms of advanced industrial countries.[2] Labor costs also account for inflation, which was originally neither imported nor triggered by internal demands,[3] and which soon became higher than in most other industrial countries, even before the oil crisis. At the same time, though the economic crisis keeps escalating, labor militancy remains undaunted. Though willing, as of the fall of 1975, to discuss what employers now perceive as urgent problems of industrial restructuring and labor mobility, unions are not ready to sacrifice, for the sake of solving these problems, either wages or full and stable employment. Thus the economic miracle has generated its own downfall and activated a social and economic malaise that the country cannot treat.

The third feature of the economic miracle is that the miracle was largely based on an expansion in the production and marketing of goods for individual consumption. It did not involve expansion and rationalization in the supply and delivery of social services. Therefore, as masses of new urban dwellers have flocked to the cities, and as the demands of an expanding economy have otherwise multiplied, the infrastructure of collective services, limited to begin with, has burst at the seams. New residents have found the cities dismal and inhospitable, while old residents have watched hopelessly the decay of their familiar environment. And if appropriate social infrastructures do not exist, no amount of increasing individual income can buy better public education, better transportation, better and cheaper housing, more efficient welfare and health services. Here, too, are the causes of social unrest. Here, too, organized labor has been extremely vocal in demanding and obtaining a greater input. But

2. Hourly labor costs in textile industries as of January 1975 were 4,258 liras in Belgium; 3,506 in Switzerland; 3,418 in Germany; 3,262 in Japan; 3,135 in Italy; 2,908 in the United States; 2,180 in France; 1,572 in England. Much of the high cost of Italian labor is a result of the social security benefits borne by the firm (48.5 percent of total cost). See *L'Espresso*, September 14, 1975.

3. Ricciotti Antinolfi, *La Crisi Economica Italiana 1969-1973* (Bari: De Donato, 1974), pp. 82-103.

when labor shows active interest not only in matters of wages and work conditions, but also in matters of full employment, of industrial restructuring, of economic development, of urban conditions, and of social services, its counterpart is no longer management but the government. And here the political roots of the syndrome are revealed: the counterpart does not respond. Just as government—by failing to encourage and adopt a concerted set of industrial policies for development—has been unable to give a different direction to the economic miracle and to anticipate its defects, so it is now unable to cure the present malaise.

THE SYNDROME AND ITALIAN POLITICS

In the last analysis, social unrest, economic crisis, the very militancy of labor organizations, are not the result of objectively unmanageable problems but the product of government ineffectiveness. It is especially in this regard that Italy differs from other industrial countries faced with their share of social and economic problems, and it is mainly ineffectiveness that explains why in Italy the problems are so much greater than elsewhere. In Italy political ineffectiveness is not new and well precedes the rapid changes of the last ten to fifteen years. It is not the social and economic crisis, in other words, that mainly explains political ineffectiveness; but the latter that mainly sustains the former. Undoubtedly the social and economic changes of the last years have further impaired the responses of the political body. But the body was ill to begin with and contaminated society.

More important, if one is interested not only in the origins of the syndrome, but also in its evolution and outcome, one must recognize that there are few if any Western countries where politics, in fact straight party politics, as thoroughly pervades (and stalemates) every single aspect of the community as in Italy. In part as a result of decades of uninterrupted rule by the Christian Democratic party, in part as a result of enduring politico-ideological divisions, little if any that is public saves itself from the smothering embrace of politics, little if any that needs solving escapes the logic of partisan gains and losses. Radio and television are strictly controlled by the government and their offices are important prizes in the equilibrium games of government partners. Bureaucracies and public agencies are similarly colonized by parties and factions in government. Political clientelism has built a spider web of partisan alliances and dealings reaching all sectors of society. It involves party factions and cliques in all sorts of economic and social endeavors, especially those connected with the building and control of infrastructures, such as welfare, education, housing, transportation, communication, services, cooperatives, and the like. The public sector, never small in Italy to begin with, has reached proportions and scope that only socialist countries can match. In the past few years, a number of large public corporations, strong of their privileged political and financial conditions, have come to dominate the advanced sector of the economy, and therefore hold the key to the economic future of the country.[4] In addition, wherever the government parties have not imposed their monopoly, all solutions to social needs and ills seem to revolve around which parties and ideologies should control what. The problem of effective regional development is often reduced to whether the opposition should govern in the periphery, though it cannot govern at the center. The problems of higher education often become problems of party balance between competing faculty constituencies. The problems of courtroom justice shade on whether the ideological progressivism of politically minded junior judges will break the conservative control of their seniors. And whether Parliament and government can take the country out of the impasse seems to rest on the partisan equilibrium of majority and opposition. Yet, for all its pervasiveness, politics remains unable to push the country beyond the impasse.

In sum, the key question in unraveling the syndrome is the response of politics. In what way, then, is Italian politics ineffective, and how can we show that the political system has failed in its responses? For years Italy, together with France, has been cited and studied as a typical example of ineffective performance. Indeed, after the advent of the Fifth Republic in France, Italy remained the classical contemporary paradigm. But for all the attention and agreement, most of the analysis is only inferential; that is, it does not offer much evidence of performance,[5] nor for

---

4. In 1963 public enterprises accounted for 17.4 percent of total sales among the first 194 Italian firms; in 1971 they accounted for 31.8 percent. Calculated from *Prodi*, op. cit., p. 21, Table I.

5. Among the few exceptions, see Giovanni Sartori, "Dove Va il Parlamento," in

that matter does it define the term and its evaluative criteria—except by vague constitutive referents, such as stability or viability. Rather, it infers performance from alleged causes, chiefly the party system, political ideology, political culture. Before proceeding with our investigation and eventually raising causal questions it is therefore necessary to define performance, to isolate the aspects relevant to us, to pinpoint the criteria for evaluation and evidence, and to explain why—having defined performance—the study will focus on the Italian Parliament. This is the object of the next two sections.

POLITICAL PERFORMANCE

The term *performance* refers to the execution and accomplishment of work and also, in a connotation relevant to us, to the manner and effectiveness with which something fulfills an intended task. That is, *performance* contains in its very definition an evaluative criterion, that of producing what is intended or expected. Performance, to put it redundantly, is effective to the extent that it produces what is intended. The point is also conveyed by *rendimento*, the Italian word for "performance," where *rendimento* literally refers to what is rendered, given back, returned, yielded, in short, to outputs. We are dealing with the obvious, but the obvious is often overlooked, and the step, though small, is valuable: it begins to pinpoint the complexities we are up against. For, if performance, and namely political performance, has to do with intended outputs, there are now two things that need investigation: outputs and their "intended" nature. Let me put aside for a while the latter and more vexing task and focus on the former.

Output is itself a concept that needs definition and rules of evidence, so that we can recognize an output when we see one. In addition, assuming that the problem of recognition is solved, the catalogue of outputs of a political system—even at one given time—is something that at first thought staggers the imagination. No matter what notion of the political system and its limits is entertained, its activities are bound to be endless. Every day,

---

S. Somogyi et al., *Il Parlamento Italiano 1946-1963* (Napoli: Edizioni Scientifiche Italiane, 1963), pp. 281-386. For France see Nathan Leites, *On the Game of Politics in France* (Stanford: Stanford University Press, 1959); Duncan McRae, Jr., *Parliament, Parties, and Society in France 1946-1958* (New York: St. Martin's Press, 1967).

judges pass sentences, parties recruit cadres or issue position statements, government agencies approve expenditure programs, parliaments enact laws, groups vent demands in a variety of forms, politicians confer with their electors. All of these can be taken in a way as aspects of what the polity does, instances of outputs. Even were we to agree on the range of outputs to be considered and on whether they are representative of the polity's performance, how can we possibly agree on a summary evaluation of such a variety of outputs, how can we possibly assess the overall performance of the system? The answer is that most likely we can't, at least not until some order is given to its activities.

Fortunately a measure of order has already been provided by many scholars, beginning, to remain within the more recent literature, with the works of Gabriel Almond and David Easton.[6] Political activities can be reduced to a few types of so-called functions typically exercised by all political systems. One advantage of this approach is that only a few separate functions rather than an inchoate range of activities need evaluation, and activities can be sampled within functions. More important, whatever the exact labeling and range of identified functions, one function emerges as central to the system, the function of rule-making. Other functions appear instrumental for evaluative purposes with respect to rule-making. If they have to do with the articulation and aggregation of demands or the political socialization and recruitment of citizens, they appear in effect as inputs within the system, to be evaluated for the way in which they interact with rule-making. If they have to do with the implementation of rules, they are evaluated for their success in this intended task. But it is rule-making that epitomizes performance, and it is rules that represent the significant outputs of the system.

In order not to generate confusion, I should stress that the above prejudges nothing about the exact causal relations between functions. Much research in recent years, especially when dealing with foreign countries, has concentrated on the functions that "precede" rule-making, to the point of reducing rule-making to a

6. Gabriel Almond, "Introduction: A Functional Approach to Comparative Politics," in Gabriel Almond and James Coleman, eds., *The Politics of the Developing Areas* (Princeton: Princeton University Press, 1960), pp. 3-64; Gabriel Almond and G. Bingham Powell, Jr., *Comparative Politics* (Boston: Little, Brown, 1966); David Easton, "An Approach to the Analysis of Political Systems," *World Politics* 9 (1957), pp. 383-400; David Easton, *A Systems Analysis of Political Life* (New York: Wiley, 1965).

simple process of translation of external inducements and pressures and of considering the institutions legally entrusted with authoritative decisions as mere sanctioners of the process.[7] It can as well be argued, as I will throughout the book, that rule-making and the institutions formally entrusted with it are themselves largely instrumental in defining the inducements, pressures, and demands to which they respond.[8] The point is that the distinction between functions does not establish a causal model; it simply arranges them in an ideal task-sequence so as to isolate the central function for performance evaluation. But if this function is rule-making, and pending an appraisal of its relations to other functions, it is with rule-making that we should start. The next section will show that having chosen rule-making (and the Italian Parliament), recognizing rules is not an unmanageable problem. But let us now turn to the evaluation of performance. What follows concerns performance in democratic systems, and some adaptation would be needed to fit the nondemocratic case.

Since performance refers to the execution of *intended* tasks, I take the task of rule-making in democracies to be the formation of at least sufficient, that is viable, agreement around decisions. Hence, rule-making is effective to the extent that it succeeds in this task. Viability does not refer to legal requirements for making decisions binding, but to what is politically feasible, and what elites can agree upon. The definition may seem perfectly acceptable to some, for it seems in fact to go to the essence of what is meant when speaking of the instability, unviability, or ineffectiveness of democracies such as Italy or France. To others it may appear truistic, narrow, trivial, question-begging, or arguable in point of fact and usefulness. Indeed, its defect is that it is only a constitutive definition. Its strength is that I have reached it through a process of elimination that needs explanation before I can expand on the definition. In essence, I have found no other manageable ways of understanding and assessing what is *intended* about decisional performance. There are many notions of decisional performance in addition to the chosen one. They can be

7. For two critiques of this approach, see Joseph LaPalombara, "Macrotheories and Micropolitics: A Widening Chasm," *Comparative Politics* I (1968), pp. 52-78; and Roy Macridis, "Comparative Politics and the Study of Government: The Search for Focus," *Comparative Politics* 1 (1968), pp. 79-90.

8. For a classical case study focusing on this perspective, see Raymond Bauer et al., *American Business and Public Policy* (New York: Atherton, 1963).

divided into three groups. Since the reader already knows that our focus will eventually be on Parliament, some of the examples that follow are borrowed from parliamentary performance.

The first group sees what is intended about decision-making as a question about the *proper* distribution of authority in a democracy, in the light of constitutional or other normative requirements. Theories about the proper division of labor between government and Parliament in parliamentary or presidential systems, between Parliament and bureaucracy, government and bureaucracy, Parliament and the judiciary, center and periphery, belong here. So do theories about the role of parties and degree of party control on decision-makers, theories about the relation between public officials and interest groups, and theories about the proper role of members of Parliament vis-á-vis their constituency. As the illustrations readily suggest, these are not the notions of performance we are looking for. The issue they raise is preliminary to ours. It is whether the map of decisional power and influence is democratically correct, not whether assigned powers are effectively used. In other words, these are constitutional theories *latu sensu,* prescribing arrangements in view of expected results (democraticity, accountability, mutual guarantees, participation). In our case, on the other hand, what we want to establish first is whether the Italian Parliament as a major rule-making body does well what it does, whatever its relative powers are. If it doesn't, it may well be because of wrong constitutional arrangements. Indeed, analyzing them may be essential to explain the system's overall performance, but it is not essential to illustrate it.

A second set of notions about performance looks beyond constitutional arrangements and beyond rule adoption to equate effectiveness with a calculus of outcomes, or costs and benefits.[9] The reasoning here is that decisions are only one probable means to some chain of ends. A law to increase farm workers' pensions, for instance, may seem at first ipso facto effective. If approved, it will increase pensions. But, if the further end were to secure earlier retirement of elderly farmers or to make farming attractive to the young, it may be nonproductive. Or an incentive of different type might have produced the same effect, perhaps at a

---

9. See a treatment of these notions in Aaron Wildavsky, "The Political Economy of Efficiency," in Austin Ranney, ed., *Political Science and Public Policy* (Chicago: Markham, 1968), pp. 55-82.

lower cost. Further, a law may not even produce its immediately intended effect. It may be easy actually to increase pensions, less easy to ensure, for instance, that a program for low income housing will be enforced. Bureaucratic conflict, standard budgetary procedures, legislative precedents, or simply routine may retard or kill a program. Finally, scarcity of resources may require that we choose between pensions and housing (or a bit of both). Shouldn't the measurement of performance be submitted to at least some of these criteria? The answer is that, for all their apparent precision, the criteria are complex and vague, the more so if entire bodies of policies are involved. Yet it is bodies of policies and general performance that we wish to evaluate. Further, they are not always the criteria that politicians adopt. Yet if the politician does not provide the social scientist with his criteria, it is difficult to see what the social scientist can assess. A brief look at some of the criteria, in ascending order of complexity, may suffice to illustrate the point. It may also begin to suggest that, if we have to deal with vagueness, it should at least be manageable.

1. When Italians say that a law is poorly made, poorly drafted, or "inelegant," they usually have in mind a criterion of legal rationality. The law is marred by legal snags, inconsistencies with other legislation, logical inconsistencies. Or it creates or relies upon procedures that are cumbersome and make coordination by bureaucracy difficult. Thus, the law is not applied, or enforcement is slow and ambiguous. An analysis of the legal rationality of legislation and decisions in general is comparatively easy. Rationality is revealed by contextual elements and by related legislation. Legal resources available to legislators are revealed by a study of the legal offices and the legal staff of Parliament, government, bureaucracy, political parties, and interest groups. But the intellectual boundaries of such a study are not fixed, and problems of legal rationality may soon appear as problems of power and control. In all fairness, for instance, legal rationality may be frustrated by insurmountable bureaucratic requirements. Its study may soon have to turn attention to political control over the bureaucracy.

2. When Italians say that a law is faulty (*sbagliata*), they usually mean that, though easily and swiftly applicable, it does not produce the desired effects, or it has negative side effects, or it is not

the most economical. A law making all corporate stocks nominative, aside from possibly causing a flight of capital abroad, may not produce optimal returns in terms of added revenues, diversification of investments, or other effects. The criterion is one of technical or means-end rationality; and cost-effectiveness or cost-benefit analysis recommend themselves.[10] But technical rationality may have different twists and is not universally definable. One may hold the objective constant and calculate the highest output for a fixed cost or the cheapest cost for a fixed output, or one may alter the objective simultaneously with costs to achieve an even higher rationality.[11] It may seem that as long as fixed and possibly monetary values are assigned to the alternatives, the approach is productive. Monetary values, however, are often conventional and artificial; they are imposed to allow an otherwise impossible calculus. The counterargument seems simple: better some values, no matter how artificial, than none at all. Provided, it should be added, they can be made explicit. And here is the rub. Often values, even the most direct ones, are not clear to decision-makers and therefore cannot be explicitly stated. Especially when higher rationality is sought, alternatives soon stretch into a chain of side costs, spillovers, trade-offs of a political nature whose value cannot be pinned down.[12] Yet we cannot evaluate decisions for what *we* think they should produce but for what *politicians* want them to produce. Some effects of a law on corporate stocks, for example, may be easy to calculate. Any economist can tell politicians with fairly reasonable accuracy, and taking into consideration a potential flight of capital, what its likely effects are on capital investments, tax returns, balance of payments, currency devaluation, and similar matters. He can estimate other ways of securing tax returns from stock owners, or ways of controlling financial side effects. The real difficulty is not here, but in drawing the balance sheet. Most politicians, even in the more technical areas, hold in a very real sense only vague—at best ordinal—sets of values. They may, for instance, be willing to pay *some* decrease in investments or *some* worsening in the balance of

10. An extensive treatment and critique of cost-benefit analysis is found in A. R. Prest and R. Turvey, "Cost-Benefit Analysis: A Survey," *Economic Journal* 75 (1965), pp. 683-755.
11. Wildavsky, op. cit., p. 56.
12. For a critique of economic models of government performance, see Richard Rose, "Models of Governing," *Comparative Politics* 5 (1973), pp. 465-496, esp. pp. 474-483.

payments, if a flight of capital occurs, to assert a *higher* principle of fair taxation or to secure *some* added fiscal returns. But it is unlikely that they have assigned more precise values to such costs and benefits. The case is clearer when the political consequences of the law are added. Prestige, popularity, political stability may be invaluable, that is nonvaluable. Which means that, even if politicians are offered a precise catalogue of costs and benefits, they may not know exactly whether the law was in fact successful. Or they may remain satisfied with a fair guess, or may not even care. Once again, the point is not that politicians should have long and complex schedules of preferences; the point is that schedules should be clear, by sacrificing complexity, if need be. Otherwise no calculus of effectiveness is possible.

3. When Italians refer to legislation as fragmented, dispersed, nonorganic, they mean that legislation as a whole does not respond to a projected plan, a set of homogeneous objectives, a program of development. Single laws are evaluated not for their contextual objective but for their fit within the government's long-range policies. Program budgeting, systems analysis, welfare economics, linear programming recommend themselves here as approaches to decisional effectiveness that go beyond the cost-benefit analysis of single alternatives, unscramble all resources, and redefine all means and objectives to optimize larger programs. These approaches are mentioned here simply to bring home the points already made. If it is difficult to evaluate single decisions in the light of their immediate objective, it becomes impossible to evaluate them in the light of larger programs. For, if politicians may hold vague values when choosing single alternatives, the question of how various alternatives fit together may not even be addressed, except in the most diffuse terms. Naturally, some governments may have programs and parliamentary agendas that they manage to carry out. But programs are usually fixed lists of legislation imposed by the routines of government, social emergencies (inflation, overcrowded schools), or distant ideological imperatives (increase growth, decrease inequality, decentralize government). They are also arranged seriatim by established areas of impact: education, agriculture, the South, law and order, foreign policy. It is doubtful that politicians consider such programs as an exercise in the optimization of resources, in which no ends and means are sacred. The reason is not only that some

aspects of a program and some expenditures must always be fixed and that certified areas of impact must be attended to, but also that when options are possible and exchange between areas occurs the criteria of re-allocation become complex and eminently political. Costs and benefits are therefore uncertain, too uncertain to be worth calculating; and politicians may find it more parsimonious to use informed guesses or, when guesses fail, to try to resort to mechanisms of adjustment. Of course, there may be differences between areas of policies (technical areas being, for instance, more amenable to a calculus), sets of politicians, departments, or countries. But for the time being it seems fair to say that politicians—especially parliamentarians and party politicians—operate in a realm of uncertainty. And, once again, if politicians do not know what to optimize, how can effectiveness, so defined, be measured?

There is a final reason for our not choosing approaches to performance that focus on the outcomes of decisions. The reason is exactly that rules and decisions are but probable means to some ends. That is, effectiveness connotes here "having an effect, causing, as intended." A legitimate notion, to be sure, for a strong argument can be made that to know about the "impact" of policies on their environment is to know one of the most important things, if not the most important, about politics. But we know that, even if intentions were specified, much of what passes for impact actually has little to do with intended policies. Much, rather, depends on external constraints or inducements, the amount of support policies receive, the symbolic or technical and administrative resources that political institutions enjoy, and other externalities. But decision-makers cannot easily control such externalities; in fact, the discussion above suggests that they often do not even calculate them. It follows that to study effectiveness by looking at impact is to risk attributing to policies consequences for which, on both grounds, they are not responsible.[13] In this sense, while policies have consequences that deserve study, the latter cannot be used to estimate effectiveness. Were we to match policies against consequences, all governments would turn out to be rather "an-effective" (neither ineffective nor effective). Yet, we believe that countries, institutions, and politicians per-

13. Harry Eckstein, "The Evaluation of Political Performance," *Sage Professional Papers in Comparative Politics* (Beverly Hills, Calif.: Sage Publications, 1971), p. 68.

form differently as to rule-making. If the answer is not in the consequences, then where is it?

Perhaps, as a third body of literature argues, it is in the capacity of decisions to respond to society's needs, inputs, demands for action. For, whatever the consequences of government's decisions, and whether or not the consequences are calculated, aren't decisions made in response to society? The case is clear and forceful with democratic systems and with the most democratic of their institutions—Parliament. It seems then that estimating decisional performance simply requires assessing whether decisions square with the inputs they receive. But how? This approach to performance derives from a variety of models of government, all stressing reciprocal linkages between governmental tasks and societal conditions.[14] Do any of them suggest exactly how decisional performance should be assessed? Some models assign government the task of managing the conflicts that arise from the objective and ideological divisions of society. Others consider government as referee and at times interested party in aggregating and balancing the interests of organized social and political groups. Others emphasize the authoritative function of government in allocating material or symbolic collective goods which, given their collective nature, cannot allocate themselves freely. Still others take popular demands, as articulated through the partisan or electoral process, to be the mainspring to governmental action and the occasion to structure and inform decisions. Others, finally, assign government the task of supervising social change, either by spurring it, or by adapting institutions to it and thus securing stability, or by controlling and slowing it when that is deemed necessary. All these models are to some extent prescriptive, but also descriptive of what government does at various times and places. Nor are they mutually exclusive, and differences may be nominal as well as conceptual. All, therefore, are useful in bringing us one small step closer to decisional performance. If, for instance, government managed conflict, performance is how well it manages it. If popular demands are what it responds to, it is how well it responds. If the syndrome of social malaise that characterizes contemporary Italy is due to anything, it is due, as I have already implied, to the inability of the government to steer and supervise social change. But, as these state-

---

14. Rose, op. cit., pp. 484-489.

ments indicate, the matter is still very elusive. Indeed, since all the views of government illustrated here see performance as "intended," in one form or another, to respond to social and political demands, performance should in all cases be assessed by matching policies to demands. The task, as Harry Eckstein puts it, "... poses vast empirical difficulties, and severe abstract problems into the bargaining."[15] Its returns, as shown by what follows, are likely to be limited and qualified.

To match decisions to demands, three steps would be required:[16]

1. The load of social and political demands should be ascertained. Recognition and relevance are the first difficulty here, as the number of articulated demands is probably infinite, and yet it may not cover the entire spectrum of social needs. That is, which are the demands that count? Only those which are expressed or also those which remain latent? We may agree intuitively that it is the former that count, and this not because of a Bentleian notion that needs that are not expressed do not exist but simply because expressed demands are likely to pose the most serious test to politicians. In fact, we may further agree that only those articulated demands should be considered that pose, in Eckstein's words, "special challenges" to the system. These are demands that, being articulated by strategic or large groups in society, being held with special intensity, being economically or politically costly, being divisive or controversial, or for other reasons, are of great consequence for society and at the same time require more than routine treatment. Hence, the manner in which government responds to them will be highly indicative of performance. The problem of empirically recognizing such demands remains, but I believe that at least a reasonable estimate of their range in contemporary Italy is possible. It should be kept in mind that the catalogue need not be complete but only indicative of the most consequential pressures.

There is another recognition problem in this stock-taking exercise. It should not be of any concern here, but it deserves

15. Eckstein, op. cit., p. 65.
16. For the analysis of the three steps I am much indebted to Eckstein's paper cited above, esp. pp. 65-73. Also very valuable, despite the deceiving title, is Maurizio Cotta, "Il Problema del Bicameralismo-Monocameralismo nel Quadro di Una Analisi Struttural-Funzionale del Parlamento," *Rivista Italiana di Scienza Politica* 1 (1971), pp. 545-594, esp. pp. 576-581.

mention. Usually demands are ascertained at a point after they have entered the political arena, after they have been aggregated in some form, after they have been appropriated by political parties or other organized groups, and as they are being considered by decision-makers. One objection to this way of proceeding is that the slicing-in should occur much before these stages, so as to capture demands in their original and raw form.[17] This is true, however, only if the objective is to discover how demands are formed and transformed and through what processes they come to decision. Only an analysis of this type can tell for instance what role government or parties have in creating or at least shaping the demands they are willing to entertain. But for purposes of measuring performance the problem does not exist. In fact, there is an advantage in slicing-in at later stages. If politicians cannot respond to the demands they entertain, the test will be most telling.

2. Having ascertained the load of significant demands, there remains ascertaining the government's response. The first and easiest approximation is to measure the number of decisions taken by government, to see how busy and active it keeps itself. The criterion is not foolproof, though we know that especially in highly industrialized countries demands for government intervention are constantly growing. A ratio of demand load to government output may therefore be at least indicative. A closer approximation, as suggested by Nelson Polsby,[18] is to calculate the importance of governmental decisions, on the basis of the number of people affected, the resources that are invested, those that are distributed, and the redistribution of resources that may result. Otherwise a government may give the impression of activism by producing a great number of decisions that respond to minor demands but are of minor importance and essentially uncontroversial, while avoiding the big issues. Even an analysis of the importance of decisions, however, remains only presumptive of effectiveness and should be used with a grain of salt.

3. Indeed, having ascertained demands and decisions, the ultimate question is how they fit each other not simply in terms of the number and the importance of the decisions, but in terms of

---

17. Cotta, ibid., p. 565.
18. Nelson Polsby, *Community Power and Political Theory* (New Haven: Yale University Press, 1963), pp. 95-96.

quality. And here is the insoluble difficulty. We know, of course, that matching does not consist of meeting every simple demand as is. Only in a society of limitless resources and, above all, limitless reciprocal tolerance and boredom would this be possible. Otherwise, some demands are not accepted, many have to be compromised. A decision not to act is per se no evidence of ineffectiveness. Action may be easier and more beneficial at a later time. Postponement may make dealing with other and more important demands easier or may secure an atmosphere of good will without which decision-making in general may stop. In some cases decisions may not even be needed, as demands may be safely reabsorbed or otherwise satisfied. On the other hand, even important and to-the-point decisions may actually avoid or complicate issues, while a government that gives just the impression of dealing with demands without actually addressing them may hold them in abeyance.[19] Symbolic and consummatory gratification is the stock-in-trade of much politics, whether modern or traditional, democratic or authoritarian.[20] In brief, there are a variety of ways in which decision-makers respond to demands, many of them successful, but none of them establishing a universal or plainly superior criterion.

Further, the use of a demand-response terminology for the purpose of evaluating effectiveness is simplistic and deceptive. Many decisions, for instance to reallocate resources to highly disadvantaged groups, may impose notable sacrifices on other parties. Other decisions, such as taxation or Churchill's promise of "blood, toil, tears and sweat," ask sacrifices of all. Yet these decisions are not only complied with but also often supported. It seems ludicrous to label them unsatisfactory; it is intuitive that Churchill did not act ineffectively. The ineffective government is not a government that asks sacrifices of some or all.[21] Also, as these examples indicate, much of what seems response to popular

19. Robert Dahl, *Polyarchy* (New Haven: Yale University Press, 1971), pp. 89-104; Murray Edelman, *The Symbolic Uses of Politics* (Urbana: University of Illinois Press, 1964).
20. David Apter, *The Politics of Modernization* (Chicago: University of Chicago Press, 1965), esp. chapters 7 and 8.
21. For the argument that there is one side of decisional effectiveness, having to do with the government's extractive and regulative capacities, that cannot be evaluated in terms of demand satisfaction, see Leonardo Morlino, "Stabilità, Legittimità e Efficacia Decisionale nei Sistemi Democratici," *Rivista Italiana di Scienza Politica* 3 (1973), pp. 282-284.

needs and demands is simply defined and initiated by government itself, and much of what government does cannot be assessed against demands.

The terminology is deceptive in another sense. The parties to a decision or those affected by it may find it satisfactory not for its correspondence to their concrete demands but for a variety of other reasons. The decision may create a desired image of each party; it may recognize a group's worth and importance; it may enforce or establish appropriate decisional procedures; or it may give a party political credit by the stand it takes on it. In sum, decisions emerge out of a process of aggregation, elimination, reformulation, deferment, give-and-take, and the conflict that often surrounds the process is not only about which demands should be entertained, which decisions should be made, which deferred, but also about how the process should be conducted, what role the contestants should have, what symbolic or tangible side rewards they should reap. It follows from everything said so far that the outcome of the process—decisions—cannot be evaluated in the light of immediate demand satisfaction alone but in the light of a more distant and aleatory calculus. It is no wonder that decisional effectiveness still escapes us. If it consists in satisfaction, we still don't know what is satisfactory and what is to be satisfied. Looking at demands provides only indicative results.

In fact, since decisions emerge from a give-and-take process, it can be stated that they are satisfactory when they are equitable. Equitable means literally and concretely even, balanced, leveled, or—figuratively—fair. Equity points to a calculus by contestants of reciprocal sacrifices and gains. The calculus varies and what may seem equitable in one context may not in another. One set of contestants may consider equitable nothing short of obtaining everything, another may be more accommodating: an important difference to explain, but one that immediately points out a simple fact. Having shifted our terminology from satisfaction to equity, it is now clearer than ever that no universal calculus can be conducted that matches demands with decisions. Decisional effectiveness requires a different definition that takes us off the conceptual and recognition hook. Fortunately, the discussion contains the seeds of a simple if restrictive solution, which is the one outlined at the outset. Only some adjustment of terminology and focus is needed, and we should keep in mind that to be defined and isolated is not the effectiveness of single decisions but rule-making and decisional effectiveness in general.

Since decisions are rarely optimal for all involved and often demand reciprocal losses, the difficult task of any constituted body of democratic decision-makers, in their quality as contestants or as officials responsible to them, is to exact convergence out of differences, to find a *concordia discors* so as to produce at least the minimum amount of agreement to sustain decisions. If, and only if, differences are sufficiently composed may the necessary agreement form and decisions be taken. Hence, if, and only if, decisions are agreed upon can it be assumed that differences have been composed and a degree of equity assured. If these statements sound convincing, then the definition of decisional effectiveness may most simply and conveniently be reformulated as the capacity to form "necessary" agreement around decisions. One advantage of this definition is that it avoids many of the conceptual and empirical difficulties of previous ones. In particular, it does not require us to match decisions against demands. But the advantage is illusory and the solution Panglossian unless we know now how to recognize necessary agreement, especially in the case of Italy; which in turn requires that we expand on the meaning of the term.

Few decisions are taken unanimously, and few decisional bodies, especially in democratic systems, follow such a decisional rule. The size of opposition is not synonymous with the extent of ineffectiveness. Most important, necessary agreement may or may not be embodied in a constitutionally prescribed decisional rule. In some established democracies, such as England, simple majority rule, formally leaving out the opposition party, regulates many government decisions. Yet this does not usually prevent the formulation of agreement, it does not make decisions inequitable in the eyes of the opposition, it does not stalemate rule-making. It can be said here that decisional authorities normally have no difficulties in operating according to the lawfully prescribed decisional rules. In other democracies simple majority, while often legally appropriate, is not always considered sufficient to secure the necessary agreement, and concurrent or qualified majorities are often sought and enforced.²² This is because in these democracies those contestants who would otherwise lose in the decisions may sooner or later consider the process inequitable and arrest it. Here too, however, decision-making operates according to commonly sanctioned if at times informal decisional rules. This is not to equate decisional agreement with procedural consensus, but simply to point out that the rules of the decisional game serve to define necessary agreement.²³ In this sense, democracies with well-formed and mutually shared decisional rules have the institutional potential for agreement; yet agreement may fail in single instances and even repeatedly. Although decision-makers abide by the decisional rules, their "majorities" may fall short of them on the content of specific decisions. That is, shared decisional rules point to a method for building agreement, but do not guarantee agreement. Many issues may remain controversial and quite divisive on their merits, or may be technically complex, or their solution may require resources that are not easily available. Hence agreement may be tardy, controversial issues may not be addressed, government action may become uncertain, and governments may even divide and fall. We may legitimately speak here of instances of decisional ineffectiveness, and we may recognize their presence by the above behaviors.

But the thrust of the above argument is also that necessary agreement cannot be formed unless there exist accepted rules of the game. Indeed, if the rules of the game are not accepted, the legitimacy of existing decisional arrangements and their capacity to provide equitable decisions are in question; and decision-makers operate most uncomfortably under such conditions.²⁴ If

22. I am referring in particular to the consociational practices of the smaller European democracies. The case of these democracies will be an important point of reference throughout the book.

23. An important formal analysis of decision rules in democratic institutions and how they relate to the size of veto groups and groups excluded from decision-making is found in Douglas Rae, "Political Democracy as a Property of Political Institutions," *American Political Science Review* 65 (1971), pp. 111-129. Notice especially Rae's point that more democratic institutions do not necessarily produce greater satisfaction with decisions: "In general, high consensus with low democracy may produce higher frequencies of satisfaction than low degrees of consensus with high degrees of democracy." (p. 118, footnote 22).

24. I should stress that legitimacy refers here to decision-makers and how they feel toward decisional rules. Nothing is said yet about the state of public opinion.

new decisional rules are not mutually evolved, the most likely consequence is that a democratic government becomes indecisive (it does not make decisions, especially when controversial) for fear of further precipitating a confrontation, and becomes itself divided over decisions. The types of ineffective behavior exemplified above become routine: decisions are usually slow, controversial issues are not decided, government partners disagree and split over decisions, government programs go unattended, decisions react to rather than anticipate pressures and emergencies. It is my intention to demonstrate that this is the Italian case, a classical case of illegitimacy of decisional rules sustaining decisional ineffectiveness. But the point to stress here is that to demonstrate the nature of the Italian case it will not be quite sufficient to demonstrate the regular occurrence of indecisive behavior. Other democracies are no strangers to it. We will also have to demonstrate the obvious point that Italian elites are uncertain and even in conflict over decisional rules.

In the light of what has just been said, we can define and recognize the effectiveness of a decisional body as follows:

1. Effectiveness is the capacity of a decisional body to form agreement necessary to sustain decisions.

2. Necessary agreement is the minimum agreement prescribed by the body's decisional rules.

3. The capacity to form minimum agreement is additively suggested by the following indicators. These are generic to all cases of effectiveness:
   a. Controversial decisions are taken and, once taken, do not divide the majority.
   b. Contestants are not compelled by indecisiveness to concentrate on small noncontroversial matters.
   c. Decisional processes are rapid and predictable.
   d. Government programs tend to be implemented into laws.
   e. Decisions are not usually imposed by the weight of circumstances, such as crises, emergencies, pressures, but tend to anticipate them.

4. Ex definition, the capacity to form minimum agreement cannot exist when there are no clearly shared decisional rules. A straightforward indicator proper to this specific case is that controversy consistently surrounds decisions and concerns their

form (how agreement should be formed, and what constitutes necessary agreement) even more than their content.

Finally, the discussion already contains the answer to one main objection, but it is worth making it explicit again. The objection is that democratic governments may well ride over strong opposition and impose lawful but perhaps inequitable decisions; in which case the government is "effective," but how can we assume the equation between effectiveness and equity? The answer is simply that this occurrence is very unlikely, that democratic governments are most unlikely to impose themselves in the face of basic opposition because, if they do, their authenticity may be in question. It is in the nature of democratic government to recognize and protect the free expression of competing interests and to rest its action on the free agreement of these interests. Its authenticity depends on it. Hence, when viable agreement fails, and as long as it is not reestablished, inaction is the most likely consequence. Effectiveness is bound by authenticity; and, even if government were ready to overlook value considerations (for instance, when opposition rejects and seriously threatens democracy), the outcome may be costly and uncertain, as the government may lack the instruments to impose itself and the opposition may be strong enough to change the game. An authoritarian government has no such problems. Its effectiveness is not hampered by the problem of authenticity; quite the contrary. Disagreement is unlikely to surface if the system is indeed authoritarian. If it develops, the most likely consequence is an effort to reassert the principle of authority. Only if this fails may the system either begin to liberalize and change or collapse. In sum, the definition of effectiveness presented here is appropriate exactly because it is bound by and incorporates the principles and practices of democratic decision-making. That is—and to repeat—in a democracy any distinction between effectiveness and democraticness is possible only in one sense: there can be democraticness, buttressed by well-rooted institutional rules, without effectiveness in single instances, but there cannot be effectiveness without democraticness.[25] And when analysts of Italian politics

---

25. For two valuable surveys by Italian scholars on the relation between legitimacy and effectiveness and on political performance in general, see Morlino, cited above, and Luciano Pellicani, "Mobilitazione Sociale e Crisi Rivoluzionaria," *Rivista Italiana di Scienza Politica* 3 (1973), pp. 317-336.

speak of its ineffectiveness as a synonym for the inability to govern consensually, they are pointing for short to a close causal syndrome which in Italy exists in fact. I myself will use interchangeably terms like "ineffectiveness," "decisional disagreement," "rule disagreement," "lack of consensus," for purposes of stylistic relief. But, unless otherwise intended, the terms will refer to the syndrome as a whole.

PERFORMANCE AND THE ITALIAN PARLIAMENT

A study of rule-making in Italian politics is a task of considerable proportions that goes beyond the capacities of a single research project. Even after stating that the particular outputs we want to consider are rules, and even after solving the evaluative problems, the range and diversity of outputs to be evaluated would still remain considerable. In addition, a variety of institutions formally entrusted with rule-making would have to be studied, each with internal processes that may in themselves account for their performance. Obviously, the fact that different institutions may perform differently and that an overall evaluation of rule-making is difficult to achieve cannot be ignored. But a study trying to cope with such difficulties could risk remaining superficial or at least preliminary. One alternative would be a case study of the enactment of one or very few rules, but the insurmountable problem would be how to establish the representativeness of such rules. If we choose them because they are representative of poor performance, it may be interesting to discover why the system performs poorly in such cases; but the study would not prove that the system performs poorly in general, which is the first thing to be established. If we choose them without knowing whether or not they are instances of poor performance, but on the basis of certain characteristics that we hypothesize will predict performance, the result would be the same. We would learn about causes of performance but not about how the system typically performs. If one objective of the research is to evaluate how the system really performs, a larger and random selection of outputs seems in order.

The intermediate strategy I have adopted is to concentrate on the Italian Parliament as one of the rule-making bodies. Why Parliament? Because, despite all that has been written about the passing of modern parliaments, their loss of power, the absorption of their functions by the cabinet and by other centers of decision, the Italian Parliament, as will emerge in due course, still remains a prominent decisional body. First, Parliament is not just an arena within which decisions taken elsewhere are registered. It has formal powers of initiative and amendment, powers to undo decisions and to revise proposals introduced by the government or single parties, of which it makes large use. Second, such powers extend over a wide range of issues, so that Parliament takes a large share of the system's rule-making. Many of the important decisions are still enacted by it (or, for that matter, fail because of Parliament's indecisiveness), and even most of the routine decisions that elsewhere are assigned to the bureaucracy or lesser representative bodies pass through it. Third, because of the powers it preserves, Parliament is an important mediating structure within which issues are raised, differences transacted, and solutions negotiated, or stalemates occur, alliances are undone, and divisions are sanctioned. That is, Parliament is not only a decisional body but, because of this, also a body within which most of the large and small issues of politics are vented, discussed, and shaped, and where most of the contenders in the political arena meet. Further, it possesses rules, mechanisms, procedures—written or informal—which guide these complex activities and contribute to shaping outcomes. Because of this, Parliament is a most convenient site within which to begin to evaluate and analyze the performance of the system and to isolate some of its immediate causes. Because of this, parenthetically, much of the discussion taking place in Italy on the ills and remedies of Italian politics revolves around Parliament and its reform.

Lest I exaggerate my point, the Italian Parliament is not all-powerful and does not oversee everything. There are important functions, such as that of political control over the government, that Parliament barely exercises. There are entire areas of important decisions, such as the area of state-controlled corporations, that often escape it. Much legislative initiative originates from the government and is approved untouched. Much of what goes as bureaucratic implementation of rules amounts to bureaucratic decisions that escape accountability. With all this, though, the simple fact remains that a large part of decisions still go through Parliament and that this body is far from a rubber stamp. It is this simple fact that makes Parliament a convenient choice for studying the performance of the political system. I should add that, given the strategic position occupied by Parliament, an understanding of its performance and its position in the system will begin to shed light on the operation of other centers of decision. To study Parliament is to study the traditional tools of representation, government, and opposition through which conflict is handled and decisions are made. By explaining how and why these tools operate poorly in Italy, we shall begin to explain why some areas of decision have escaped Parliament and fallen in other hands. In sum, even though different institutions may perform differently and generalizations should be guarded, attention to the role of Parliament as a pivotal institution in the distribution of decisional powers should give us at least a preliminary picture of the system's overall performance.

The choice of Parliament presents another advantage. It takes us out of a conceptual difficulty, the definition of rules. Supposing that we define them as authoritative decisions allocating national resources and shaping national policies in general, the definition would probably be as good or bad as most others: it immediately presents its host of conceptual and recognition problems, beginning with the very notion of what constitutes a decision and what makes it authoritative. But even without knowing what the genus "rule" looks like, we are satisfied that formally enacted laws belong to the genus and that legislatures make laws. Pending, therefore, systematic studies designed to identify and weigh various forms of rules, laws appear convenient entities to deal with, easily recognizable, quantifiable, and comparable.[26]

But, aside from this methodological justification, why should we focus on laws? Parliament also makes other rules and significantly contributes in a variety of ways to decisions affecting the country. The substantive justification is that laws, at least within the Italian Parlament, are the most common form of rule-making, especially on the most important issues. The reasons, as we will see, are constitutional requirements and, perhaps even more, habit.

26. See a discussion of these points in Jean Blondel et al., "Legislative Behaviour: Some Steps towards a Cross-National Measurement," *Government and Opposition* 5 (1969-70), pp. 70-71.

The point may seem controversial and needs clarification. In the light of years of study and research in informal political processes and group influence, my choice of legal outputs may strike at first as being naively formalistic. It has been argued by Giovanni Sartori, for instance, that the Italian Parliament is primarily an important center for negotiation between parties, governments, bureaucracies, and parliamentary leaders, and that most of the real decision-making does not take place on the floor of Parliament or in the committee rooms but in informal settings.[27] And since decisions are taken in informal settings, attention to official legislative activities is largely misplaced. This criticism, however, says nothing about the end product of negotiations and informal processes. In Italy what is negotiated is often legislation. My choice of laws, on the other hand, says nothing about processes and influences in law-making; it is dictated only by the need to have easy outputs with which to assess performance. If the choice of Parliament as a site of important decisions is correct, it follows that the choice of laws is also correct, in that to evaluate legislation is to evaluate a good part of important decisions. What the emphasis on negotiations and informal dealings simply tells us is not that we should disregard laws as significant outputs, but that in explaining them we should look at what lies below official processes. Negotiation, after all, points to a method, not to a result.

THE INSTITUTIONAL PERSUASION: EXPLAINING POLITICAL PERFORMANCE IN ITALY

As mentioned before, much has been written on the ineffectiveness of Italian politics, but most of the literature is only inferential; that is, it infers performance from probable political causes. A brief analysis of the status of these explanations will serve to orient our causal search.

Many authors have pointed out that the Italian party system, with its innumerable parties and cumulative ideological contrapositions, seriously undermines the operation of government. The sheer number of parties and the fact that no party alone controls an absolute majority of parliamentary seats makes coali-

---

27. Sartori, op. cit., pp. 378-382.

tion government necessary. But coalitions tend not to endure, especially if partners are ideologically divided.[28] The presence of a strong Communist party, the strongest in the West and the second party in the country, further complicates matters. Some scholars see in the party the power to arrest the system because it is a repository of widespread and deep-seated discontent and the chief source of polarization and confrontation.[29] Other scholars, while recognizing the antigovernment role of the Communist party, stress the fact too that the party is also capable of exercising ideological influence on some of the coalition partners, chiefly the Socialists and the left factions of the Christian Democratic party, thus undermining party and governmental cohesiveness.[30] Still others accent the fact that, despite the strength of the Communist party, the presence of an even stronger Christian Democratic party has created a sort of "imperfect two-party system"[31] in which two great parties dominate the political scene and poll approximately two-thirds of the votes, but only one continues to control government. The lack of a serious alternative stalemates the system, slows down governmental action,[32] and confines the

28. On multiparty systems and the stability of coalitions, see Michael Taylor and V. M. Herman, "Party Systems and Governmental Stability," *American Political Science Review* 65 (1971), pp. 28-37; Jean Blondel, "Party Systems and Patterns of Government in Western Democracies," *Canadian Journal of Political Science* 1 (1968), pp. 180-204; Eric Browne, "Testing Theories of Coalition Formation in the European Context," *Comparative Political Studies* 3 (1971), pp. 391-412. For a critique of theories linking coalition instability to multiparty systems, see Lawrence Dodd, "Party Coalitions in Multiparty Parliaments: A Game Theoretical Analysis," *American Political Science Review* 68 (1974), pp. 1093-1117. Ample references to the large literature on coalitions are found in Adriano Pappalardo, "L'Analisi delle Coalizioni," *Rivista Italiana di Scienza Politica* 4 (1974), pp. 197-230.

29. For an early and in many ways naive view of the phenomenon by a social psychologist, see Hadley Cantril, *The Politics of Despair* (New York: Basic Books, 1958).

30. The most important version of this view is in Giovanni Sartori, "European Political Parties: The Case of Polarized Pluralism," in Joseph LaPalombara and Myron Weiner, eds., *Political Parties and Political Development* (Princeton: Princeton University Press, 1966), pp. 137-176.

31. The term is Giorgio Galli's. See Giorgio Galli, *Il Bipartitismo Imperfetto* (Bologna: Il Mulino, 1966) and *Il Difficile Governo* (Bologna: Il Mulino, 1972). In the latter book Galli argues that both major parties have consistently worked to cut to size the smaller parties around them and in so doing have contributed to the minute fragmentation of the party system.

32. In the work cited in footnote 26, Jean Blondel musters evidence in support of his thesis that multiparty systems dominated by one party give origin, as in Italy, to the least stable coalitions.

Communist party to a mixture of sterile opposition and limited everyday compromises.

A somewhat different approach to the performance of the Italian political system moves from political culture, both mass and elite. At the mass level Italian political culture has been characterized as the most apathetic, alienated, and fragmented among Western democracies. Political apathy, when, as in Italy's case, it stems from long-standing feelings of mistrust for politics, disaffection, and personal political ineffectiveness, questions the legitimacy of the political system, erodes support, and therefore weakens the performance of the system itself.[33] For one thing, support is likely to sustain performance, especially when the system is faced with controversial and potentially divisive issues. A system that lacks credit and good will may become indecisive in the face of basic choices and further lose its capacity for responsiveness. For another thing, alienation from the system signifies *incivisme*, that is, the absence of a network of root-and-branch intermediate associations through which citizens participate responsibly and autonomously in the political process and address, inform, and shape political decisions. Hence, as the responsibility for decisions falls exclusively on the central government, the loading of demands and the government's isolation from society undercut its performance.

The predicament is made more serious when the extreme fragmentation of Italian political culture is also considered. The argument here is that Italy has for many decades been divided into a number of quite isolated and stable political and social subcultures reflecting the various cleavages of society. Such cleavages stem from the class divisions of a country long characterized by strong inequalities, the religious divisions over Catholicism, the disparities between North and South, as well as a more generalized tension between center and periphery, and the survival of local and parochial identities following the country's political unification.[34] When

33. For a classical comparative investigation of the phenomenon, see Gabriel Almond and Sidney Verba, *The Civic Culture* (Princeton: Princeton University Press, 1963). See also Giuseppe Di Palma, *Apathy and Participation* (New York: Free Press, 1970).

34. The classical statement is found in Joseph LaPalombara, "Italy, Fragmentation, Isolation, and Alienation," in Lucian W. Pye and Sidney Verba, eds., *Political Culture and Political Development* (Princeton: Princeton University Press, 1965), pp. 282-329.

such cleavages give origin to strong political subcultures, organized around political parties and related mass organizations, as is especially the case with the Catholic and the Communist subcultures, little communication, understanding, and compromise is possible across divisions. The country, quite literally, becomes ungovernable, that is, unsteerable, the more so if those who are supposed to steer don't know how.

Much has also been written about the defects of Italian political elites, although mostly in a partisan or journalistic rather than a scholarly vein.[35] Among the various cultural characteristics of Italian elites a few have to do with their orientation toward problem-solving and are particularly significant for political performance. While Anglo-Saxon political culture values pragmatic solutions, informed by facts and experience, tentative and adjustive in style, and validated by empirical testing, Italian political culture values rationalistic solutions, informed by ideas and abstraction, definitive and fixed in style, and validated by logical consistency.[36] More simply, for many Italian elites the test of a policy is not so much whether "it works" as whether it fits a set of ideas. If we add to this the fact that Italians in general appear significantly less trustful and cooperative in interpersonal relations than citizens of other Western democracies,[37] the prognosis seems serious. A country like Italy, so divided ideologically and so politically fragmented, especially needs political elites that share and practice the values of pragmatism, compromise, and adjustment, and are skilled in the search for agreement. Instead its political class reflects and compounds the defects of mass politics and thus further slackens the performance of the political system.

To summarize the asserted defects of Italian politics, they consist of a fragmented party system, an alienated and apathetic political culture, the presence of strong political subcultures, and a political class that values ideology over pragmatism. These are old and traditional defects that threaten political performance, and they are the main reason for the syndrome of malaise that has more recently affected the country. The new demands generated by rapid growth

35. For the most recent and significant exception, see Robert Putnam, *The Beliefs of Politicians* (New Haven: Yale University Press, 1973). Relevant aspects of Putnam's analysis will be considered in later chapters.
36. Giovanni Sartori, *Democratic Theory* (Detroit: Wayne State University Press, 1962), pp. 232-33. For empirical support see Putnam, op. cit., Part I.
37. Almond and Verba, op. cit., chapter 10.

have aggregated with old and unresolved ones and fallen upon a political system already unable to respond; hence the crisis of the last years. Substantial parts of this thesis will reappear in due time, but they will need considerable refining and ordering. Indeed, if I may play the devil's advocate for the rest of the paragraph, there are some questions about the compelling theoretical and factual status of these explanations for political performance, and even about the real quality of performance. To begin, let me suggest that the drama or comedy—as the preference goes—that surrounds Italian politics is as much shadow as substance and that in sum the system, for all we know, may work better than is generally thought. Granted, the political debate in Italy is still characterized by much ideological and partisan verbiage. But this may be adopted mostly for public consumption and to maintain party cohesion. It may be a strategy to build and preserve strength for bargaining. It may also reflect an old penchant of Italian political elites for intellectual display. Nor should one forget that the symbolic weight of marxism, catholicism, or for that matter anticlericalism is naturally difficult to dispel, though its impact may be reduced to verbal pronouncements. All these factors, in sum, do not necessarily prevent action and decisions being taken in the routine of government.[38] We also know, in fact, that the term *trasformismo*—to signify nonpartisan, unprincipled, and even base log-rolling—is Italian, and that *trasformismo*, which marked prefascist politics, is still often used to describe the Italian political process. Granted, government coalitions are short-lived; but they continue to draw from the same personnel. Governments fall, but ministers (and programs) often remain.[39] Granted, the existence of strong subcultures that accumulate and freeze the old lines of division of Italian society. But it is a mass-level phenomenon, maintained by local and lower political cadres.[40] National elites, especially if young, seem more and more part of a national

38. Two significant studies challenging the notion that ideology was at the root of the problems of French politics during the Fourth Republic are Leites, op. cit., and Macrae, op. cit.
39. For evidence that, because of the game of musical chairs, Italian ministers actually have longer experience in office than their British colleagues, see Percy Allum, *Italy—Republic Without Government?* (New York: Norton, 1973), pp. 119-121.
40. For an analysis of Italian subcultures at the mass and elite level, see Alessandro Pizzorno, "Introduzione allo Studio della Partecipazione Politica," *Quaderni di Sociologia* 15 (1966), pp. 235-87, esp. p. 276. See also Pizzorno, "Elementi di uno Schema Teorico," in Giordano Sivini, ed., *Partiti e Partecipazione Politica in Italia* (Milano: Giuffré, 1969), pp. 5-40.

political culture that reflects in part the integrative forces of an expanding economy and society,[41] in part the experience of governing together.[42] Nor should one forget that older elites, which began their political socialization during fascism, are often tied by personal friendships that developed in the common struggle against fascism and survived the trials of postwar party politics.[43] Granted, finally, the *incivisme* and political disaffection of the Italian electorate. But their threat to the political system and capacity to undermine performance seem diffuse and elusive. One obvious way of punishing the political system would be for voters to withdraw electoral support from the system and/or reward antisystem parties. But Italian voters regularly turn out in numbers unparalleled in any other Western democracy, are the least sympathetic toward maverick parties, and have been—until June 1975—among the most stable in their party preferences. Also, on the strength of its progressive adjustment to the rules of the parliamentary game, it is doubtful whether the large Communist party is an antisystem party and whether its mass support is motivated by antisystem feelings.[44]

41. For a treatment of age and political culture among Italian political elites, see Putnam, op. cit., chapters 5, 11, and pp. 220-225. See also Robert Putnam, "Studying Elite Political Culture: The Case of 'Ideology,'" *American Political Science Review* 65 (1971), pp. 673-675.

42. There is an ample if uneven literature on Communist-controlled local government and the consequences of local government for the integration of the Communist party. See, for example, Gianluigi Degli Esposti, *Bologna PCI* (Bologna: Il Mulino, 1966); Robert H. Evans, *Coexistence: Communism and Its Practice in Bologna, 1945-1965* (Notre Dame: University of Notre Dame Press, 1967); Robert Leonardi and Gianfranco Pasquino, "Le Elezioni in Emilia-Romagna," *Il Mulino* 24 (1975), pp. 559-582.

43. The dissimilarity with the experience of most emerging nations, where national elites came to blows in the wake of the successful struggle against colonialism, has been pointed out to me by a prominent Communist deputy. Undoubtedly, the sense of unity that characterized the antifascist struggle and the guarded behavior of the Communist party before and after the fall of Fascism has much to do with the preservation of common antifascist bonds. How persuasive these bonds can be for saving the system is (if I can step briefly out of my devil's advocate role) something rather different.

44. For the most recent statement to this effect, see Luciano Pellicani, "Verso il Superamento del Pluralismo Polarizzato?" *Rivista Italiana di Scienza Politica* 4 (1974), pp. 645-674. For American views on the accommodation of the Communist party, see Donald Blackmer, *Unity in Diversity: Italian Communism and the Communist World* (Cambridge, Mass.: MIT Press, 1968); Sidney Tarrow, *Peasant Communism in Southern Italy* (New Haven: Yale University Press, 1967); Thomas Greene, "The Communist Parties of Italy and France: A Study in Comparative Communism," *World Politics* 21 (1968), pp. 1-38; Robert Putnam, "The Italian Communist Politician," in Donald Blackmer and Sidney Tarrow, eds., *Communism in Italy and France* (Princeton: Princeton University Press, 1975), pp. 173-217; Norman Kogan, "The French Communists and Their Italian Comrades," *Studies in Comparative Communism* 6 (1973), pp. 184-195.

As to the neofascist *Movimento Sociale,* its appeal, even when in the ascendant, has always remained limited. If the political culture of Italian voters is a threat to the system, the threat remains in some ways latent and potential.

It is the task of this book to clarify these assorted doubts, on three points. First, on the point of decisional ineffectiveness and disagreement, something which, I will try to show, is not contradicted but in fact buttressed by the practice of *trasformismo.* Second, on the empirical status of some of the alleged explanations for performance, especially elite political culture which, I will try to show, is sensitive to the need for compromise but is unable to transform the need into an operative set of decisional rules. Third, on the theoretical validity of some of the explanations, something puzzling enough to deserve further attention in the rest of this section. The central reason for the puzzle is that performance—more precisely the decisional effectiveness of the Italian Parliament—is an institutional phenomenon ultimately and directly regulated by Parliament's internal rules. Analytically the *explanandum* belongs to a different level than some of the alleged *explanantia*—such as the party system, its mass ideological appeals, subcultural fragmentation. Linkages between the two levels may or may not exist and, because when they exist they are at a distance, they take some effort to pinpoint and verify. Variables like cleavages and party system, in other words, lie metaphorically at the opening of a funnel of causality.[45] The puzzle is whether and how they come to be funneled through and to impinge upon decisional effectiveness, and whether Parliament cannot protect itself from their influence.

Out of metaphor, if effectiveness consists of building necessary agreement around decisions, it stands to reason that a country deeply cleft ideologically, burdened with an assortment of political parties competing for space, has a problem. Divisions make the search for agreement that much more difficult. But it also stands to reason that divisions make it that much more urgent and desirable to achieve agreement;[46] at one condition, which Italy by and large meets—that no significant contestant is bent upon destroying the system. Then how is it that all the defects of Italian politics seem to funnel through, in fact seem to find their ideal breeding ground in,

---

45. For the metaphor of a funnel of causality, see Angus Campbell et al., *The American Voter* (New York: Wiley, 1960), pp. 24-32.

46. Arend Lijphart, *The Politics of Accomodation* (Berkeley: University of California Press, 1968), chapter 10.

Parliament? How is it that the virtues and good intentions (and they exist) but pave the road to their frustration? Here is the puzzle again. For to say that Parliament is representative of its society is of limited help. So are the parliaments of a number of democratic countries close to Italy and afflicted by political problems similar at first inspection to Italy's. I am speaking of the so-called Small European Democracies: Belgium, the Netherlands, Switzerland, Austria. They too have deep cleavages, entrenched subcultures, or fragmented party systems in various but always potentially dangerous combinations. Yet for most of their history, in the past or in the present, their elites have managed to mold agreement out of division.[47] Italy alone presents a persistently negative syndrome. Why? The Italian traditions of *incivisme* and the tensions of uneven development are surely unknown to Switzerland and the Netherlands. But Italy has never known the linguistic confrontations of Switzerland and Belgium and the denominational *verzuiling* of the Netherlands. Nor have its class-religious subcultures ever been as encapsulating as Austria's.[48] The key to what will funnel through and whether agreement is still possible doesn't seem to be in these differences.

One reason, it has been said and documented, why some of the Small Democracies have managed to build agreement lies in the political culture of their elites, a culture based on accommodation and compromise, aware of the costs of confrontation, committed to the maintenance of the system, willing to transcend the divisions of the system to forge mutually equitable solutions.[49] But the statement strikes me as somewhat tautological, and whether elites are able to forge agreement may not be so much a question of how badly they want it (Italian elites at least understand its importance) as a

47. Among the most significant analyses, see Lijphart, ibid.; also Lijphart, "Typologies of Democratic Systems," *Comparative Political Studies* 1 (1968), pp. 3-44, and "Consociational Democracy," *World Politics* 21 (1969), pp. 207-225; G. Bingham Powell, *Social Fragmentation and Political Hostility; an Austrian Case Study* (Stanford: Stanford University Press, 1970); Rodney Stiefbold, "Segmented Pluralism and Consociational Democracy in Austria: Problems of Political Stability and Change," in Martin O. Heisler, ed., *European Politics* (New York: McKay, 1974), pp. 117-177; Val Lorwin, "Segmented Pluralism," *Comparative Politics* 3 (1971), pp. 141-176; Jürg Steiner, *Amicable Agreement Versus Majority Rule* (Chapel Hill: University of North Carolina Press, 1974); Eric Nordlinger, *Conflict Regulation in Divided Societies* (Cambridge, Mass.: Harvard University, Center for International Affairs, Occasional Papers in International Affairs, No. 29, January 1972); Kenneth MacRae, ed., *Consociational Democracy: Political Accommodation in Segmented Societies* (Toronto: McClelland and Stewart, 1974).

48. Stiefbold, op. cit., passim.

49. Lijphart, "Typologies of Democratic Systems," op. cit., pp. 22-24.

question of what Belgians call *optimisme institutionnel* or what I will call institutional persuasion. To put it in another and imperfect metaphor, political institutions work like dams, regulating and selecting the flux of what lies upstream. In democracies where society is fragmented and heterogeneous, it is essential that they be built well. The point was well understood by Madison and the American Founding Fathers. Indeed, more than England, it is the American republic—a new, diverse, and rapidly growing nation with new elites and an uncharted future in front—that represents the most remarkable incarnation of the institutional persuasion.[50] The metaphor simplifies the issue but brings home the point. It is this institutional persuasion that Italian political institutions lack. Parliament lacks it, and so does the party system, if we correctly think of the latter as a crucial intermediate structure between society and political elites.

The purpose of our looking at institutional arrangements is not simply to refine and extend the chain of causality, so that distant causes can more precisely be linked to decisional performance. If this were the only function, there would be no real puzzle. Causality exists, and distant causes would need only tracing back. Further, the image of a chain of causality—like that of the funnel—conveys the impression that distant causes act by shaping and affecting closer ones. According to it, the political institutions and rules that regulate decisions—and more generally any and all intermediate political institutions—are the product and reflex of extant social conditions. But this is a gross and vague hypothesis, which allows no variance and hence no disproof and which often flies in the face of reality. Nor is the hypothesis much improved if re-stated in terms of the people, and especially elites, forging the institutions and rules they want. Aside from the fact that more often they are stuck with the artifacts of past generations, what elites want, in what sense, and why is much in question. Institutions and rules may be adopted and wanted as lesser evils, or to try them out without initial commitment, or because of self-interest and the desire to preserve a measure of power in the face of change. The history of older democracies is replete with examples of such adaptive, perhaps grudging, engineering.[51] As to its consequences, it is doubtful that institution -

50. Seymour Martin Lipset, *The First New Nation* (New York: Basic Books, 1963), esp. chapter 1.
51. Dankwart Rustow, "Transitions to Democracy: Toward a Dynamic Model," *Comparative Politics* 2 (1970), pp. 337-364.

building could always imagine the shape of things to come. Once rules and institutions are created, for whatever purpose, elites may not always be total master of them, and their behavior may have to adapt significantly.

In sum, political institutions and rules guiding and influencing decisions may or may not reflect extant social conditions, may or may not be purposely designed by political elites; but their existence establishes a system of incentives and disincentives, rewards and punishments, which controls the flux of demands and within which decision-makers act. If appropriately turned out, institutional arrangements may successfully control centrifugal forces within society or among elites and sustain the formation of agreement. This is the meaning of the institutional persuasion. In explaining decisional effectiveness, first things must come first.

But how strong is the institutional persuasion? In the case of the Italiam Parliament I shall try to demonstrate that decisional effectiveness—that is, the capacity to create necessary agreement—is marred by conflict over the very rules that regulate the formation of agreement and by an elite culture ambivalent about elite roles. Cultural ambivalence and conflict are in turn sustained by a failure in institutional engineering, that is, by a system of parliamentary incentives and disincentives that rewards centrifugal forces and most "transformistic" deals and that punishes responsible cooperation. It is not so much that Italian political elites do not want to agree, as that they find agreement neither possible nor convenient. Nor is it that Parliament reflects the centrifugal forces of society so much as that it has been designed to sustain and even create such forces. As we move further upstream, it will appear clear that the task of forming agreement and controlling dispersive impulses does not fall on Parliament alone. If control fails upstream, Parliament is only in small part responsible; and agreeing becomes that much more difficult. The role of the party system is crucial here. Its defects are classically in the sheer number of parties and in their mass-level ideological contrapositions; its centrifugal effects are even greater than those produced by Parliament. We will also see that, despite some superficial morphological similarities, the party systems of the Small Democracies do not have the same effects on their countries.

But I shall conclude that ineffectiveness has also played a

function. Paradoxically, it has been one of the factors contributing to survival. Is the function exhausted? What lies ahead?

THE DATA FOR THE STUDY

The following quantitative data have been employed for the study:

1. A random sample of 359 enacted laws drawn by Professor Franco Cazzola (University of Catania and Committee for Political and Social Sciences in Rome) for his study of legislative behavior in Italy, kindly made available to the author. The sample represents approximately 4 percent of all enacted laws for the five Parliaments from 1948 to the summer of 1971. The sample will be referred to as the "Cazzola" sample.

2. A random sample of 1975 legislative proposals, stratified by government and private members' initiative, covering the first four Parliaments from 1948 to 1968. The sample is the basis for a large-scale quantitative analysis of legislative outputs in Italy conducted by Professor Alberto Predieri (University of Florence), Professor Vittorio Mortara (University of Calabria), and others. Partial data from the sample have been kindly made available by Professor Mortara. The sample will be referred to as the "Predieri-Mortara" sample.

3. A random sample of 400 legislative proposals, stratified by government and private members' initiative, drawn by the author expressly for this study. The sample covers the period from 1963—beginning of the Fourth Parliament and of the Center-Left coalitions—to early 1972—presidential dissolution of the Fifth Parliament. It will be referred to as the "Di Palma" sample.

4. Interviews, partially open-ended, with a stratified sample of 160 members of the Fifth Parliament from the three major parties: the Christian Democratic, the Communist, and the Socialist. For each party, rosters from the Senate and the Chamber of Deputies were combined and a random sample of 70 was drawn. Each parliamentarian received a letter from the author, indicating the scholarly purpose of the interview, and a covering letter from his or her parliamentary group clearing the interviews and inviting coopera-

tion. The latter was necessary as a matter of courtesy toward the parties. As the difficulties involved in obtaining interviews from Italian parliamentarians were known beforehand, a high limit of four recalls was set.[52] Sixty Communists were interviewed (average number of recalls 2.2), but only 48 Socialists (average number of recalls 2.9), and 52 Christian Democrats (average number of recalls 3.1). The lower rate of Socialist response may be explained by the smaller parliamentary contingent, which increases the work-load of each parliamentarian. There were 98 Socialists in the Fifth Parliament, but 254 Communists and 403 Christian Democrats. Differences in response rates between Communists and Christian Democrats have most likely to do with the greater cohesiveness and institutional accessibility of the former. Communists revealed in general greater cooperativeness than respondents from the other parties. No significant difference was found between respondents and nonrespondents in terms of age, education, region represented, seniority in Parliament and politics, as well as in terms of indices of political professionalism and political prominence. The indices were developed from the interviews in the case of the respondents, and from background data published by Parliament in the case of nonrespondents.

Interviews were conducted and recorded, partially by the author and partially by a team of trained social science graduate students from the University of Rome and the "Luigi Sturzo" Institute of Sociology, in the spring of 1970 and the fall of 1971. The interview schedule covered perception of legislative roles and legislative procedures, government-Parliament relations, relations with parties and the electorate, inter-elite relations, values and attitudes toward politics, conflict, conflict resolution, and background data on the respondents. Modal length of the interviews was two hours, but many lasted as little as one hour, others as much as five.

One reason why a stratified sample of the three major parties was preferred over a random sample of all parties is that the three parties hold the key to parliamentary behavior and to the pattern of decisional disagreement the study intends to explore. What is therefore important is to show not the overall distribution of attitudes

---

52. Because of their heavy schedule, and to preserve representativeness, no limit on the number of recalls was set in the case of state ministers and undersecretaries. Exhaustion and politeness set the ceiling.

and roles, as reflected by the relative strength of the parties, but rather the typical attitudes and roles of the three key contestants.

In addition to the above data, structured interviews were also conducted with the permanent secretaries (a civil service position) of seven of the fourteen standing committees of the Chamber of Deputies, to obtain information on various aspects of committee behavior. Interviews similar to those with members of Parliament were also conducted with a number of national and provincial party leaders from each of the three parties. They are not employed in the study for a simple reason, quickly explained in Chapter VI.

II

Legislative Behavior: Effective or Ineffective?

As we begin the evaluation of the decisional effectiveness of the Italian Parliament and its legislative output, it is appropriate to recall very briefly some of Parliament's constitutional features. The reason is not to explain legislative outputs but to place them in their institutional and procedural context. To the extent that some of these features have explanatory relevance, they will receive closer scrutiny in Chapter V.

Parliament is composed of the Chamber of Deputies and the Senate of the Republic, both popularly elected every five years through slightly different but essentially proportional electoral systems.[1] The two bodies sit in permanent session throughout the year, save for summer recess and national holidays. They share basically identical legislative powers, as bills may be presented in any of them but must be approved by both. There is practically no limit to what Parliament can legislate upon and, since no matter that has been acted upon by law can be further regulated without a new act of Parliament, legislative proliferation is likely.[2] Except for budgetary laws, no limits are placed upon the right of individual members to initiate legislation and to introduce amendments. The government has no veto power

---

1. Electoral colleges for the Chamber of Deputies are multimember, and seats are allocated proportionally by party list. Senate colleges are single-member; but unless a candidate receives 65 percent of the votes (a very rare occurrence), seats are allocated proportionally in regional colleges.

2. According to most legal doctrine, there is no "riserva di atto amministrativo" in the Italian legislative system. That is, any matter for which the Constitution does not prescribe otherwise can be object of formal law. Hence, much of what in other legislations is regulated by administrative act, in Italy is regulated by law. And what is regulated by law cannot be changed except by an act of at least equal legal standing. See Costantino Mortati, "Sui Limiti della Delegazione Legislativa," *Jus* 3 (1952), pp. 214 ff.

upon private bills and amendments, unless it asks for a vote of confidence, and no formal power to close discussion. Nor does the law grant government bills any priority in the parliamentary agenda, except when the budget is to be approved or when the government asks for emergency decree powers. Parliament autonomously sets its internal rules, and the president of each branch fixes the agenda for his own branch and assigns bills to its standing committees. If the government intends to secure priority for its own bills, it can do so only by influencing the presidents and the committee chairmen. Finally, a most important characteristic of the Italian Parliament is the fact that each standing committee may act as a legislative body of its own. That is, the president of each branch, in assigning each bill to a committee, decides whether the committee shall report the bill to the floor or shall take final action on it. In fact, as we will see, most legislation is directly enacted in this fashion by the committees.

COUNTING LAWS: GOVERNMENT AND PRIVATE

If one relies on these constitutional characters alone, the Italian Parliament seems to enjoy a degree of legislative power and independence from the executive unparalleled by most other legislatures. As a minimum, constitutional norms do not stand in the way of an active and autonomous Parliament, though, by the same token, they scarcely channel its activities either. Even so, in sheer numbers, Parliament's legislative output may surprise the unaware. Simply, the number of laws passed by Parliament is in absolute terms very high and in relative terms considerably above other Western legislatures. During the twenty years from the adoption of the new constitution in 1948 to the end of the Fourth Parliament in 1968, Parliament approved 8,010 laws, or an average of about 400 per year. Nor is there evidence that the output is declining. In the First Parliament (1948–53), 2,317 laws were passed; in the Second Parliament (1953–58), 1,897; in the Third (1958–63), 1,785, and in the Fourth (1963–68), 2,011.[3] These figures compare with 545 laws passed by West Germany's First Bundestag (1949–53), 510 by the Second Bundestag (1953–57), 424 by the Third (1957–61), and 426 by the Fourth

---

3. See Table 1 below.

(1961–65).[4] Lower outputs are similarly reported for 1966 in England (98 laws), Ireland (34), Sweden (285), France (147), and India (51).[5] Predieri reports the following average yearly outputs: England, 68.6 (1945–51), Denmark, 129 (1960–65), and Belgium, 100 (1948–58).[6] Some of these comparisons may seem unwarranted on many grounds, given the disparity in years and constitutional background. But it is exactly the fact of disparity that lends value to my point: Whatever the reasons, and irrespective of context, Italy produces by far more laws than any of the countries on which I found data.

This level of "productivity" is even more remarkable if, leaving aside comparisons with other countries, one matches output against the limited time and organizational resources at Parliament's disposal. It is true that Parliament sits in permanent session through the year and that the committees' power to enact laws substantially increases output. But it is also true that time is severely curtailed by a variety of factors.[7] Committees do not normally meet when there is debate on the floor (which is usually every afternoon). Parliament meets only from Tuesday to Friday, provided there are no national holidays, with which the Italian calendar is filled. It does not usually meet during the formation of a new government, a process that often lasts several weeks and has occurred on the average every eleven months. A substantial amount of the meeting time is taken up by discussion of the yearly budget, by political debates during government crises and the formation of new coalitions, by question time, by internal activities, etc. Data for the 1953–56 period indicate that, if we leave out time spent on budgetary laws, Parliament devoted an average of 34 percent of its actual meeting time to legislation.[8] As to individual sources, suffice it to say at this point that individual members of Parliament are not entitled to offices and secretarial

---

4. Gerhard Loewenberg, *Parliament in the German Political System* (Ithaca: Cornell University Press, 1967), p. 270.

5. Jean Blondel et al., "Legislative Behaviour: Some Steps towards a Cross-National Measurement," *Government and Opposition* 5 (1969-70), p. 75, Table 1.

6. Alberto Predieri, "Aspetti del Processo Legislativo in Italia," in *Processo allo Stato* (Firenze: Sansoni, 1971; Atti del Convegno sulla Riforma dello Stato, a Cura del Centro di Ricerca e Documentazione "Luigi Einaudi"), p. 55.

7. Giovanni Sartori, "Dove Va il Parlamento," in S. Somogyi et al., *Il Parlamento Italiano 1946-1963* (Napoli: Edizioni Scientifiche Italiane, 1963), p. 363.

8. Predieri, "La Produzione Legislativa," in Somogyi et al., op. cit., p. 234, Table 5.

assistance unless they are high officers of Parliament. Most of them literally live out of a suitcase. And as to common technical and organizational resources, the Italian Parliament, to make a decidedly conservative estimate, is at least no better off than other European parliaments.

In view of these considerations, one may be tempted to conclude that the Italian Parliament is an active and busy body that gets things done and spares no energies—limited as they are—in the process. The conclusion might well be warranted if quantity were a satisfactory criterion for judging the scope of decisions, decisional effectiveness, and the capacity to reach agreement. But hopefully the reader is well aware from the previous chapter that counting output is at best a preliminary and primitive form of assessment. It tells us something, and accurately so, but we don't know what. Why, then, did we spend time counting? The reason is double. In the first place, it begins to give us a picture of the salient characteristics of the legislative process. In the second place, as I intend to show when the relevant criteria are finally considered, a high output, far from signifying effectiveness and agreement, may be a symptom of the opposite. The same ambivalence is revealed by other quantitative aspects of legislative performance. These too may suggest agreement and effectiveness at first, but eventually acquire quite a different meaning.

GOVERNMENT AND PRIVATE INITIATIVE: RATES OF SUCCESS

Another criterion of effectiveness may seem to be the percentage of proposed bills that become laws: the higher the rate of approval, the higher the agreement should be. Here a distinction imposes itself immediately, that between government and private bills. The success of the former presumably assesses the capacity of the government to hold together a parliamentary majority around preestablished programs. Private bills, on the other hand, especially if they come from the opposition, neither commit the parliamentary majority nor are they preceded by the degree of extraparliamentary negotiation and agreement among parties, interest groups, and bureaucracy that makes the acceptance of government bills more likely. Hence, the success of private bills

TABLE 1. Legislative Output in Four Parliaments[1]

	First Parliament (1948-53)			Second Parliament (1953-58)			Third Parliament (1958-63)		
	Introduced	Passed	Percent Passed	Introduced	Passed	Percent Passed	Introduced	Passed	Percent Passed
Government	2287	2054	89.8	1667	1414	84.8	1569	1300	82.9
Members of Parliament	1375	260	18.9	2514	480	19.1	3688	481	13.0
Total	3662	2314	63.2	4181	1894	45.3	5257	1781	33.9
Percentage: Members' bills of total	37.5	11.2		60.1	25.3		70.2	27.0	

TABLE 1. (Continued)

	Fourth Parliament (1963-68)			Total (1948-68)		
	Introduced	Passed	Percent Passed	Introduced	Passed	Percent Passed
Government	1569	1240	79.0	7092	6008	84.7
Members of Parliament	4414	771	17.5	11,991	1992	16.6
Total	5983	2011	33.6	19,083	8000	41.9
Percentage: Members' bills over total	73.8	38.3		62.8	24.9	

[1] Sources are the *Resoconto Generale dei Lavori Legislativi*, published by the Chamber of Deputies, and the *Resoconto Generale dei Lavori del Senato*. The table does not report 10 laws initiated by voters or regional councils.

should be a distinctively valuable measure of Parliament's transactive skills when majorities are not prearranged. A sharper but not necessarily more precise way of putting it is that, while the success of government initiative may reveal nothing more than the extent to which Parliament acts as a rubber stamp, that of private initiative is a more telling test of Parliament's own decisional skills.

As to government bills, the story is quickly told. Table 1 shows that their percentage of success in the first four Parliaments is consistently and safely around 80 percent, and finer time-data indicate that, except for very short-lived governments, no government ever went below 70 percent.[9] The picture, when it comes to private bills, is more complex and needs a good deal of interpretation. Their success is considerably lower, around 16-17 percent, but this is by no means an insignificant figure. What accounts for the difference, in addition to the political factors just mentioned, is in some part the fact that government bills are disproportionately assigned to committees for final action. This procedure, as Chapter V will show, is speedier and more likely to lead to approval than the procedure requiring final action on the floor.[10] Referral to committees for final action, in other words, is often used by the president of either house in order to further secure passage. Also, many private bills are presented for propaganda purposes or as a gesture to please local and special interests, with little intent to press for their approval. Many other bills are in competition with similar proposals, possibly from the government, which intend to regulate the same matters and with which they form legislative clusters. The fact that a private bill is not approved, then, does not signify that the matter has not been regulated.[11] Some private bills are so similar to each other that they can be construed as functional equivalents of mutual amendments, and the absorption of one bill by another or its withdrawal signifies at least partial success. Another important consideration here is that hundreds of private bills are proposed every year,

---

9. Predieri, "Aspetti del Processo Legislativo in Italia," op. cit., p. 77; Vittorio Mortara, *L'Analisi Quantitativa del Processo Legislativo* (Bologna: Il Mulino, 1970), p. 302.

10. Mortara, ibid., p. 173.

11. Pierre Ferrari and Herbert Maisl, *Les Groupes Communistes aux Assemblées Parlementaires Italiennes (1958-1963) et Françaises (1962-1967)* (Paris: Presses Universitaires de France, 1969), p. 48.

accounting for an increasingly greater majority of proposed legislation. It may be the simple fact that so many are proposed that, almost physically, limits their success. More important, whatever their rate of success, private bills still represent one-fourth of all enacted legislation and, here too, the ratio is increasing. In sum, the space that Parliament reserves for private bills not only indicates that there are no constitutional restrictions on the matter and that the formal powers of parliamentary initiative are considerable, but it plainly means that Parliament makes ample use of this power and invests a good part of its resources in developing the appropriate negotiating skills.

A comparison with private initiative in other parliaments is appropriate at this point, provided we know the grounds for comparing. Postwar data for various democratic countries reported in Table 2 indicate not only that the proportion of approved bills that are of private initiative is, with the exception of West Germany, lower than in Italy,[12] but also that their absolute number is small and even minimal.[13] The point of difference is not so much that these parliaments make more limited us of their powers of initiative then the Italian Parliament, or that they lack the necessary negotiatory skills, but that their initiative is severely curtailed, formally or in fact, by the government. Even in the case of West Germany, where 37 percent of the private bills introduced from 1949 to 1965 became law, it is very

12. It should be noted, however, that, as in Table 1, this proportion is increasing in Italy, while it is possibly decreasing in Germany. The proportion was 27 percent and 26 percent in the First and Second Bundestag, but went down to 17 percent and 23 percent in the Third and Fourth. The figures have been calculated from Loewenberg, op. cit., p. 270.

13. These data are confirmed by many comparative studies of legislatures. Various if scattered evidence reveals that—with the most notable exception of the American Congress, operating under a presidential system, and of the Fourth French Republic—private bills are few in number, an average of 5 to 15 percent are passed, and they represent 5 to 10 percent of all legislation. See K. C. Wheare, *Legislatures* (London: Oxford University Press, 1968), pp. 101-105; Gerhard Loewenberg, ed., *Modern Parliaments* (Chicago: Aldine-Atherton, 1971), esp. chapters 4 and 5; Michel Ameller, *Parliaments* (London: Cassell, 1966), pp. 140-151; Jean Blondel, *Comparative Legislatures* (Englewood Cliffs: Prentice-Hall, 1973), pp. 109-113; S.A. Walkland, *The Legislative Process in Great Britain* (London: Allen and Unwin, 1968); Philip Williams, *The French Parliament (1958-1967)* (London: Allen and Unwin, 1967), chapter 4; Kenneth Miller, *Government and Politics in Denmark* (Boston: Houghton Mifflin, 1968), p. 132; M. van Impe, *Le Régime Présidentiel en Belgique* (Bruxelles: Etablissement Emile Bruylant, 1968), p. 214; Hans Daalder, "Cabinet-Parliament Relations and Party Systems" (mimeographed, 1967).

TABLE 2. Annual Legislative Output in Selected Legislatures and Years[1]

	U.K. (1966-67)	Ireland (1965)	Sweden (1966)	France (1966)	India (1966)	West Germany (1949-65, annual average)	Italy (1948-68, annual average)
Total bills passed	98	34	285	147	51	121	400
Private member bills passed	14	0	11	14	0	27	100
Percent the latter are of total	14.3	--	3.9	9.5	--	22.3	25.0

[1] Sources are: For U.K., Ireland, Sweden, France, India: Blondel et al., op. cit., p. 75; for West Germany: Loewenberg, *Parliament in the German Political System*, op. cit., p. 270; for Italy: see Table 1.

likely that the high rate of approval is due to the bills' limited number (a yearly average of 68 introduced in the Bundestag, compared with 556 in Italy)[14] and to the fact that the government has in one form or another suggested, accepted, or tolerated them. In Italy the sheer dimensions of parliamentary initiative prevent such a system of government screening. In fact, and by their own admission, most members of Parliament wishing to introduce legislation do not even bother to clear it with their own parliamentary group,[15] let alone with the government. Hence, the success of private initiative is largely left to the skills of the proponents.

Naturally, private bills are more likely to succeed if they originate with members of the majority. But this is not because of the fact that once proposed such bills are more likely to obtain a government sanction. By common agreement of the members of Parliament and the parliamentary staff interviewed, the government takes usually limited interest in them, either by opposing or especially by supporting them. Private bills are mostly left to find their own constituency through their own devices, and proposals by members of large parties have an added advantage in this game, as have proposals by members of several parties. It is in this light that the evidence reported in Table 3 should be read. The bills with the greatest record of success are "grand coalition" bills, that is, bills by Christian Democrats together with Communists and/or with a coalition of members from most other parties of the Right and Left. They are followed very closely by bills initiated by Christian Democrats alone or together with members of the small secular parties which traditionally have formed government coalitions with the Christian Democrats. According to the sample data reported in the table, approximately one-fourth of these bills become law. In third position, with a 13 to 14 percent rate of approval, are bills by Communist and/or Socialist proponents.

Of great interest also is the fact that Christian Democratic bills make up approximately 60 percent of all private bills approved. The reason is a combination of the fact that Christian Democrats

---

14. Calculated from Loewenberg, *Parliament in the German Political System*, op. cit., p. 270, and from Table 1.

15. The significant exception is the Communist party. See Predieri, "Aspetti del Processo Legislativo in Italia," op. cit., p. 81, footnote 184.

TABLE 3. Private Members' Bills Proposed and Passed in Four Parliaments[1]

PARLIAMENT

	First				Second			
	Proposed	Passed		Percent of total passed	Proposed	Passed		Percent of total passed
		Number	Percent			Number	Percent	
PCI-PSI[2]	32	4	12.5	8.3	47	3	6.4	7.5
PSI	14	3	21.4	6.25	10	0	—	—
DC-Center parties[3]	102	31	30.4	64.6	85	26	30.6	65.0
Center parties[4]	9	0	—	—	9	1	11.1	2.5
Right[5]	2	0	—	—	23	0	—	—
Grand coalitions[6]	29	10	34.5	20.8	35	10	28.6	25.0
Other coalitions	1	0	—	—	2	0	—	—
Total	189	48	25.4	100.0	211	40	19.0	100.0

PARLIAMENT

	Third				Fourth			
	Proposed	Passed		Percent of total passed	Proposed	Passed		Percent of total passed
		Number	Percent			Number	Percent	
PCI-PSI	49	9	18.4	21.4	34	7	20.6	14.6
PSI	17	2	11.8	4.8	20	3	15.0	6.25
DC-Center parties	123	24	19.5	57.1	130	27	20.8	56.25
Center parties	27	0	—	—	55	2	3.6	4.2
Right	25	1	4.0	2.4	21	2	9.5	4.2
Grand coalitions	20	6	30.0	14.3	32	7	21.9	14.6
Other coalitions	2	0	—	—	0	0	—	—
Total	263	42	16.0	100.0	292	48	16.4	100.0

Table 3 (Continued)

PARLIAMENT

All

	Proposed	Passed		Percent of total passed
		Number	Percent	
PCI-PSI	162	23	14.2	12.9
PSI	61	8	13.1	4.5
DC-Center parties	440	108	24.5	60.7
Center parties	100	3	3.0	1.7
Right	71	3	4.2	1.7
Grand coalitions	116	33	28.4	18.5
Other coalitions	5	0	—	—
Total	955	178	18.6	100.0

[1] The analysis is based on the "Predieri-Mortara" sample.
[2] Bills by Communist (PCI) members, alone or together with Socialist (PSI) members.
[3] Bills by Christian Democrats (DC) alone or (14 bills) together with members of one or more of the other center parties (Republican, Social-Democratic, and Liberal party).
[4] Bills by members of the center parties, excluding DC.
[5] Bills by members of the Movimento Sociale (MSI) and/or the Monarchist party.
[6] Bills by DC members together with PCI members and/or members of both center and right-wing parties.

make greater use of the initiative than other parties, even after accounting for party size, and that their bills have a higher rate of success. Forty-five percent of the private bills in the sample are introduced by Christian Democrats *alone*, and their party has controlled on the average 45.9 percent of all seats in the first four Parliaments. Communists and Socialists have controlled an average of 36.8 percent of the seats but have introduced only 24 percent of the private bills. Similar or even lower rates, relative to party size, characterize smaller parties. In explaining Christian Democratic predominance one cannot discount the fact that Christian Democrats have been uninterruptedly in power for thirty years, thus providing the representatives of the party with unparalleled resources. But this is not to say that cabinet backing has anything to do with predominance. If cabinet support were to count, one would expect members of the minor parties belonging to the government coalition to obtain a degree of success in their initiatives if not equal to the Christian Democrats then at least respectable. Instead Table 3 shows that when these parties act alone their success is minimal—3 percent—and actually not even comparable to that of the PCI which, while numerically more consistent, still represents the opposition. If cabinet support were to count, one would also expect that a party's entry into or exit from the coalition area changes the chances of success of its members' legislative initiative. But the data belie the expectation. The relevant cases are the Liberal and the Socialist parties, the former leaving and the latter joining the government coalition at the outset of the Fourth Parliament, as the country moved from the Center to the Center-Left coalition formula. Since the sample contains only one approved bill presented by Liberals alone, I have chosen, in order to extend the data bases and reduce random error, all bills presented by Liberals, whether alone or with other members of Parliament. Contrary to the "cabinet counts" expectation, the Liberals' rate of success remained at 10 percent during the Third *and* Fourth Parliaments, and the Socialists' actually slightly decreased from 22.7 percent during the Third Parliament to 19.0 during the Center-Left. One may argue that an analysis of the initiative of the Liberals in alliance with other parties is not appropriate, as it hides the personal input of the former. But this is in a way what makes the evidence revealing. The success of the smaller parties is always very limited, unless they join with other parties, a strategy that seems to bear equal fruit whether they are in the government or the opposition. Thus the success of smaller parties does not depend on their standing vis-à-vis the government, but more likely on their capacity to find informal alliances within Parliament. And the advantage Christian Democrats enjoy in this game is simply a function of their party's size, of their transactive resources and skills, and thus of their ability to elicit the support or the "senatorial courtesy" of their many party colleagues and of the other members of Parliament.

In conclusion, the analysis of legislative initiative points so far to two characteristics: the existence of two initiatives—by the government and by private members of Parliament—side by side, and the concurrence of the majority and opposition parties (especially the PCI) in the formation of private legislative will. As to the first characteristic, what government initiates is most often enacted, but considerable room is also left for parliamentary initiative. As to the second, while the lion's share of parliamentary initiative goes to the Christian Democatic party, there are a few signs that much initiative also cuts across the government coalition lines and is the product of special and broad parliamentary alliances. More than one-third of successful private legislation originates from the extreme Left and from "grand coalitions" but very little from the smaller government coalition partners.

VOTING AND AMENDING: THE BEHAVIOR OF THE OPPOSITION

This concurrence of government and Parliament and of majority and opposition emerges more clearly when we consider two more aspects of legislative performance: roll-call and amending behavior. As to the former, an analysis of the party composition of the majorities supporting legislation reveals explicitly what was implied in the previous discussion; i.e., that support often goes beyond the proponents and their parties. What is of particular importance here is the favorable behavior of the PCI in regard to legislation initiated by the government or by members of the parliamentary majority. The "Cazzola" sample has been used to explore these propositions. To begin with, a first indication that most laws are passed with composite majorities, which include members of opposition parties, emerges by computing the average percentage of votes cast in favor of enacted legislation in each Parliament.[16] As can be seen from Table 4, in no Parliament has legislation *on the average* obtained less than 75 percent of the votes cast, an average that could not be matched by the parliamentary majority alone, assuming—which was not always the case—that such majorities were always and solidly behind every bill.[17]

As to the behavior of the major opposition party—the PCI—it is well known to insiders and students of the Italian Parliament, if not to the general public, that the party often adds its votes to those of the majority. It is also well known that such convergence occurs especially within the standing committees. The supporting

TABLE 4. Average Percentage of Favorable Votes in a Sample of Laws in Five Parliaments[1]

PARLIAMENT					
First		*Second*		*Third*	
Number of Laws	Percent "Yes"	Number of Laws	Percent "Yes"	Number of Laws	Percent "Yes"
102	78.4	75	83.9	79	88.3

PARLIAMENT					
Fourth		*Fifth*		*All*	
Number of Laws	Percent "Yes"	Number of Laws	Percent "Yes"	Number of Laws	Percent "Yes"
70	76.6	33	75.3	359	81.3

[1] Figures for the first four parliaments are taken from Franco Cazzola, "Consenso e Opposizione nel Parlamento Italiano. Il Ruolo del PCI dalla I alla IV Legislatura," *Rivista Italiana di Scienza Politica* 2 (1972), pp. 71-96. Figures for the Fifth Parliament are calculated directly from the sample. The number of laws for the Fifth Parliament is smaller than for the others because the sample was drawn before its end.

16. In this and following computations of parliamentary voting behavior, it should be kept in mind that individual roll-call analysis is impossible, since voting in the Italian Parliament is normally by show of hands or secret. Roll call is rarely asked for (usually for the purpose of imposing party discipline) and can be easily offset by a counter-request for a secret or division vote. Since, on the other hand, party discipline is very strong—especially in the Communist group—and cases in which discipline is broken are well known, I have used declarations of voting intention by party whips as safe indicators of party vote. These, in turn, have been checked against figures reporting present and voting members by party and aggregate voting results.

17. Except during the First Parliament, when the elections of 1948 gave the DC more than half of the parliamentary seats and the center parties together controlled approximately 64 percent of the seats, the government coalition area has usually included no more than 55 percent of the seats.

evidence, presented in Tables 5 and 6, speaks for itself. More than 70 percent of the bills initiated by the government or by Christian Democratic members *alone* are approved with the vote of the Communist party. If we add to this the instances of abstention, it can be said that four out of five majority bills are, as a minimum, not contested and in fact most often supported by the Communist Left. Further, while this behavior is most typical in the committee rooms, where legislation is often enacted, it occurs rather frequently on the floor as well, despite the fact that debate is public and formalized, and ideological confrontations should more likely occur.[18] What is perhaps less appreciated is the degree to which the PCI extends its support not only to the private initiative of the majority, but also to government initiative itself. It is true, again, that bills presented by Christian Democratic members are supported by the PCI more often than government bills (Table 7). But even for the latter, support is quite high, close to 70 percent of the government bills.[19] Nor is this rate of support a result of approval procedure, as one might surmise from the fact reported previously that in the Italian Parliament government bills tend to be enacted by committees more often than private bills.[20] In point of fact, in the "Cazzola" sample it is Christian Democratic private bills, not government bills, that are more likely to follow this approval procedure, and once we account for this (Table 8) the behavior of the PCI toward private and government bills becomes more alike. That is, the behavior of the PCI changes as between the committees and the

---

18. A breakdown of the figures in Table 4 according to where laws are enacted reveals that even on the floor laws are approved with very large majorities:

	I	II	III	IV	V	All
	Percent "Yes"	Percent "Yes"	Percent "Yes"	Percent "Yes"	Percent "Yes"	Percent "Yes"
Committee	90.0	91.6	96.2	89.3	84.6	91.0
House	74.6	78.2	84.9	71.6	73.5	76.5

P.A. Allum similarly reports that 90 percent of all legislation enacted in the committees is approved unanimously but does not quote the source of his information. See Percy Allum, *Italy—Republic Without Government?* (New York: Norton, 1973), p. 133.

19. Data similar to Tables 5, 6, and 7 are reported in Franco Cazzola, "Consenso e Opposizione nel Parlamento Italiano. Il Ruolo del PCI dalla I alla IV Legislatura," *Rivista Italiana di Scienza Politica* 2 (1972), Table 4. However, they include all bills, rather than only government and DC bills, and are limited to the first four Parliaments.

20. See Table 47, Chapter V.

TABLE 5. PCI Vote on Government and DC Members' Laws in Five Parliaments in Percentage and Absolute Figures[1]

Parliament	Yes	No	Abstention	Total Laws
First	61.5 (59)	35.4 (34)	3.1 (3)	100.0 (96)
Second	78.4 (58)	12.2 (9)	9.5 (7)	100.0 (74)
Third	87.5 (63)	6.9 (5)	5.6 (4)	100.0 (72)
Fourth	69.0 (40)	20.7 (12)	10.3 (6)	100.0 (58)
Fifth	50.0 (15)	16.7 (5)	33.3 (10)	100.0 (30)
All	71.2 (235)	19.7 (65)	9.1 (30)	100.0 (330)

[1]"Cazzola" sample.

TABLE 6. PCI Vote (Percent "Yes") on Government and DC Members' Laws in Five Parliaments and by Approval Procedure[1]

	House Floor		Committee	
Parliament	Number of laws	Percent "Yes"	Number of laws	Percent "Yes"
First	20	30.0	76	69.7
Second	7	42.8	67	82.1
Third	11	72.7	61	90.2
Fourth	9	33.3	49	75.5
Fifth	9	33.3	21	57.1
All	56	41.1	274	77.4

[1]"Cazzola" sample

TABLE 7. PCI Vote (Percent "Yes") on Government and DC Members' Laws in Five Parliaments and by Proponent[1]

	Government		DC Members	
Parliament	Number of laws	Percent "Yes"	Number of laws	Percent "Yes"
First	90	60.0	6	83.3
Second	59	74.6	15	93.3
Third	47	89.4	25	84.0
Fourth	42	61.9	16	87.5
Fifth	28	50.0	2	50.0
All	266	67.7	64	85.9

[1]"Cazzola" sample

TABLE 8. PCI Vote (Percent "Yes") on Government and DC Members' Laws by Approval Procedure and Proponent[1]

	Government		DC Members		Total	
	Number of laws	Percent "Yes"	Number of laws	Percent "Yes"	Number of laws	Percent "Yes"
House floor	51	41.2	5	40.0	56	41.1
Committee	215	74.0	59	89.8	274	77.4
Total	266	67.7	64	85.9	330	71.2

[1]"Cazzola" sample

floor of the house, but within these institutional settings its attitudes toward government and parliamentary legislation do not seem to vary much.

It is worth pointing out, incidentally, that such behavior on the part of the Communist party is in keeping with another aspect of its legislative performance. As may be guessed, given the composite majorities behind most legislation, much of the legislation that does not clear Parliament—in fact, almost all of it—fails not because it is formally rejected, but simply because it does not complete debate before Parliament is dissolved.[21] This is the fate of fully 84.5 percent of the unapproved bills contained in the "Predieri-Mortara" sample, while only 2.4 percent were actually rejected.[22] A way of avoiding rejection is for the president of either branch of Parliament to assign a bill to one of his committees for final action, since the procedure makes approval more likely and faster. But it is in the power of one-fifth of the members of the committee or one-tenth of the members of the branch considering the bill to reverse the decision and have the bill referred to the full house. This is a power that the Communist party could easily use to clog the floor agenda and stalemate the majority, but that the party hardly uses. Thus the PCI not only supports a substantial part of majority legislation, it also, if

---

21. Until the 1971 reform of the Chamber of Deputies' standing rules, bills that failed to be enacted before the dissolution of Parliament could not be carried through in the next Parliament but had to be introduced as new bills.

22. Mortara, op. cit., p. 146. Similar figures from our sample are reported in Table 52, Chapter V. Failure without rejection is especially typical of Communist bills. For instance, only one of the 523 bills presented by the party during the 1958-63 Parliament was rejected, while fully 323 never initiated or completed debate, and 66 were approved. See Ferrari and Maisl, op. cit., p. 48.

by omission, helps legitimize committee processes favoring such legislation.

The reader should not draw hasty conclusions from the evidence just presented as to the reasons for the opposition's legislative behavior and as to its implications for Parliament's legislative performance. We are still merely assembling a broad quantitative sketch of legislative output and its sources, and much more must be said before its significance is established. The fact, for instance, that the PCI does not, as in principle it could, stalemate government and majority legislation should not come as a revelation or, by the same token, as proof that the marxist left has adopted an ameliorative role in legislative decision-making. All that can be said at this point is what the evidence tells us, namely, that government, Parliament, and opposition have each maintained an influence of their own and often concur in the formation of the legislative will. As to the quality of influence and concurrence, it is too soon to tell.

The same caution should finally be observed in assessing the last aspect of legislative performance, the use of amending powers. While the power to propose legislation points literally to initiative, assigned to and recognized for various actors, amending powers point to reaction and control, in response to somebody else's initiative. Both, however, can also be construed as resources that legislators employ in different ways to negotiate decisions and influence legislation. Hence, an analysis of amending behavior, no less than the analysis of the legislative initiative just conducted, can reveal the extent to which legislators may bargain their way through decisions and the extent to which final legislation carries the imprint of different hands. It may reveal the extent to which proponents may want or may have to adjust decisions, and the extent to which those who offer amendments are capable of affecting decisions.

As in the case of legislative initiative, the use of amending powers seems also to point toward a concurrence of government, Parliament, and opposition in the law-making process. This begins to emerge when comparing amending by different parties, on different types of bills, and in different decisional contexts, and is confirmed when comparisons are made with the legislatures of other countries. The "Cazzola" sample reveals that most amendments (57.5 percent) are introduced by members of the smaller parties. The Communists and Christian Democrats, with 18.4 and 24.1 percent respectively, take a smaller share, especially in consideration of their size. By far the largest number of proposed amendments, in absolute and relative terms, concerns "floor bills"—that is, bills enacted by the whole house—especially when they are initiated by the government (Tables 9 and 10). In fact, the single most common type of amendment (four out of ten) is one introduced by members of the smaller parties to a government bill that has been passed on the floor of the house. This distribution of amending behavior may not be surprising. There are a number of good reasons why floor bills are more likely to be exposed to revisions, the more so if they are also government bills, not the least of which is their importance and the publicity of the debate. Similarly, the smaller parties may find amending the least burdensome way, given their size and hence limited capacity for legislative initiative, to claim their legislative function.

But how successful are amendments and which are the least and most successful? In the aggregate, it is exactly those bills on which the amending efforts concentrate that seem most difficult

TABLE 9. Amendments Presented to Government and Private Bills by Bills' Approval Procedure, in Percentage of All Amendments[1]

Government Bills		Private Bills		Total	
Number	Percent	Number	Percent	Number	Percent
953	50.4	100	5.3	1053	55.7
560	29.6	277	14.7	837	44.3
1513	80.1	377	19.9	1890	100.0

[1]"Cazzola" sample. Each percent entry is a percentage of the grand total.

TABLE 10. Average Number of Amendments Presented per Bill Controlled for Bill's Proponent and Bill's Approval Procedure[1]

Government bills	Private bills	Total
18.3 (52)	12.5 (8)	17.55 (60)
1.9 (219)	3.5 (80)	2.8 (299)
4.2 (271)	4.3 (88)	5.3 (359)

[1]"Cazzola" sample. In parenthesis is the number of bills.

to revise, especially if amending is at the hands of the smaller parties (Table 11). Fourteen percent of the amendments to floor bills are approved, compared to 72 percent for committee bills. Government bills are, in general, rather difficult to amend, and clearly much more difficult than private bills (31 percent of amendments succeed against 74 percent for private bills), and the difficulty is greater on the floor of the house (10 percent success), the more so if the amendments come from the smaller parties (4.2 percent are passed).[23] Yet this is not the whole story. As the examples indicate, there are interaction effects at work among the various factors, and when they are fully explored, as in Table 11, it appears that Parliament—with its special decisional organization emphasizing committee legislation—does leave some room for smaller and opposition parties, even when it comes to government legislation.

Amendments by members of the majority party, as the table shows, have a relatively uniform and rather high rate of success, even for those types of bills that are, on the whole, most difficult to amend. For instance, 77 percent of majority amendments to government floor bills are approved, compared with 86 percent of all majority amendments. As to the other parties, it is true that their amendments are not nearly as successful as those of the majority. It is also true that their amendments to floor bills are mostly doomed to failure, especially if the bills are proposed by the government and the amendments are by the smaller parties. But rates of approval, especially for the latter two categories, increase quite drastically in the committees, and at times come close to the rates for Christian Democratic members. Even in the case of Communist amendments to government bills, which remain clearly less successful than similar amendments by other parties, rates of approval in the committees almost treble, from 11 to 29 percent. Very simply, with parties other than the Christian Democratic, amendments are much more likely to pass if the committees act as legislators. Compared with this procedural factor, whether amendments concern private or government bills is not quite as important. The case is clear with the smaller parties, where the overwhelming factor remains the site where

---

23. The cases are too few for a more detailed analysis, but whether a smaller party is a supporter of the government or has joined or left the government seems to make no clear difference for the success of its amendments.

TABLE 11. Percentage of Amendments Accepted of Total Voted on, Controlled for Party of Amendment, Bill's Proponent, and Bill's Approval Procedure[1]

	PCI			DC		
	Government bills	Private bills	Total	Government bills	Private bills	Total
Floor bills	10.9 (110)	34.2 (38)	16.9 (148)	76.7 (73)	100.0 (26)	82.8 (99)
Committee bills	29.3 (157)	41.9 (43)	32.0 (200)	83.1 (225)	92.4 (132)	86.6 (357)
Total	21.7 (267)	38.3 (81)	25.6 (348)	81.5 (298)	93.7 (158)	85.7 (456)

	Smaller Parties			Total		
	Government bills	Private bills	Total	Government bills	Private bills	Total
Floor bills	4.2 (770)	16.7 (36)	4.7 (806)	10.5 (953)	45.0 (100)	13.8 (1053)
Committee bills	77.0 (178)	93.1 (102)	82.9 (280)	66.1 (560)	84.8 (277)	72.3 (837)
Total	17.8 (948)	73.2 (138)	24.9 (1036)	31.1 (1513)	74.3 (377)	39.7 (1890)

[1] "Cazzola" sample. Figures in parentheses are the number of amendments voted; percentages are percent of amendments approved.

bills are approved. As to the PCI, the difference between government and private bills is substantial on the floor of the house, where the Communists' capacity to amend the former is limited, but is much narrower in the committees. Which is another way of saying that what sustains the Communists' ability to influence government legislation is still the fact that most of it is enacted in the committees.

In conclusion, the committees are not only the place where most legislation is enacted, but also the place where the smaller parties, and to some extent the PCI, have the best opportunity, through amending, to influence even government legislation.[24] This is not entirely to say that influence is strictly a function of the committees' legislative powers.[25] It is rather to recognize where, given the present decisional organization of Parliament, influence is more easily exercised.

At present, there is a last quantitative question that deserves to be answered, namely, to put it as narrowly and neutrally as possible, how many single amendments per "bit" of legislation does Parliament pass? It is clear that even if all amendments were passed, this might still mean very few amendments overall, as amending may be an activity in which Parliament seldom engages. The question is of particular importance when it concerns the opposition's attitude toward government legislation, and it can best be answered through a comparison with other legislatures. If we compare the behavior of the PCI alone to that of all opposition parties in selected Western democracies (Table 12), the Communists turn out to be neither more nor less likely to make use of amending powers than oppositions in other coun-

24. This does not mean that government bills are more heavily revised if they are also committee bills. Given the greater number of amendments proposed to floor bills, the average number of amendments passed per government bill is, as shown by the following, somewhat higher on the floor.

	PCI	DC	Others	Total
Floor	.23	1.08	.62	1.93
Committee	.21	.85	.63	1.69

The statement in the text means only that revisions by the PCI or the smaller parties are more easily *accepted* in the committees.

25. As I shall document in Chapter V, what affects the behavior of parties in the committees is not only the setting but the fact that the legislation assigned to them tends to be less controversial. Convergence, aided by the committee setting, tends to occur on less controversial legislation.

TABLE 12. Opposition Amendments to Government Bills, Proposed and Approved, in Selected Legislatures

	UK (1966-67)	Ireland (1965)	Sweden (1966)	France (1966)	Italy[1] (1948-71)
Amendments per article[2]	.232	.086	.206	.514	.196
Percentage of amendments passed	3.9	7.0	2.9	13.6	21.4
Amendments passed per article	.009	.006	.006	.070	.042

[1] Only PCI.

[2] As bills from the various countries differ considerably in length and number of articles, with Italy's being the shortest, and as longer bills attract more amendments, we have used articles rather than bills as a more appropriate basis for calculation. Figures for all countries except Italy have been calculated from data contained in Blondel, "Legislative Behaviour," op. cit., Tables 1 and 4. In the case of Sweden and France, the length of bills reported by Blondel refers also to private bills (2 out of 28 in the Swedish sample; 8 out of 49 in the French). Figures for Italy have been calculated from the "Cazzola" sample.

tries. Since their attempts to revise government legislation, however, are much more successful, the Italian Communists alone are able to revise more "bits" of government legislation than the pooled oppositions in every other country, excepting France. The French exception (which refers to the Assembly of the Fifth Republic) is an interesting one, since, as we shall see, it goes to the question of the quality of revisions and the weight of influence in general. Indeed, to know all the above is not quite to know how much influence is exercised through amending powers. Influence depends also on the importance of the revisions introduced, and in a way even more on the importance of legislation. I shall be able to deal with the matter in a few pages, and then only in an indirect fashion.

EFFECTIVENESS OR INEFFECTIVENESS?

Here I conclude my quantitative excursus through legislative output. In broad outlines, we have seen that the Italian Parliament produces a large amount of laws, often approved by great majorities that go as far as the Communist party. We have also seen that such support goes not only to private bills but also to government ones. We have seen that the principal legislator is the government, as most of what Parliament approves is initiated by the government, but we have also seen that some space is left to parliamentary initiative, even from the opposition. We have just seen that amending too leaves some room for smaller and opposition parties. Further, these characteristics, some of which have become stronger with the passing of time, make the Italian Parliament quite different from the legislatures of other representative democracies.

This may appear to be evidence of decisional effectiveness, in the basic sense in which we understood it in the first chapter: the capacity to sustain agreement among political contestants on a variety of issues and to compose differences in an equitable fashion. A huge legislative output, supported by composite majorities and originating from various legislative sources, may seem a fitting instance of how equity between competing claims and views is attained and how agreement is manipulated. In particular, the behavior of the Communist party fits well with this interpretation. The party concurs in many of the majority decisions, preserves a degree of legislative influence through its amending and initiative powers, and by its hands-off attitude on procedural matters allows Parliament to act. In fact, many analysts of the Italian parliamentary scene interpret the legislative behavior of the Communists and Christian Democrats as evidence that an implicit compact exists between the two which, whether planned or historically necessitated, gives Parliament a chance to endure and operate.

It would be, however, a considerable error to confuse conditions of survival with conditions of decisional effectiveness. To begin with, the fact that Parliament produces a large amount of legislation may mean that it drives itself hard; but, beyond this, what it works at is not yet clear. Quantity doesn't stand for quality, and "many laws" doesn't mean important laws and extensive agreement. A legislature may give the impression of action by keeping itself busy with a host of trivial and essentially undivisive matters on which a minimum common denominator can be found, while never addressing itself to the crucial issues that divide the political society. The defect is in seeing laws as decision units of equal value in the nature of the matters they regulate. Since they are not, a large legislative output might well appear as suspicious, on the principle that the more laws produced, the pettier their objects and the more superficial the agreement. The prodigious legislative output of the American Congress may be one thing, quite another the equally prodigious output of the Italian Parliament. Hence, a closer evaluation of the matters that Parliament regulates and of the way it regulates is in order. As the proverbial tip of the iceberg, what appears on the surface and is agreed upon may hide and, at the same time, suggest what remains "hidden," that is, the extent of disagreement.

Similarly, the mere fact that Parliament enacts its own laws, as well as those initiated by government, and that the opposition maintains some legally recognizable influence in both cases, is per se no more a sign of agreement among diverse legislative sources than if all the power of initiative were in the hands of the majority or the government. There may certainly be cases in which strict government control over the initiative constrains the oppositions, deprives them of any input, leaves little room for bargaining, and reduces Parliament to nothing but the sanctioning hand of the government. Or there may be cases in which the executive exercises all the initiative by default because parliamentary oppositions have no interest in playing the parliamentary game and in sharing legislative responsibilities. But these seem extreme cases. In genuine parliamentary democracies, government initiative, even when exclusive, usually incorporates, by a rule of anticipated reactions, concurrent solutions or at least solutions with which the oppositions can live, thus making recourse to parliamentary initiative less likely. This compensates for the legal restraints on parliamentary initiative and makes it in fact less urgent. In such a case, it can well be said that agreement, though not always visible, goes beyond the formal majority.

If, on the other hand, a legislature makes extensive use of the initiative, this too may mean many things from the viewpoint of agreement. It may mean that the rule of anticipated reaction has not operated or that, to use more familiar terminology, demands have not been aggregated sufficiently by government before entering Parliament, so that the legislature is left with the task of forging agreement where it did not exist, or is at any rate left free to fill the political vacuum. In turn, the outcome of this situation may not be successful, as Parliaments are cumbersome decisional bodies, and the weakness of previous agreements further complicates matters. The result is not the absence of legislation, but most likely the multiplication and fragmentation of its sources, and the confinement of agreement to marginal and therefore less divisive issues. In essence, this is a scenario of mutual weakness in which significant decision-making is thwarted. A less realistic variant is a scenario in which a cohesive government majority confronts in Parliament an opposition it can neither curb nor accommodate, so that whatever agreement is worked out within the majority is threatened and offset in Parliament. Parliamentary and government initiative still coexist, yet they work not only disjointedly but at cross-purposes. In essence, this is a most unenduring and transitory condition, as there is not even agreement sufficient to maintain equilibrium in a mutual political vacuum. Alternatively, the presence of parliamentary initiative may be a commonly engineered way of forming agreement through concurrent majorities, whereby parliamentary powers have been preserved to protect and institutionalize political diversity, and various forces genuinely if disjointedly share in the formation of the legislative will. As a last possibility, government may be too busy making important decisions outside Parliament to care what Parliament does. In this sort of sandbox theory of parliamentary initiative, Parliament is left free to make its own legislation, and indeed indulges in it, as the matters it can autonomously decide are only rarely of relevance. Agreement within Parliament may exist, but it does not concern the important issues.

The same considerations, with suitable adjustments, can be made when interpreting the evidence on Parliament's amending powers, since these are, like parliamentary initiative, a way of sharing in legislation. It should be clear, for instance, that amending is but one formalized way of influencing legislation, which may be used in lieu of informal negotiations accompanying the preparation and drafting of legislative proposals. Amendments, therefore, may not capture the whole extent to which decisions adjust competing views, and their absence may not signify lesser adjustment. In fact, to go one step further, the opposite may be argued, on the ground that the choice of one or another strategy of influence is not a matter of indifference, and that recourse to amendments signifies that previous adjustments have not been successful. Further, amendments, being a rather formal device, may be a rather ineffective and mechanical way of achieving adjustment, and a high rate of success may indicate centrifugal tendencies among parliamentary forces. For a researcher, the advantage of amendments as compared with informal negotiations is, of course, that the latter are not always visible and not easy to study in the aggregate. But in studying amendments, these cautionary notes should be heeded.

A somewhat related problem emerges when assessing the impact and success of amendments per se. I compared above the Communist party with oppositions in other countries, and I used a head-count criterion to conclude that Italian and French oppositions revise government legislation more often and more successfully than others. But "more often and more successfully," I warned, does not mean more thoroughly and significantly, as we don't know yet about the quality of the influence and the quality of what is influenced. Therefore, even if we take success to mean that the government accepts or at least does not resist amendments, we cannot consequently claim pervasive and significant concurrence between government and opposition. In fact, France exemplifies exactly the opposite case. Blondel points out that the relative ease with which opposition amendments are passed in the Assembly of the Fifth Republic appears to be nothing but a small concession to a weak legislature by a strong executive that makes most of its important decisions outside of it.[26] But the case of Italy, as it is known, is quite different. At least, compared with the French Assembly, the Italian Parliament is the site where most government decisions must be discussed and sanctioned. What does the high impact of amendments by an opposition like the PCI mean in this context? We will be put on the right track immediately if we stay with Blondel's analysis a bit longer. Blondel's point about the marginality of the French Assembly in decision-making is corroborated by an index which he and his co-authors constructed to compare the "importance" of legislative outputs in various countries, where importance refers to the number of people affected by a bill, the number of distributed resources, and the amount of resource alteration. Blondel reports that French bills score clearly the lowest on the index. If we adapt and apply the same index to Italy (Table 13), we find that legislation by the Italian government scores even

26. Blondel et al., op. cit., pp. 76-77, 79, and 84.

TABLE 13. Importance of Legislation in Selected Countries[1]

	UK	Ireland	Sweden	France	India	Italy
Number of bills	49	28	28	49	15	129
Average importance	3.2	3.1	2.1	1.3	3.1	.99
Average number of articles	19	35	16	7	15	5

[1] Eight of the 49 French bills and 2 of the 28 Swedish bills are private bills. Data for Italy are from the "Di Palma" sample, from which approved government proposals were taken.

lower than France's.[27] And the consequence is that—in indirect answer to the question raised at the end of the previous section—amendments by the PCI are themselves very likely to be on limited matters.

But the consequence is now much less interesting than the finding. The point of difference between the two countries is clear. To exaggerate and bring out the contrast, in France

27. Blondel et al., ibid., intend *important* to mean the extent to which bills "appear to be designed to affect the community and constitute elements of departure from the current situation" (p. 73). They use four criteria for their index: (1) How many people are affected by the bills; (2) How large is the amount of resources they distribute; (3) How drastically present resource distributions are altered; and (4) How long bills are. They assign a maximum of 10 points per bill, 2 or 3 per criterion, depending on the criterion. No other information on how the scoring was done, however, is supplied in the paper or is otherwise available. I decided, nevertheless, to try the comparison. To stack the cards against me, I eliminated the last criterion, knowing already that Italian laws are shorter. I further allocated 0 to 3 points for each remaining criterion, on the assumption that a somewhat wider range would have inflated the Italian scores. However, it was impossible to second-guess how the authors actually scored each bill on these criteria. I therefore asked eleven Italian judges, mostly law students, to score the bills on intuitive grounds, but did not inform them of the purpose of the test. The procedure should again favor inflating the scores toward the mean, as a scorer instructed to use intuitive grounds tends to rely on internal comparisons with the overall legislative production. As it turned out, the unreliability of the procedure was offset by the fact that the great majority of bills appeared at their face value to be of very limited importance. Interscorer reliability for each of the three index-criteria was almost perfect (.93, .86, .84, respectively). The coefficients were calculated through an extension of the Spearman-Brown split-half reliability formula

$$\text{(Reliability} = \frac{11r}{1 + (11-1)r})$$

in which "11" is the number of judges and "r" is the mean of paired interscorer r's for the specific criterion.

government decides literally elsewhere; in Italy, it decides largely through Parliament. If important decisions are taken, most of them should constitutionally show up in Parliament.[28] And if the government does not take them, there is no need to belabor the point to show that Parliament doesn't either. In terms of the number of people affected, number of resources distributed, and amount of alteration in resources, we find that laws initiated by members of Parliament, with an average of .91 on the index, are hardly different from government laws. In fact, what is still really surprising is that the former are not clearly lower than the latter. In sum, legislative initiative in Italy now shows the following characteristics: it is very abundant; it is shared, if unequally, by government and parliamentary forces; it is supported by concurrent majorities; but it concerns relatively limited matters. The latter characteristic in a way explains the others. I have contended that legislation concerns mostly limited matters for the simple reason that Parliament cannot form the necessary agreement on the important ones. But the proof is not yet with us.[29] In the next section the contention will first have to pass two serious objections.[30] Only as the objections are cleared and the quality of legislation is more closely scrutinized will the case for disagreement acquire strength.

RESOURCES, INCREMENTALISM, AND *LEGGINE*

The first objection stems from a series of recent studies of state and local policy output in the United States, which tend to show that the extent of the areas impacted by policies, the extent of the resources allocated, and the extent of the impact have little to do with political and institutional variables, and much more with the

---

28. I have indicated in the opening chapter and I will show in the closing chapter that there is a realm of important decisions that escapes Parliament. But in a parliamentary system in which Parliament as a matter of fact still occupies a large space this is not sufficient to explain the limited nature of formal legislation.

29. This is so also in view of the tentative way in which the index of legislative importance for Italy was built and compared with Blondel's.

30. The two objections are briefly but insightfully considered in Robert Salisbury, "The Analysis of Public Policy: A Search for Theories and Roles," in Austin Ranney, ed., *Political Science and Public Policy* (Chicago: Markham, 1968), pp. 163-164. I am greatly indebted to this paper for some of the insights, to be found in the rest of the chapter, on the way in which decisional capabilities affect type and content of decisions.

poverty or abundance of local resources.[31] In simple words, more societal resources available means more policies and greater impact. Transferred to our case, this literature may lead to speculation that the detailed and minor nature of Italian legislation has little to do with defects in the Italian Parliament, in its political class, in decisional and influence structures, and in sum little to do with the incapacity of Parliament to form agreement on the important issues. It may just have to do with a cluster long fallen into disrepute, not least because it justifies political stagnation; i.e., the shortage of national resources—gross and per capita national product, urbanization, social mobility, or any other aspect of modernity likely to increase system capabilities—as well as the difficulty of mobilizing and linking resources to each other.

But the objection loses plausibility because it cannot explain why Italy's decisional outputs differ as they do from those of the other countries examined in Table 13. While Italy's legislation is, on the average, less important than that of all the other countries, it cannot be claimed by any stretch of the imagination that this is because its system resources are so inferior to those of India and Ireland or, for that matter, to those of England, France, and Sweden.[32] One probable reason for this lack of fit is that, as Robert Salisbury notes, studies linking American local policy outputs to system resources take as their dependent variable not the average amount of expenditures and outputs of each decision but the *aggregate* amount of all decisions. This means that in the aggregate a rich country can outlay and distribute considerable resources, and yet the type of policies usually adopted may be such that each policy distributes little and operates at a low level

---

31. Richard Dawson and James Robinson, "Inter-Party Competition, Economic Variables, and Welfare Policies in the American States," *Journal of Politics* 25 (1963), pp. 265-289; Richard Hofferbert, "The Relation between Public Policy and Some Structural and Environmental Variables in the American States," *American Political Science Review* 60 (1966), pp. 73-82; Phillips Cutright, "Political Structure, Economic Development, and National Social Security Programs," *American Journal of Sociology* 70 (1965), pp. 537-550; Thomas Dye, *Politics, Economics, and the Public: Policy Outcomes in the American States* (Chicago: Rand McNally, 1966); Ira Sharkansky, "Economic and Political Correlates of State Government Expenditures: General Tendencies and Deviant Cases," *Midwest Journal of Political Science* 11 (1967), pp. 173-192.

32. Also very important is the fact that while obviously the country's resources have grown tremendously since the war, we found no clear increasing trend in the average importance of legislation over the five Parliaments.

of aggregation. In fact, one consistent criticism of the politics of expenditure in Italy is exactly that individual policies are highly fragmented and that enormous resources are merrily wasted to satisfy a myriad of highly sectorial and parochial demands. In sum, if the wealth of system resources can explain alone how much is spent and distributed, it cannot explain how resources are distributed and in response to whose claims.[33] Hence I can assert with some confidence that differences between Italy and the other countries in the importance of single legislative decisions are not due to variance in system resources, because the latter have little to do with the weight of single policies.

If the reader is not convinced by this reason for the lack of fit, he may consider another: The importance of system resources for decisional outputs varies with the level of resources, in the sense that, in countries that have reached a rather high level (Italy and most Western countries), the latter are no longer paramount in explaining policies, and other factors of otherwise limited importance step in.[34] Whichever argument suits the reader better, the fact remains that the case of Italy's decisional outputs cannot be explained by the country's resources. By the process of elimination, the notion that the case is political acquires some strength.

Similar arguments will be used now to counter the second objection. This is the objection of "incrementalism," according to which policies are adopted by small adjustments upon previous policies.[35] It would follow from it, as from the previous objection, that political factors are of little use in explaining the importance

33. Three empirical analyses showing the importance of political variables, alone or in combination with resource variables, and variation with policy areas are Ira Sharkansky and Richard Hofferbert, "Dimensions of State Politics, Economics, and Public Policy," *American Political Science Review* 63 (1969), pp. 867-879; Brian Fry and Richard Winters, "The Politics of Redistribution," *American Political Science Review* 64 (1970), pp. 508-522; Virginia Gray, "Innovation in the States: A Diffusion Study," *American Political Science Review* 67 (1973), pp. 1174-1185.

34. Guy Peters has collected evidence to show that the level of welfare expenditures in democratic countries is at first affected by the amount of resources available to them, but that, as their resource basis expands, differences among countries are more appropriately accounted for by political factors. Guy Peters, "The Development of Social Policy in France, Sweden, and the United Kingdom: 1850-1965," in Martin O. Heisler, ed., *Politics in Europe* (New York: McKay, 1974), pp. 257-292.

35. Otto Davis, M.A.H. Dempster, and Aaron Wildavsky, "A Theory of the Budgetary Process," *American Political Science Review* 60 (1966), pp. 529-548; Ira Sharkansky, *Spending in the American States* (Chicago: Rand McNally, 1968).

of legislation. In fact, according to this objection, legislation would always tend to be of limited importance in terms of the extent and intensity of its impact, and political factors would have little room to maneuver. Thus, the limited importance of Italy's legislation should not be taken to signify ineffectiveness, unless the term is expanded to the point of meaninglessness. The objection, however, falls because, if incrementalism is largely a constant—and there is solid evidence for it—it cannot explain why Italy appears more "incremental" than other countries.

It is tempting to find the explanation by combining the two objections in one very appealing hypothesis: that within a common propensity toward incrementalism countries exemplify variations that are best accounted for by the level of their societal resources. But once resources are joined with incrementalism, their role acquires a new and quite different twist such that, again, it does not seem intuitive why Italy's resources should make its policies more "incremental."

Presumably incrementalism is not only the inescapable result of decisional constants, but also, as it has been asserted, a necessity-made-virtue, whereby change is best pursued through decisions that are marginal in scope and adjustive of many demands.[36] In this sense, a large number of relatively "unimportant" decisions are likely to effect more change for more people than fewer "important" ones. This is not a mechanical and additive claim, but a claim that each incremental decision has spillover and multiplier effects triggering other decisions and expanding outcomes beyond immediate impact. If this be the case, incrementalism should be most appropriate as a strategy of change—and perhaps also most likely—in countries with considerable, diversified, interdependent, and easily mobilizable resources. One reason is that, where resources are plentiful and interdependent, even decisions that marginally readjust them are likely to trigger further adjustments and substantial final changes. Another is that, whatever their multiplier effect, incremental decisions are more likely to be requested by the proliferating groups and interests that accompany the expansion of resources. If we now take the matter from the other end, it then seems that incrementalism should be discouraged in countries with scarce and unmo-

36. David Braybrooke and Charles Lindblom, *A Strategy of Decision* (New York: Free Press, 1963); Charles Lindblom, *The Intelligence of Democracy* (New York: Free Press, 1965).

bilizable resources, in the sense that small decisions would not produce a spillover, would not trigger larger changes, and would essentially disperse and intolerably waste resources. Such countries should try to offset the otherwise limited overall impact of their policies by concentrating on few decisions with multiplier potentials.

But where, along this continuum of incrementalism, should Italy belong? Certainly not where it is found, at the lowest end. Italy's resources are not so special as to recommend, on rational grounds, extreme incrementalism as the most appropriate approach to change. In sum, the two objections still leave us with the conviction that the case of Italy cannot be adequately explained by levels of resources or by a universal if locally extreme propensity to take decisions in small doses, and is not at all a case of incrementalism, but one of political ineffectiveness.

Under incrementalism, decision-makers, to trigger change, *do not need* and are not pressured to effect substantial reallocation of resources. Incrementalism, the very word, implies that decisions, no matter how limited, produce a degree of gain and amelioration. In Italy—and here is the basic difference—decision-makers are often pressured by large groups to pursue but *cannot afford* substantial reallocations, in the sense that, by the definition of ineffectiveness, they cannot find the necessary agreement. Reallocations would be perceived as threatening aggregate conflicting interests. In other words, the scenario is not one in which decision-makers can afford to allocate resources according to reasonably constrained, ameliorative, cost-benefit guesses, but one in which they cannot afford (but they may not avoid either) confrontation over policies. And the rule in this scenario is that, if policies and choices create problems, decision-makers will displace them in favor of administration. That is, a few things intimate themselves as the sort of things the Italian Parliament should invest most of its energies in, without in the short range hurting anybody. It can keep up the country's huge administrative machinery, and it can respond to benefit demands by special groups as the need arises, the better so if the groups are organized but not so large as to appear a threat to others. These are essentially "due" housekeeping chores, implying reaction and conservation more often than initiative and change, but once adopted they have a way of imposing themselves on both government and opposition.

Support for these points can be teased out of the political debate surrounding Parliament and its legislative activities, as well as out of a further qualitative analysis of legislative output. Italian politicians and political analysts have a simple and effective way of labeling the inflated but essentially minor legislative output that their Parliament mostly produces. They call them *leggine*, or small laws. And there is hardly an article, study, debate, or round table on the "disfunctions of Parliament" that does not bemoan the inflation of *leggine*, point to it as the best evidence of the expanding crisis of representative institutions, and argue about the remedies.[37] Hardly another aspect of parliamentary behavior, except for the role of the Communists in Parliament, attracts the attention of parliamentary analysts as much. Nor are politicians themselves less sanguine about it. Despite the fact that our interview schedule did not mention *leggine*, few respondents failed to volunteer extensive remarks on the subject. Further, politicians may disagree on the immediate causes and remedies of *leggine*, but they are basically unanimous in condemning them in one form or another and in arguing that Parliament produces far too many of them.

For all the agreement, however, it is less easy to say offhand what, in the opinion of the insiders, *leggine* are and why they are bemoaned. The term is subjective and evaluative, rather than legal and analytical. In point of law, there is no such formal category either in legislation or in doctrine. Analytically, it does not always receive refinement, as it is often used to gratify personal convictions. Even its scholarly usage is often and inescapably marred by serious definitional problems.[38] At best, it is a composite concept, receiving different meanings from different sources. In one meaning, for instance, *leggine* seems to be used simply as a derogatory term for incremental legislation. While the country needs basic structural reforms to adapt its social institutions to a rapidly expanding economy and to increasing rates of

---

37. Good examples can be found in Leopoldo Piccardi, Norberto Bobbio, and Ferruccio Parri, *La Sinistra davanti alla Crisi del Parlamento* (Milano: Giuffrè, 1967).

38. See for these difficulties Mortara, op. cit., pp. 93-95; Predieri, "La Produzione Legislativa," op. cit., pp. 228-229.

social mobilization, in reality—thus goes the argument—the country is left to its own devices as neither government nor Parliament enacts the required "great laws," which are laws that, by the extent and the importance of the sector they affect and the large amount of resources they mobilize, substantially alter the previous equilibrium and change society. *Leggine*, on the other hand, affect marginal changes in limited sectors of society, and hence remain inconsequential. A good example of this meaning comes from the interview with a Christian Democratic member of the Chamber of Deputies.

> Of course we need the *Riforme*, and we need them in the seventies. We owe them to our voters, because we are a popular party, the largest party, the party of government. . . . You can teach me, the South, the reform of the penal code, university reform, the problem of housing, health, education, every citizen knows what our country needs. These are in sum the great reforms of which we have been talking for years. All the rest does not count. . . . [It] has to do with a legislation of detail—the *leggine*—which basically does not change . . . the social framework and which will have to be delegated to the regions, local government . . . the very civil service. With this I am not suggesting that we should have no *leggine*. It is understood that many of them may even be deleterious . . . but there are many others that are necessary and deserve to be passed. But it is not with them that we qualify the work of a modern Parliament. (DC 51)

The respondent may be quite right in advocating more comprehensive reforms for his country, and delegation of much legislation to lesser bodies. This is not the point. But his analysis of everyday legislation does not indicate defects more serious than incrementalism. Further questioning did not help dispel the impression:

> Of course many *leggine* contribute to changing society in some fashion. That is why we make them. But it cannot be in this way that we build a newer and more dynamic society. (DC 51)

Hardly more helpful was the answer of a Socialist deputy, unusually prone, by the astringent standards of Italian politicians, to sportive imagery.

> The *leggine*, it is very simple. It is like using the Queen Mary for coastal navigation without ever venturing on the open seas. Or like a [soccer] player . . . who dribbles in midfield and never scores. (PSI 30)

And that was that. But it would be wrong to read the debate on *leggine* as strictly an ideological or normative one on the appropriateness of incremental approaches in the Italian situation. While the line is not always easy to draw, and the term suffers from contaminations that frustrate analytical use, the literature and the interview answers on *leggine* also reveal the more important view, although never stated in such "Anglo-Saxon" terms, that much legislation is not even incremental, that it is designed to maintain the machinery of administration or to distribute narrow benefits, and that its existence depends on the extreme fragmentation of political forces in Parliament and their inability to come together.[39]

A Socialist senator:

> Our party doesn't make a question of grandiose reforms. For years Nenni [the senior statesman of the party] has preached a "politics of things" ... concrete policies. But even these need a firm commitment of the majority [party]. ... But a party like the DC, which is a party so divided in factions and minifactions, can't even afford this luxury. ... Take the bureaucracy ... the unchallenged domain of the DC. For how many years has the DC promised a reform of the civil service? We even have a Minister for Bureaucratic Reform. ... Well, we have today the most overgrown and most inefficient civil service in the civilized world. We are not even able to cut its red tape, its oppressive ... legalism. And all these are small things that cost nothing. Instead, Parliament continues to pass *leggine* upon *leggine* as they come, tailor-made for this or that special category of civil servants; to add ... fringe benefits ... upon fringe benefits. ... I am not saying that our civil servants are overpaid, because the great majority is not. ... But, in this way, we waste the public money without results, while the government makes itself an accomplice of the interests of the [higher civil servants]. ... This has nothing to do with the "welfare state" of the English or Scandinavian type; it is always the usual old story of the benefactor state. (PSI 13)

A DC deputy:

> But the PCI, too, uses Parliament to benefit its own clienteles. These are things that cannot be hidden. ... We are the first to advocate a delegation of *leggine* to other public bodies, but it is the PCI that

---

39. In addition to Piccardi, Bobbio, and Parri cited above, see for various articles and notes by constitutionalists, social scientists, and politicians, the following edited volumes: *Processo allo Stato*, op. cit., Parts I and II; Istituto per la Documentazione e gli Studi Legislativi (a cura di), *Indagine sulla Funzionalità del Parlamento* (Milano: Giuffrè, 1969), Vol. 2; Istituto Antonio Gramsci (a cura di), *La Riforma dello Stato* (Roma: Editori Riuniti, 1968).

opposes it because, naturally, it is a very powerful tool of electoral clientelism. It isn't so much that the PCI, in this way, keeps a foot in the door of Government... because the things you can do with *leggine* are little things.... Nevertheless, this attitude has very grave consequences for our Parliament... because, in this way, Parliament is transformed into an administrator, and, to tell the truth, a very improvident administrator. In sum... Parliament is becoming more and more unable to exercise its traditional function of sovereign legislator.... This is what causes today's crisis in our parliamentary institutions. Or, if we want to look at greater distance, let us well say that the prime cause... is the lack of cohesion among the democratic forces. But let us not say here that the fault is our party's. For years we have governed, with high sense of duty,... together with the other democratic parties, but, unfortunately, the same cannot always be said of some of our friends. Too often they have been more concerned with criticizing us, as the principal party of the coalition, than with holding together the unity of the majority.... Then, naturally, much legislation becomes trivial and corrupt, and doesn't take into account the real exigencies of the country. (DC 3)

A PCI senator and leader of the party:

It is not the *leggine* that cause the crisis of Parliament.... Certainly our party recognizes the problem. As you have learned as a law student, the task of Parliament is to legislate, the task of the executive and the bureaucracy is to apply [the laws] and to answer for them to Parliament. In reality, instead, the parts have inverted themselves... and Parliament has become an administrative agency.... But let us be wary of the treatment. One doesn't recover from the flu by lowering the fever. Things would get worse if we were to delegate legislation even further... [to] the bureaucracy. We would lose what little control we have on it, and the character of our legislation would not improve at all. You can't make intelligent legislation without the contribution of the Communists. This is what the leadership of the DC... has still failed to recognize, and it is this that makes our legislation so parochial and dispersive. As to depriving... Parliament of its powers to turn them to the bureaucracy, it is clear what would happen. It happens that the DC leadership would continue to do within it what it tries to do in Parliament. But at least here the democratic forces can control it.... [It would] keep unaltered the bureaucratic machinery... favor the narrowest corporate interests... postpone the needed social and economic reforms, [all of this against] the demands of the country's great productive categories. (PCI 39)

The quotes may still impress a jaded reader as mere ideology on the merits of different parties and different legislative output, revealing little of the actual status of Italian legislation. But beyond their obvious partisanship there is a surprising degree of coincidence in these analyses, in their view of legislation, its defects, and its general causes. Legislation is consistently presented as minimal and unproductive, not just because it does not address itself to large social categories and to advocated reforms, but because it is consistently and further degraded by centrifugal forces. Little does it matter that no party, as expected, is willing to take the blame for it. What counts is that the reported syndrome remains the same. I am therefore inclined to take the responses not just as partisan views but as reliable information. After all, these are legislators and should know what they produce.

ITALIAN LEGISLATION: EFFECTS AND LEVEL OF AGGREGATION

For those who remain skeptical as to the nature of Italian legislation, a look at the major types of legislation considered by Parliament should complement well the words of those who enact them. If we are in the right so far, legislation should, in fact, have the following characteristics:

1. It should distribute benefits to the subjects to which it is immediately addressed. It should not deprive them of benefits. The reader appreciates that legislation may, in fact, be directly depriving. An increase in taxation, while possibly anti-inflationary, is objectively and immediately depriving for bona-fide taxpayers. The imposition of import quotas negatively affects importers. The request that university professors reside where they teach may please, at least in Italy, few of those who teach in small university towns. But if depriving policies are painful for any decisional system to adopt, they should be especially painful when it comes to ineffective ones. The reason is the policies' unpopularity with the groups immediately affected, which will tend to divide legislators further and to foster avoidance of responsibility. By the same token, legislation should have no negative consequences for outsiders either, that is, for those whom legislation may indirectly affect. But how can an ineffective Parliament produce legislation that benefits immediate recipients without hurting others? The double feat is most likely achieved by an extreme disaggregation of the benefits, both

internal and external, and for two reasons. First, benefits bestowed on large social categories or complex organizations are a mixed blessing, since they may involve internal conflict as to their appropriate distribution. Second, the larger the category affected by the benefits, the more likely that the legislation will be perceived as externally depriving. Extreme disaggregation, however, has one side cost. If it avoids external deprivation, it also produces narrow or no external benefits. In sum, legislation under the hypothesis should be beneficial for its immediate subjects but externally neutral.

2. In the light of the above, legislation should concern small and homogeneous group interests, especially if they are of a middling character, such as to make the groups politically acceptable to most parties.

3. Since the largest and the best organized group in society is the bureaucracy and since, given the extreme compartmentalization of its legal roles, it is the most capable of disaggregating its demands, most legislation should concern its sectorial benefits and regulation.

4. Conversely, legislation should be scarce whenever it cannot be easily disaggregated to the point where outsiders are not hurt *and* where specific organized interests to benefit from it are identified. This is likely to occur with constitutional or aggregate economic issues.[40]

I have tested the propositions by means of our sample of legislative proposals, first used in Table 13. The advantage of considering proposals and their originators, rather than only enacted laws is to show, as will briefly appear, what may be called anticipatory socialization: It is not so much that Parliament rejects legislation that does not fall in the above categories, as it is that Parliament is simply rarely asked to consider it, even by the opposition.

The first proposition is the most difficult to test, given the fact that no objective criteria for judging whether legislation is bene-

40. An important theoretical exploration of how types of policies (distributive, redistributive, regulatory) relate to political processes and relations between political actors can be found in Theodore Lowi, "American Business, Public Policy, Case-Studies, and Political Theory," *World Politics* 16 (1963-1964), pp. 677-715. See especially Lowi's notion that distributive low-aggregation policies avoid mutual interference, and therefore avoid conflict and do not require compromise (pp. 692-693). See also on the point E.E. Schattschneider, *Politics, Pressures and the Tariff* (Englewood Cliffs: Prentice-Hall, 1935).

ficial or depriving can be established, especially when it comes to its "external" effects. Also, much legislation does not so much deal with the explicit allocation of material or symbolic resources as with the regulation of collective behavior, whose "benefit" value escapes assessment. It was necessary, therefore, to employ a panel of judges. Eleven Italian judges (mostly law students) were used.[41] They were instructed to classify the proposals according to whether they had beneficial, mixed, or depriving effects on their immediate subjects. They were also asked to say whether or not the proposals had consequences for other than the immediate subjects, and whether these, too, were beneficial, mixed, or depriving. They were further alerted to the need to classify even proposals that concerned the legal status of institutions or the legal definition of procedures and behavior. Only those proposals were preserved on which seven or eight of the eleven judges—depending, as indicated in the Appendix, on the specific classification—finally agreed. The others (about 15 percent of the total, equally distributed between government and parliamentary proposals) were submitted to two other judges to see if they differed from the rest and in what way.

The analysis in Tables 14 and 15 confirms our expectations. Both government and parliamentary proposals are overwhelmingly of the direct beneficial type, but more than half are judged to have no external consequences and very few to have detrimental or mixed external consequences. There still remain a good and, perhaps, unexpected number of proposals with beneficial external consequences, but an analysis of their content gives

TABLE 14. Effects of Government Projects, As Percentage of All Government Projects

| | OTHERS | | | | |
	Beneficial	Neutral	Mixed	Depriving	Total
SELF Beneficial	20.3 (35)	47.1 (81)	8.7 (15)	4.1 (7)	80.2 (138)
Nonbeneficial[1]	4.7 (8)	4.1 (7)	--	11.0 (19)	19.8 (34)
Total	25.0 (43)	51.2 (88)	8.7 (15)	15.1 (26)	100.0 (172)

Note: Numbers in parentheses are raw figures from which percentages are calculated.
[1]Contains also projects with "mixed" effects, as too few fell into the class.

41. See Appendix for criteria of classification.

TABLE 15. Effects of Parliamentary Projects, As Percentage of All Parliamentary Projects

		OTHERS				
		Beneficial	Neutral	Mixed	Depriving	Total
SELF	Beneficial	24.6 (41)	53.9 (90)	7.8 (13)	1.8 (3)	88.0 (147)
	Nonbeneficial[1]	3.6 (6)	7.2 (12)	1.2 (2)	--	12.0 (20)
	Total	28.1 (47)	61.1 (102)	9.0 (15)	1.8 (3)	100.0 (167)

[1] Contains also projects with "mixed" effects, as too few fell into the class.

some interesting answers to the puzzle. Of the *government* bills producing external benefits, about four out of ten are bills falling in the category almost by definition. That is, they are general regulatory laws addressed not to special classes of citizens but to all citizens likely to engage in a given behavior (hence, incidentally, the distinction between direct and external consequences was impossible). Few of them, however, involve some major regulatory change, such as the legislative enforcement of a principle embodied in the Constitution or the reform of a body of norms of the civil or penal code. Mostly they involve partial modifications of isolated regulatory norms. The remaining 60 percent are harder to classify, but they are, by and large, either proposals for expenditures by government agencies (none above three million dollars), or proposals regulating special sectors of the civil service and judged to be beneficial to the sectors' clienteles. As to the *parliamentary* proposals with external beneficial effects, about one-third belong to the latter category, and the rest are mostly either expenditures or general regulatory laws, with the same characteristics as above.

In sum, it can be said that, even when proposals are judged to have external benefits, these seem to have limited import, either in terms of size of the categories they affect or in terms of the impact. In a way, it is the very size of the external benefits that makes them an unmixed blessing. They marginally benefit a few or even many, but, in so doing, they do not touch other interests. That external benefits are often limited also appears from the unclassified proposals. Their two judges could not detect anything that made them different from the image the judges had of normal legislative production. But they did not know that in seven out of ten cases disagreement among the original judges was on whether the proposals had externally neutral or beneficial effect, i.e. that the two modes in the classification were "neutral" and "beneficial." The reason is simply that these were typically bills regulating or benefiting special civil service categories, public agencies, or related interest groups; but their level of aggregation was low enough so that the judges, while implicitly agreeing that they had no externally depriving consequences, could not quite see favorable effects either.

But what about the proposals with mixed or depriving external consequences? They are mostly of the fiscal variety, or they directly regulate/benefit somewhat larger social categories than the other proposals. At times, they impose fees, duties, and the like in favor of the government or a branch of it and appear as depriving for the whole community or parts of it. At times, they recognize rights for special categories that impose reciprocal restrictions on others, as in the extension of copyright laws. Interestingly, only in few cases are their external consequences far-reaching, as with the recognition of extensive workers' rights within the plant or with the enforcement of some broad constitutional principle (regional decentralization, for example), both staunchly opposed by some parties. It would have been advantageous—were it not for "depriving" restrictions on research funds—to have more proposals with mixed or depriving consequences in the sample, so as to examine their exact nature and distribution. Clearly the class is a heterogeneous one in which, next to some intimations of broader social reform, are found many proposals of a more limited redistributive nature. But here is exactly the strength of the finding: despite the fact that the proposals in the class have, by and large, manageable redistributive implications, probably not unlike most proposals of the same class in other political systems, our sample catches few of them. The reason we find so few is that the overwhelming majority of legislation prefers to devote itself to the distribution of narrow benefits.

Finally, one point in the evidence deserves emphasis: government and private bills essentially cover the same categories and duplicate each other, even though—given the government's responsibilities and somewhat greater aggregative capacity—the latter has an edge on redistributive legislation.

I have anticipated throughout the discussion of the two tables that, as stated in the second proposition, much legislation is narrowly sectorial, and that this is what accounts for the legislation's special pattern of immediate benefits and avoidance of wider deprivations. The evidence is laid out in Tables 16 and 17. After having terminated the assessment of the proposals' effects, the eleven judges were asked to divide the proposals according to whether the immediate subject was the national community, a composite and large sector of it, organized around broad but recognizable activities and institutions, or smaller and more homogeneous groups, involved in unique and specialized activities and institutions.[42] As it appears in Table 16, government proposals are more aggregative than parliamentary ones, but the

TABLE 16. Level of Aggregation of Government and Parliamentary Projects, in Percentage and Absolute Numbers

	National	Sectional	Microsectional	Total
Government	28.0 (56)	26.5 (53)	45.5 (91)	100.0 (200)
Parliamentary	22.5 (45)	21.0 (42)	56.5 (113)	100.0 (200)

TABLE 17. Effects of National/Sectional and Microsectional Projects, in Percentage and Absolute Numbers[1]

National/Sectional		OTHERS		
	Beneficial	Neutral	Mixed Depriving	Total
SELF Beneficial	33.1 (59)	29.8 (53)	16.3 (29)	79.2 (141)
SELF Nonbeneficial	5.6 (10)	5.6 (10)	9.6 (17)	20.8 (37)
Total	38.8 (69)	35.4 (63)	25.8 (46)	100.0 (178)

Microsectional		OTHERS		
	Beneficial	Neutral	Mixed Depriving	Total
SELF Beneficial	10.6 (17)	73.3 (118)	5.6 (9)	89.4 (144)
SELF Nonbeneficial	2.5 (4)	5.6 (9)	2.5 (4)	10.6 (17)
Total	13.0 (21)	78.9 (127)	8.1 (13)	100.0 (161)

[1] Entries are absolute numbers and percentages of national/sectional and microsectional projects falling within each class of effect.

42. See Appendix for criteria of classification.

differences are small and, in both cases, approximately half of the proposals are of the microsectional kind; that is, they concern narrowly specialized groups and institutions with a limited and homogeneous membership. In turn (Table 17), microsectional proposals have beneficial effects on their immediate subjects but are overwhelmingly without external consequences.

But something interesting and rather unexpected emerges from the table. The original proposition was that, by disaggregating legislation, Parliament and government would avoid getting entangled in broadly redistributive policies, around which agreement is difficult to form and maintain. The table does show that disaggregated proposals more consistently avoid redistributive effects, but it does not seem to show that redistribution is *typical* of national and sectional proposals. It is true that external consequences are more often produced by proposals that are national or sectional in scope. But this still leaves more than one-third with no external effects. Further, approximately another 40 percent is judged to have external beneficial effects but, as it will be recalled from the discussion of Tables 14 and 15, these benefits seem of a limited kind, designed to please larger constituencies marginally without disturbing the existing allocation of resources and symbols. Only the remaining quarter, at best, seems to involve policies with more serious redistributive and mixed effects.

One good reason for this distribution of effects among more largely aggregative legislation is revealed if we now move to the third proposition; namely, that a legislature and a government unable to aggregate would devote much of their energies to civil service propositions, since these are the most disaggregable and the civil service is a most natural and most powerful client of politicians. In fact, our eleven judges evaluated exactly 37 percent of all proposals, about equally divided between government and Parliament, as having to do either with the granting of financial and career benefits to members of the civil service or with the internal regulation of civil service procedures and the legal status of its branches and offices.[43] This 37 percent *does not include* budgetary allocations other than for wage and fringe-benefit improvements, nor does it include proposals aimed at

---

43. 25.7 percent of government proposals and 32.4 percent of parliamentary proposals in the "Predieri-Mortara" sample deal with the legal, career, and financial status of state and local government employees. See Mortara, op. cit., p. 142, Table IV-13.

creating new administrative units or new competences and realms of activity. The category, in other words, is mostly concerned with the upkeep of the administrative machinery, the preservation of the interests and prerogatives of its members, and only in smaller part with broader matters of branch reorganization. That is why (Table 18) its scope is typically microsectional, more so than the rest of legislation. These proposals are more likely to concern, let us say, librarians employed by the state than retrieval systems for state documents; more likely to concern national archives' librarians than all librarians; more likely to concern the computation of their pension levels at retirement than their entire wage and fringe-benefit package. In turn, as it can be seen from Table 19, these proposals are also and predominantly without external consequences, much more so than the rest of legislation.

Interestingly, however, the lack of an external impact is only in part a function of the low level of aggregation, since even civil service legislation of a broader sectional kind lacks this impact.[44]

TABLE 18. Level of Aggregation of Proposals Regulating or Benefiting the Civil Service, in Percentage and Absolute Numbers

National/Sectional	Microsectional	Total
37.8 (56)	62.2 (92)	100.0 (148)

TABLE 19. External Effects of Proposals Concerning the Civil Service, by Level of Aggregation in Percentage and Absolute Numbers

	Beneficial	Neutral	Mixed Depriving	Total
National/Sectional	21.3 (10)	72.3 (34)	6.4 (3)	100.0 (47)
Microsectional	8.2 (6)	86.3 (63)	5.5 (4)	100.0 (73)
Total	13.3 (16)	80.8 (97)	5.8 (7)	100.0 (120)

44. The finding is so extreme that it suggests the operation of a "halo effect." Even though the judges were not told to sort out proposals concerning the civil service until after they had completed their assessment of external effects, they obviously recognized them as such as they were assessing them. Their harsh assessment may be a function of a cultural habit of considering civil service legislation as automatically wasted. Notice, however, for a partial correction, that Table 19 has 28 cases fewer than Table 18. These, as stated at the outset, are all proposals which the judges could not agree to classify as either externally neutral or beneficial.

And this is what partially explains why, when we looked at all national/sectional proposals in Table 17, we found them unexpectedly short on redistributive effects. Indeed, civil service proposals make up 26.4 percent of all national/sectional proposals, but 54.0 percent of those with no external effects. If civil service legislation is left out, the pattern of external effects is somewhat improved (Table 20).

In sum, civil service legislation, given its relatively large incidence, contributes to dampening redistributive policies in two ways:

1. By being more highly disaggregated than other legislation, as stated in the third proposition.

2. But also by being externally neutral and essentially of an internal-benefit type, even when broad branches of the civil service are regulated.

There remains now to test the fourth and converse proposition. Much of the legislation described so far has to do with benefiting and regulating the civil service or specialized interest groups in some form connected to it. Conversely, as I have implied, little room should be left for legislation that cannot be easily disaggregated and can easily divide interests and parties, such as ordinary legislation required to implement many of the provisions embodied in the Constitution, or legislation directly allocating economic resources of a broad aggregate variety. For the latter, only the existence of a vast public sector of the economy and of powerful public corporations, partially self-financed and specially budgeted, can offset the indecisiveness of Parliament. Little room should also be left for fiscal policies, especially if they increase rather than decrease imposition. Little

TABLE 20. External Effects of National/Sectional Proposals, Civil Service and Other, in Percentages and Absolute Numbers

	Beneficial	Neutral	Mixed Depriving	Total
All proposals	38.8 (69)	35.4 (63)	25.8 (46)	100.0 (178)
Civil service proposals	21.3 (10)	72.3 (34)	6.4 (3)	100.0 (47)
Other proposals	45.0 (59)	22.1 (29)	32.8 (43)	100.0 (131)

room should be left for legislation that does not find a ready and organized clientele to support it, or whose innovative character may rub against established interests and conventional value priorities, as in the the case of penal and educational reform or ecological, urban renewal, and conservation plans.

This picture of omissions and inaction has surfaced here and there in the discussion of the previous findings. But the smallness of our sample cannot do complete justice to the claims. Some evidence is supplied by the Italian study based on the much larger "Predieri-Mortara" sample and is reported in Tables 21 to 27.[45] Undoubtedly many of the proposals whose low incidence is reported in the tables are of such kind that, in most political systems, they will necessarily occupy a relatively limited space, the more so if the system, as in Italy, has a propensity to give any minute decision the form of law. How many constitutional implementation provisions can, after all, a Parliament become involved in or how many times can it legislate on national

TABLE 21. Percentage of Constitutional Implementation Proposals

	Constitutional	Others	Total
Government	.5 (5)	99.5 (937)	(942)
Parliament	2.4 (23)	97.6 (932)	(955)

TABLE 22. Percentage of Economic Planning Proposals

	General planning	Sectorial planning	Local planning	Others	Total
Government	.6 (6)	.5 (5)	.4 (4)	98.4 (927)	(942)
Parliament	.1 (1)	.5 (5)	.4 (4)	99.0 (945)	(955)

TABLE 23. Percentage of Civil and Penal-Code Revision Proposals

	Code revision	Others	Total
Government	1.0 (9)	99.0 (933)	(942)
Parliament	3.1 (30)	96.9 (925)	(955)

45. The tables are adapted and recalculated from Mortara, op. cit., pp. 138-144, Tables IV-7 to IV-17.

TABLE 24. Percentage of Proposals Protecting Monuments and the Environment

	Environment	Others	Total
Government	1.4 (13)	98.6 (929)	(942)
Parliament	.7 (7)	99.3 (948)	(955)

economic planning? The point is, however, that these proposals seem to occupy a space that is too obviously limited to be comfortably explained away by those considerations, especially if one keeps in mind that the matters which they propose to regulate are central to the continuing debate among political elites. If action does not follow expression, I suggest that it is also because it would flounder or divide. How else to explain that proposals for the implementation of constitutional norms, all economic planning projects, including local planning, projects to revise norms of the penal and civil codes, and environmental projects, all hover around the one percent mark? And how to explain that government is almost as inactive as Parliament on these issues?

Proposals with a direct economic impact, as well as fiscal and public education proposals, fare somewhat better. But, after all, economic proposals touch upon what should be a vast area of government intervention. They include state subsidies to private and public economic activities, the creation and strengthening of institutional infrastructures of economic import, support for state economic monopolies (electricity, airlines, radio and television, etc.) and subsidies to local governments to offset their constant and huge budgetary deficit. Fourteen percent of government proposals and 9 percent of private ones falling in this class are, to say the least, not impressive figures. Consider also that these are *not* enacted bills. In view of the rates of approval reported below and in Table 1, and given the total number of government and private bills passed by Parliament since 1948 and reported in the same table, this means that Parliament probably passed a yearly average of 7 private and 48 government bills falling into this class. With all due regard for the chance of a nonrandom sampling error, the figures seem small indeed, even by absolute standards. Here the propensity to give every minute decision the

TABLE 25. Percentage of Economic Proposals

	1	2	3	4	5	Total
Government	5.3 (50)	6.3 (59)	1.1 (10)	1.2 (11)	86.2 (812)	(942)
Parliament	3.2 (31)	3.5 (33)	.5 (5)	1.4 (13)	91.4 (873)	(955)

Column 1: State cash contributions to private economy, sectorial and local, above 95 million dollars.

Column 2: Establishment and consolidation of public economic infrastructures; contributions to local governments to balance budget; matching funds for public works by local government and government agencies.

Column 3: Support for state monopoly activities (electricity, airlines, radio-television, railroads, oil and natural gas, etc.).

Column 4: State economic concessions to private and public agencies.

Column 5: Other proposals.

TABLE 26. Percentage of Fiscal Proposals

	Fiscal imposition[1]	Fiscal exemption	Others	Total
Government	5.9 (56)	10.2 (96)	83.9 (790)	(942)
Parliament	3.7 (35)	9.7 (93)	86.6 (827)	(955)

[1] Includes projects modifying but not increasing imposition.

TABLE 27. Percentage of Public Education Proposals

	Public education	Others	Total
Government	5.4 (51)	94.6 (891)	(942)
Parliament	10.5 (100)	89.5 (855)	(955)

form of law cuts both ways: why, then, so few economic laws? The same argument can be made for fiscal and public education proposals. In addition, the preponderant majority of fiscal proposals are exemptions, not impositions. And proposals having to do with public education, it may be easily surmised, deal not so much with educational reform as with benefits for the single largest category of government employees, school teachers. Parliamentary proposals here outstrip in percentage government ones by two to one. School teachers are the most cherished "clientele" of senators and deputies.

I have dealt so far with typologies of legislative proposals to show that the disaggregation of legislation begins even before

Parliament acts. But evidence concerning the rate of approval of the various types raises a question about our analysis which deserves immediate clarification. We find that 74.5 percent of the government projects in our sample and 18.0 percent of private projects became laws. These compare with, respectively, 82.0 percent and 18.4 in the "Predieri-Mortara" sample. But, within each type of proponent, the various types of legislation have about the same success, almost irrespective of their content. That is, it makes little difference whether proposals are sectional or microsectional, beneficial or depriving, aimed at fiscal relief or at benefiting public employees. If they originate from the government, their success is very high and consistent; if they originate from Parliament, success is much lower. There is a tendency for microsectional and nondepriving projects to be somewhat more successful, but the differences are small enough to warrant aesthetic relief from additional tables.

This lack of differences may appear suprising at first: if disaggregation of proposals should favor their passage, why is there no evidence of it? There are three answers to the puzzle. In the first place, it is true that government and parties put their major efforts into producing the kind of minute legislation that is most likely to pass. The logic of disaggregation is inescapable, and not even the opposition can avoid it. For instance, while there is a moderate tendency for Communist proponents to prefer more aggregated proposals and for Christian Democrats to concentrate on narrower benefits and on public employees, especially teachers, what is most impressive is the essential duplication of efforts by the various parties. Nevertheless, the same principle of anticipatory socialization previously illustrated may also be applied, if with greater difficulty, to the rarer instances of aggregative legislation. We have already seen that much of it is designed so as to avoid, perhaps at the cost of its relevance, controversial external consequences and to insure readier support. The point of the difference is not so much that aggregative legislation is less likely to pass, as that it requires a greater amount of preparatory work to make it acceptable. That is why less of it is presented. The real difference, in other words, is that the major efforts in preparing legislation go more easily elsewhere and that, especially in the case of government initiative, much legislation on which some form of previous consensus does not exist is simply not submitted to Parliament. This in no way alters, and is in fact consistent with, the original proposition that disaggregation is the most effective way to build legislative success. Wherever disaggregation is not operative, successful legislation is harder to design. That is why in cases where disaggregation is practically impossible and consequences of legislation are mixed—as in constitutional and economic planning proposals and others of similar character—we have found almost complete inaction.

The second explanation of the puzzle concerns government projects more closely. Compared to more minute legislation, the obvious disadvantage of aggregative legislation presented by the government is that it touches very closely on the government's program commitments. The success of minute legislation is in a way checked by the fact that, since it responds to narrower interests often extraneous to each other, it is left to its own devices to compete for physical space in a glutted field. Each proposal is uncontroversial enough to pass, provided it can find suitable room on the agenda. The success of aggregative legislation, on the other hand, is helped by the fact that, by touching on the government's program commitments, it is more likely to enjoy the consensus of the coalition partners and to obtain priority in parliamentary debates. It is true that such consensus may be difficult to build, but it would be naive to ignore its advantages when present.

Thirdly, there are ways in which aggregative legislation *is* penalized in Parliament. These, however, do not surface through a broad aggregate analysis of legislative typologies and their rates of approval. What would be required at this point is a closer analysis of what happens to legislation when it enters Parliament. I am postponing, however, this analysis till Chapter V, where the procedures and rules of the game employed by Parliament in decision-making will be discussed. Briefly to anticipate, Parliament uses some of its procedural resources—especially for what concerns the agenda and the assignment of legislation to the committees for final or reporting action—so as to speed up and ease the passage of the less "difficult" and more palatable legislation, thus contributing to that progressive "degradation" of legislation initiated before its entrance in Parliament.

But more of this later; it now seems appropriate to conclude the chapter by recalling and restating what it was designed for and what remains to be accomplished.

CONCLUSIONS

The chapter was designed to prove decisional ineffectiveness, but the proof—in view of the recognition criteria outlined in Chapter I—has proceeded circumstantially. As in removing the layers of an onion, I have progressed from the outer layers, where evidence is indirect and its meaning (its "measurement validity") questionable, toward the inner core, where the required evidence is derived in more straightforward form from the definition of ineffectiveness. We have found in the first layers that Italian legislation, more than that of other democracies, seems to be produced in concurrent fashion. It is abundant, approved by large majorities, more heavily amended than in other countries, and it includes a good share of private initiative. The meaning of these findings has remained obscure until, moving to an inner layer, we have found that legislation is also highly fragmented and disaggregated and, therefore, essentially uncontroversial. The connection between the two sets of findings is easily found if we reflect that, insofar as legislation is uncontroversial, it can also be produced in a concurrent fashion. Everyday legislative production, in other words, prospers on narrow transactions which do not penalize any political party and in fact coopt even the opposition.

Next I have theorized that extreme proliferation and disaggregation of the legislative product is peculiar to Italy, cannot be satisfactorily explained by other factors, such as system resources or incremental practices common to most countries, and therefore bears witness to Parliament's decisional ineffectiveness. An institution unable to form agreement around decisions does not stop making them; it rather adapts its processes and products to the circumstances. It disaggregates decisions, it falters and slows down on more divisive issues, it responds rather than initiates, it postpones government programs, etc. It remains still to demonstrate that the legislative behavior of the Italian Parliament is, as anticipated, a case of disagreement not only on the content of important decisions but on the decisional rules of Parliament. That is, there are countries in which commonly shared decisional rules operate, and in which nevertheless legislation may be fragmented and legislative processes may be slow, cumbersome, and reactive. England in the last few years seems an instance of this case. Here the institutional conditions for effective performance exist, yet they may be constrained by disagreement on the content of many decisions, which suggests or imposes decisional strategies of avoidance or postponement. It is possible that the cumulation of disagreement on the content of decisions sets conditions for an eventual breakdown of the decisional rules themselves. I have argued that the latter is Italy's case, that the Italian political class cannot see eye to eye, not only on the content of decisions, but especially on how and by whom decisions shall be made. That is why legislation is fragmented in the extreme, and that is how basic disagreement oddly spawns legislative proliferation. But the fact that Italian legislation shows these symptoms in the extreme does not yet prove that its case is different in kind. If the thesis is that the Italian Parliament lacks clear decisional rules, it is this lack we now have to prove. This is the task of the next chapter, where the last "layer" will be removed.

III

*The Uncertain Compromise:
Parliament's Decisional Rules*

DECISIONAL RULES IN ITALY: AN INTERPRETATION

To know the interests and preferences of a set of decision-makers in a decisional unit is not sufficient to predict their policies. We also need to know their decisional rules, that is, the number and composition of decision-makers whose agreement is required before a policy is imposed. We have offered examples of decisional rules in the previous chapters; they are best summarized by Jürg Steiner's distinction between "majority" and "proportionality."[1] A closer look at the two should illustrate how a decisional body may fail to operate according to any one or to any consistent combination of the two, and may therefore fail to decide. Majority rule is rather straightforward: it does not recognize special minority inputs and denotes the authoritative settlement of issues by a simple majority of decision-makers. Proportionality, as the rule by which each group of decision-makers with special interests is entitled to influence decisions in proportion to its size, is intuitively more complex and less straightforward in its applications.[2] When formalized in a vote-counting rule, it requires composite majorities by concurrent groups, and it therefore verges on unanimity, where each group has veto power, *irrespective of its size*. If the rule is relaxed, proportionality simply requires participation by all significant groups

---

1. Jürg Steiner, "The Principles of Majority and Proportionality," *British Journal of Political Science* 1 (1971), pp. 63-70. For a definition of decisional rule, see Douglas Rae and Michael Taylor, "Decision Rules and Policy Outcomes," ibid., pp. 71-90. Both articles have been useful in thinking through the opening remarks of the chapter.

2. Proportionality is more easily applied to the distribution of elected and appointed offices, where it means proportional representation and the assignment of posts so as to reflect group composition.

in the bargaining over decisions. But it then becomes difficult to assess whether the bargaining produces decisions accommodating groups in proportion to their size. We can only say, with Steiner, that the presence of a bargaining process is a rough indicator that proportionality is ideally operative.

Neither proportionality nor majority is an easy rule to live by. Proportionality, by extending the scope and diversity of legitimate preferences to be accommodated, severely restricts the range of options that are available and complicates their identification. Though solutions may exist,[3] they require a higher level of aggregation, an often greater amount of mutual sacrifices, a greater commitment of resources and skills, and a greater forbearance than in the case of majority rule. The accommodative policies that should ensue, as Steiner and many other authors have indicated, are most appropriate for segmented political systems, on the double grounds that they are especially designed to close their deep subcultural divisions and that they prevent minority subcultures from otherwise "opting out" of the system.[4] But their appropriateness is not sufficient cause for their adoption. In fact, if anything, they may be the exception among segmented systems, on the ground that the qualities required by proportionality are intuitively often lacking in systems that most need them. As Eric Nordlinger and Arend Lijphart have shown, even elite commitment to proportional practices is not sufficient for their adoption, and a host of other conditions must accompany it, which make proportionality a rare if theoretically significant occurrence.[5] And even when proportionality is adopted, its high demands for restrained partisanship, reciprocity, and mutual tolerance, as well as the high premium it puts on the capacity to aggregate in complex or inventive ways, may make its success dubious. Quite literally, the majorities that can be mustered may fall short of the decisional rule, in which case proportionality degenerates into a sort of spoils system. If it is difficult to

3. See Rae and Taylor for the relative demonstration.
4. See the literature listed in footnote 47, Chapter I. See also Giuseppe Di Palma, "The Study of Conflict in Western Society: A Critique of the End of Ideology" (Morristown, N.J.: General Learning Press, 1973; a Module in the Political Science Series).
5. Arend Lijphart, "Consociational Democracy," *World Politics* 21 (1969), pp. 207-225; Eric Nordlinger, *Conflict Regulation in Divided Societies* (Cambridge, Mass.: Harvard University, Center for International Affairs, Occasional Papers in International Affairs, No. 29, January 1972), chapter 4.

compose *different* interests through collective policies that increase mutual tolerance, it is easier to divide and distribute spoils and offices on proportional grounds without disturbing existing equilibria. Such degeneration of proportionality is helped by the fact that the disaggregation of the spoils makes the interests of the various segments *indifferent* to each other.[6] The armistice between segments, thus engendered, need not be usually broken except when, by mutual accord, elections are called to verify each group's claims to a share of the spoils.

Majority rule restricts ideally the range of interests and the number of parties to be accommodated, and in so doing expands the chances of accommodation. There is less emphasis on restrained partisanship and on the "unnatural" practice of political tolerance and forbearance, more on implementing what the majority has been democratically entitled to do. In this sense, majority rule is objectively easier to administer, *assuming*, however, *that the "external" interests tolerate the arrangement*. And the other side of the coin is that majority rule, by replacing coalescence with a politics of strict competition that approaches formally a zero-sum game, requires that the external interests accept the logic of insiders-outsiders and cast themselves in the role of loyal opposition. If this condition is not met—and especially if the external interests are cohesive or centered in one major party—the rule of majority does not function that easily anymore. This is not simply because the opposition may disrupt, in more or less illegal ways, its operation, but also because the arrangement will tend to divide the majority itself: it will tend to reproduce within it that very span of divergent interests truncated by the adoption of the rule. As stated of democracies in Chapter I, majorities are unlikely to impose themselves in the face of basic opposition. On one side the legitimacy of their rule may be impeached, on the other they may lack the resources, institutional and attitudinal, to enforce the strict logic of government and opposition. Hence, viable internal agreement may fail and inaction ensue.

In sum, neither proportionality nor majority, the two ideal types of democratic decision-making, are easy to operate. There are countries that have adopted a version of one or the other, or

---

6. E.E. Schattschneider, *Politics, Pressures and the Tariff* (Englewood Cliffs: Prentice-Hall, 1935), pp. 135-136.

more often a mixture of the two, and have managed to function with relative success. There are others—and Italy is one—which have settled for neither, have wavered between the two, and in the process have altered the basic traits and sharpened the defects of both.

As in the case of Italy, Weimar Germany, the Fourth French Republic, these are countries in which political fragmentation has originally advised or plainly imposed a version of proportionality designed to avert confrontation and to preserve recognition of political diversity, but in which the choice has never been thoroughly implemented and has increased those negative consequences of fragmentation it was supposed to check. The risk of failure may be intuitive, but the specific reasons for it are not, at least not yet. It can however be said (and this is not quite an explanation but rather an indication of where the explanation has to be found) that proportionality has worked well as a rule for distributing offices, mainly elective ones, but less well as a policy rule. In Italy, proportionality, as a system of popular representation, is by and large mutually agreed upon. Few at least take lightly the consequences of changing it and seriously advocate the change. Proportionality as a policy rule, on the other hand, is far from being a settled issue, and efforts at operating it have always foundered on recriminations and unaltered distrust. Two things should be anticipated in this connection. One is that the operation of proportionality would mean, in the Italian context, dealing with the Communist party as a partner in decisions. The second is that the political system, while incorporating many constitutional features bearing on proportionality, has never institutionalized the kind of top-elite negotiating mechanisms that seem crucial for the successful operation of proportionality as a policy rule. The site within which proportionality should operate remains by exclusion Parliament, a most unwieldy institution for the task. Thus proportionality, by serving its expressive function well and allowing the proliferation of interests, and by failing at the same time as a policy rule, has in fact increased the decisional difficulties of the system.

Nor can majority rule provide a corrective, for the fact is that it is itself very controversial. Opposition to Communism and the attractiveness of strong and active government have converted some in the governing parties to the idea of majority. But resistance to it comes not only from the Communists, who see in it a device to maintain their party out of power; it also comes from inside the majority itself, sectors of which are sensitive to the solicitation of the PCI and feel wary of the kind of strong executive that is required for the successful operation of the rule. In sum, both proportionality and majority have exercised their own attraction on the Italian political class, but both demand a degree of acceptance of reciprocal decisional roles and a degree of centralized management of diversity which have not been obtained. In its place the system has realized an easier-to-develop halfway house in which, as mentioned, the basic traits of both rules have been altered. Instead of proportionality solidly administered by top-elites, we have fragmentation of decision sites—even within Parliament—increasing reliance on the distribution of spoils, and the parceling out of offices and disaggregated resources according to partisan criteria that often include the opposition. Instead of majority rule in which government and opposition each uphold its function, we have majorities that falter and oppositions that have never quite resigned themselves to their role. Indeed the PCI looks back to its traditional role as a fundamental opposition, looks forward to the prospective of a grand coalition, and in reality often settles for everyday spoils. As Gianfranco Pasquino has recently put it, the Italian political system has never—since the unification of the country—resolved its conflicts either through a clarifying confrontation or through an explicit compromise accepting the limits of the system.[7] As a result, two defects—as two sides of the same coin—have characterized Italian politics: the continuing practice of nineteenth-century *trasformismo*, and the incapacity of the opposition to play its role. The former term refers to the practice of absorbing and appeasing the opposition by parceling out spoils and resources and to a logrolling conception of government, the latter to the inability of the opposition to play the game of alternance in government.

7. Gianfranco Pasquino, "Il Sistema Politico Italiano tra Neo-Trasformismo e Democrazia Consociativa," *Il Mulino* 22 (1973), pp. 549-566.

DECISIONAL RULES: THE POLITICIAN'S VIEW

The rest of the chapter is meant to document this interpretation of the operation of decisional rules in Italy. We will first look at what decision-makers have to say about decisional rules, then at constitutional and political developments since the war. As to the former, a first-hand impression that uncertainty surrounds the operation of decisional rules clearly emerges from our interviews with members of Parliament. The respondents were presented with the two ideal rules and asked which they preferred and whether, in view of their preference, they were on the whole satisfied with the type of decisional rule operating in Parliament. The most interesting side of the results is not the differences among political parties, though these are rather clear, but the sense of general unease and dissatisfaction exhibited by many of the answers.

On the point of personal preference (Table 28), Socialists and Communists preferred mixed or proportionality rule more often than Christian Democrats.[8] But there are two other findings of greater interest. One is that Socialists and Christian Democrats are each divided as to their preferences. The other is that, on the whole, a large number of respondents found the alternative between majority and proportionality unwarranted and inappropriate, and opted for some balance of the two rules. Furthermore, the justifications for the latter choice tended to change with party. Christian Democrats who offered comments presented this

TABLE 28. Percentage Preferring Three Different Decisional Rules

	DC (52)	PSI (48)	PCI (60)
Majority	55.8 (29)	27.1 (13)	8.3 (5)
Proportionality	17.3 (9)	27.1 (13)	51.7 (31)
Mixed	25.0 (13)	45.8 (22)	40.0 (24)

8. The question reads: There are ideally two ways in which parties in Parliament should participate in legislative decisions. Which do you prefer, and *why*?
  1. Decisions should be reached by the majority parties and should reflect the will of the government coalition.
  2. Decisions, at least important ones having serious consequences for the country, should be reached by majorities that go beyond the government coalition and should always reflect the interests of the major oppositions.
  3. Neither alternative is alone appropriate. They must be balanced with each other.

choice as mainly a way to avoid the dangers of proportionality. They stressed that proportionality meant in effect giving the PCI a voice in governing and that, while in "a system like the Italian" this cannot or should not be entirely avoided, it should not lead to a "confusion of roles" and should not deprive the majority of its final right to govern. They also emphasized, however, that strict majority rule would endanger the autonomy of parliament vis-à-vis the government and its ability to keep in close touch with the complex reality of the country. Communists *and Socialists* who chose a balance of the two rules tended to come at it from the other side. Their emphasis was on checking the power of the majority (it should be remembered that since 1963 the Socialists *are* part of the majority). They pointed out that the "proper distinction between majority and opposition" is often a "sterile alibi for preconceived anti-Communism" (PCI 27). They stressed the elements of pluralism contained in the constitutional framework, and the need to make room for the great popular forces represented by the PCI, so as to strengthen the system. But their emphasis was also on the fact that advocating greater room for the PCI does not mean advocating its immediate entry into government, nor even the formation of stable "top-alliances" among parliamentary elites. The objective can be attained through "methods that leave each part a degree of autonomous choice and responsibility." (PCI 16). This mixture of sentiments and justifications is present also among those respondents who clearly opted for one of the rules. Even those Communists who indicated preference for proportionality justified it as merely an ideal one, and explained it in terms not dissimilar from their party colleagues who had opted for a balance of the two rules. In the comment of a young Communist deputy:

> In my view it is the . . . [proportional] alternative which is the most appropriate, because of the complexity and diversity of our country. But here I am speaking of an understanding among parliamentary forces, not of the fact that the Communists should bail out the government as it is today. Many times it is just necessary that the government takes responsibility for its own action, and that we as opposition active in Parliament intervene to correct government action. (PCI 9).

Only those Christian Democrats and a few of the Socialists who had preferred majority rule were very adamant about their choice. They made it clear that in their opinion the only way to run a Parliament is according to the "classical British canons." It is for the majority to govern and for the opposition to oppose. This is the way in which the best democracies operate, and the best way in which the PCI can fulfill its democratic function.

In sum, attitudes toward the proper decisional rules of Parliament are quite mixed, and the mixture does not originate only from the fact that attitudes differ across parties as also from differences within parties and from the balanced personal posture of most politicians. The finding per se does not yet say that such pattern of preferences makes the operation of Parliament difficult. Many of the preferences strike at first as quite moderate and reasonable, especially when they are qualified and explained by the respondents. It is typical of most elites at most times in most countries to give qualified responses to most questions. And the very fact that Italian parliamentary elites show qualified decisional preferences may actually suggest that a conciliation of preferences is possible. Further, even if the disagreement between die-hard majoritarians and others cuts across the government parties themselves and may seem the most difficult to reconcile, it may still coexist with the operation of a firm decisional rule. Those who oppose it will show dissatisfaction, yet possibly abide by it.

That such firm rule may however not exist, and that it may not exist because diversity of preferences involves more than reasonable doubt, begins to surface only when we compare the respondents' preferences with their satisfaction at the existing decisional rules. What impresses at first in this regard is that, whatever the personal preferences, the Italian political class is not satisfied with what it sees (Table 29).[9] But what is most important is that the reasons for dissatisfaction are not so much that the opposite rule operates, as that there is no clear rule. It is true that the least satisfied are the Christian Democrats who prefer majority rule. And the partisan point of their disappointment is clear from most of the answers they volunteer: They believe the PCI has invaded the sphere of the majority and is in effect imposing its will on it by successfully dividing and blackmailing it in Parliament, often with the assistance of elements of the majority itself. The dissatisfac-

9. The question reads: In view of your answer above, do you consider yourself mainly satisfied or mainly dissatisfied with the way in which major decisions are made in Parliament today?

TABLE 29. Percentage Dissatisfied with Present Decisional Rules, by Rules Preferred[1]

	DC	PSI	PCI
Majority	79.3 (23)	61.5 (8)	40.0 (2)
Proportionality	66.7 (6)	76.9 (10)	74.2 (23)
Mixed	69.2 (9)	63.6 (14)	70.8 (17)
Total	73.1 (38)	66.7 (32)	70.0 (42)

[1] Percentages are calculated on absolute numbers in Table 28.

tion of most Communists is also clear, though of opposite sign: Three out of five volunteered statements to the effect that the DC leadership is monopolizing power and curbing that "constructive dialogue" between majority and opposition for which Parliament is the most appropriate site.

But beyond the die-hard majoritarians and most Communists, both of whom—by expressing extreme and divergent preferences—seem to know what they want, and what exists, there is a sizable middle ground that includes members of all parties. Their comments indicate that their dissatisfaction does not reflect a predictable discrepancy between partisan aspirations and fulfillment—compatible in theory with a steady decisional system—but a more detrimental uncertainty about what should and what does exist. Most illuminating here are the responses of those politicians—especially Christian Democrats and Socialists, but also Communists—who chose mixed or proportionality rules. Approximately half of them explained that they were dissatisfied at the way decisions are actually made, not because the system had adopted a clear decisional model contrary to theirs, but because—if I may splice together strands from various answers—what they advocated was quite a novel and unexplored way of conceiving the relations between majority and opposition. Hence, while the constitutional framework for it existed, a combination of "objective difficulties," improvidence, and extreme political differences had prevented this model of governing from coming to life, and no decision about what system to follow had ever been made. Each party and faction remained free to press its own brand of solution and had enough strength to restrain the others, but no combination of parties had enough strength to govern. As a Christian Democrat bluntly stated it: "Here there are neither rules nor methods—majority, grand coalition, grand compromise, or whatever. Even in Parliament the temptation to indulge in the Italian game of outsmarting each other is too strong. In the end we are all fooled." (DC 42).[10] An important variation on this theme, and one that illustrates the counterintuitive nature of many of the answers, was the answer of some of the Socialist politicians who, having advocated mixed or proportionality rule, were dissatisfied with current decisional arrangements. Given their advocacy, it seemed reasonable to predict that their source of dissatisfaction would be an alleged abuse of majority rule by the Christian Democratic party. In fact their concern was of a different and perhaps more topical kind. It had to do with the feeling that Communists and Christian Democrats were already using the crisis of decisional institutions to run ahead of the other parties and call for a direct alliance between DC and PCI that would, in their view, betray the purpose of proportionality. The task of the PSI, especially after entering the government—these respondents argued—was not to pave the way to a "conciliar pact" between Communists and Catholics but to work for a "larger majority" of *all* democratic parties.[11]

Once again, the jaded reader may find these answers to the questions on decisional rules as mere ideology not very revealing of the actual state of affairs. He may be wary of playing along with the intricacies and nebulousness of the Italian ideological discourse and of searching for substance that may turn into shadow. My point is that, when it comes to decisional rules, the actual state of affairs is what politicians believe in, and it may be useful to bank on it for a while longer. Underneath the self-justifications and the peculiarly Italian indulgence in the intricacies of the political game, what develops from the above answers is a simple reality, if we are willing to stick to the core of what politicians say: Italian politicians cannot agree on proper decisional rules and are above all dissatisfied with present decisional arrangements. Further, these attitudes are not simply a

10. The term the respondent used for "outsmarting" and "fooling" is *far fesso*. The expression is strictly Italian and culturally untranslatable.

11. The expression "conciliar pact" or "patto conciliare" was coined by Professor Giovanni Spadolini, historian, publicist, and senator for the Republican party. It ironically evokes an ecumenical embrace between Catholics and Communists in the spirit of Pope John XXIII's Second Vatican Council, or "Concilio."

matter of partisan divergence, but also one of genuine ambiguity about what should, could, and does exist. And if this is so, there is one simple reason for it—there are no established, consistent, easily recognizable decisional rules according to which the system operates. A Communist senator and party leader put the latter in the sharpest way:

> These categories [majority and proportionality] have no meaning for me in abstract. I am a politician and my party experience has taught me to make choices in a precise political context. In Italy the immediate goal of my party is to achieve according to the occasions a proper balance between the majority and the democratic opposition. . . . In reality, though, this balance has not been found yet, and our system lives a dangerous day-by-day existence, with governments . . . unable to formulate a political will of their own, on which the popular forces can exercise a leverage. We can say that this is the situation after De Gasperi . . . At least De Gasperi, when he was at his best, did hold his majorities together. Our party, on the other hand, has not always been able to achieve those alliances with the non-Communist masses without which larger and more solid majorities cannot be formed. (PCI 36).

I have essayed in these paragraphs to give a "hard" empirical image of the disagreement on decisional rules. But, in a way, the attitudes I have investigated are nothing except condensations *in corpore vili* of political events. The nature of these attitudes, as well as the way they affect decision-making, become clearer if we now cast them within a pertinent reading of constitutional and political developments since the end of World War II. What these developments show is that a series of institutional choices after the war combined proportional representation of interests with decisional rules and structures that failed to congeal and hence to "persuade" and organize interests around decisions.

DECISIONAL RULES: CONSTITUTIONAL AND POLITICAL DEVELOPMENTS

The story begins in rather conventional fashion and closely resembles the well-known story of the French Fourth Republic as it emerged from the war.[12] As in France, and even more so given Italy's Fascist interlude, the war wiped the slate clean of the old

---

12. Stanley Hoffmann, "Paradoxes of the French Political Community," in Stanley Hoffmann, ed., *In Search of France* (Cambridge, Mass.: Harvard University Press, 1963), esp. pp. 34-60.

liberal oligarchies, in part compromised with the previous regime, and signaled the emergence of the mass parties legitimized by the struggle against dictatorship. These parties—the Socialist, the Communist, and the Christian Democratic—established themselves through the Resistance and in the first postwar elections as the dominant parties in the country. It fell upon them to give Italy a new democratic setup, and to work out a mutual modus vivendi. On the last point, however, one fact, which became decisive in institutional restructuring, dominated the postwar scene: No party and no homogeneous coalition could safely count on monopolizing the political scene and on governing on its own. In the first national elections for the Constituent Assembly, in June 1946, the Christian Democrats barely matched the strength of the long-allied Socialists and Communists, despite the wide appeals of organized Catholicism and the party's capacity to absorb substantial sectors of the traditional liberal electorate.[13] Further, the DC was from the beginning internally uncohesive and fragmented, attractive as it was to a broad spectrum of radical to conservative Catholic strata. Socialists and Communists, on the other hand, despite the latter's organizational strength, their dominant role during the Resistance, and their control of strategic public offices and organizations at the end of the war, could hardly count on ruling alone in a Catholic country already assigned, in the postwar balance of power, to the Western sphere of influence. Further, the end of the Resistance and the gathering conflict between East and West brought out the ideological differences between Catholics and Marxists, and led in 1947 to the splitting of the Socialist party over the alliance with the Communists and to the ejection of the two parties from the government. In sum, uncertainty dominated the phase of political reconstruction, and interest in self-preservation advised against a resolving confrontation and for a compromise between the two forces. Examples of significant compromises, at least on the Communist side, are: (1) Communist approval of Article 7 of the Constitution, recognizing the 1929 Lateran Pacts with the Vatican; (2) Togliatti's decision, as Minister of Justice, not to press for "defascistization" in the bureaucracy and the military; (3) the

---

13. For the results of national elections since 1946, see Table 55, Chapter VI.

decision of the party to dismantle its Resistance apparatus and to revert to normal.[14]

But the compromise never went so far as to build the sort of institutional persuasion needed for an effective modus vivendi that would reach beyond mere survival. This would have required a degree of strict political engineering and of closer and more intense bargaining in which the parties, because of mutual distrust or partisan calculations of costs and benefits, were not willing to engage. Instead, the compromise chose the easiest way out. It consisted in a representation and constitutional structure long on expressiveness and promises of collective social and economic regeneration, but short on the tools with which the parties could bring the latter about. In effect, the adopted constitutional framework was left open to all possible contents, handled confrontation not by channeling but by postponing it, and gave each party the illusion that, if it mustered enough strength, it could after all fill the vacuum with its political weight.

As to representation, the adoption of proportionality in local and national elections was the most obvious choice, in view of preserving the strength of the major parties and protecting their respective claims for the future.[15] Also, as in France in the same period, proportional representation, coupled with and in turn favoring the emergence of organized mass parties, seemed to most politicians the most appropriate and least costly way to do away with the prefascist clientelistic politics centered on single-

14. On the period of reconstruction and its political and constitutional issues, see Giuseppe Mammarella, *L'Italia dopo il Fascismo 1943-1968* (Bologna: Il Mulino, 1970), Part II, chapters 1, 2, 4, and 6; F. Catalano, *L'Italia dalla Dittatura alla Democrazia* (Roma: Lerici, 1962); Norman Kogan, *A Political History of Postwar Italy* (New York: Praeger, 1966), chapters 3 and 5; Giorgio Galli, *Il Difficile Governo* (Bologna: Il Mulino, 1972), chapters 1 and 2; Adolfo Battaglia et al., *Dieci Anni Dopo, 1945-1955, Saggi sulla Vita Democratica Italiana* (Bari: Laterza, 1955); Federico Chabod, *L'Italia Contemporanea, 1918-1948* (Torino: Einaudi, 1961); Antonio Gambino, *Storia del Dopoguerra dalla Liberazione al Potere DC* (Bari: Laterza, 1975); Enzo Piscitelli, *Da Parri a De Gasperi: Storia del Dopoguerra 1945-1948* (Milano: Feltrinelli, 1975); G. Quazza (a cura di), *Italia 1945-1948* (Torino: Giappichelli, 1974); Aurelio Lepre, *Dal Crollo del Fascismo all'Egemonia Moderata* (Milano: Guida, 1974); Stuart J. Woolf, ed., *The Rebirth of Italy, 1943-1950* (London: Longmans, 1972).

15. As indicated in Chapter II, elections to the Senate are based on a system of regionally centered single-member constituencies, but since few seats are allocated in the first ballot and remaining seats and votes are allocated proportionally in regional colleges, the system basically worked as a proportional one.

member constituencies and parties of notables. It would build a responsible party system and would effect a democratic regeneration. The first consequence of proportional representation was actually to allow the survival and appearance of many smaller parties, soon to occupy a key role in coalition politics. Furthermore, once proportionality gave its first results, the awareness of the major parties that none of them could monopolize a majority of the electorate, and the instability of their constitutional compromise, made the presence of smaller potential allies indispensable to their game. In complex and not always conscious ways, Communists and Catholics favored and maintained party proliferation.[16]

But the weaker link in the chain, and the one that eventually failed to operate, was the decisional structure imposed upon the system of representation. Barring a presidential model, unacceptable to most politicians as "extraneous" to the Italian tradition and potentially "authoritarian," there were two parliamentary models, if we recall Steiner's distinction, which postfascist Italy might have adopted. One was the British model—in part a reality, in part a polemical point of reference—where the emphasis is on centralization of authority, effectiveness of executive action, preeminence of the executive over Parliament, and alternance in power over time. It is a model in which the opposition is strictly confined to the role of political stimulus, criticism, and control, but in which the role is balanced and made acceptable by alternance over time and by the operation of unwritten norms of reciprocal tolerance. It is easy to surmise, given the emphasis on alternance and tolerance, why the adoption of such a model in Italy was problematical. Most politicians had a genuine dislike for strong government, stemming from the feeling that the country had fallen prey to Fascism because of a prefascist semiauthoritarian structure, and that any reform calling for the strengthening of the governing institutions would favor authoritarian revivals in new disguises. There were serious misgivings about how any governing party might use strong executive powers, and there was uncertainty about which party would control government. Hence, there was a feeling that, whoever controlled power,

---

16. This is the ingenious thesis of Giorgio Galli's most recent work on the crisis of Italian government and parties. See Galli, op. cit., esp. pp. 9-41.

the system would not provide for alternance in government and for tolerance of oppositions. The Constituent Assembly—elected to give the country a new constitution—sat from 1946 until the elections of 1948, and the political events of the period did not completely clarify the future balance of party strength. It is true that there was a significant growth in the power of the Christian Democratic party, and a progressive political isolation of Socialists and Communists. And the DC tried to take advantage of its increasing political clout by soft-pedaling some of the dispersive decisional characteristics of the new Constitution. But the main features of the Constitution had already been settled by the existing balance of power in the Assembly, and the menacing organizational growth of the PCI, even as its isolation increased, advised against any final alteration of the constitutional framework.[17]

Failing the first model, what emerged from the Assembly was a model that closely replicated prewar continental parliamentarism, that is, a limited compact among the dominant parties with a function of mutual guarantee. This model has been interpreted by some constitutionalists and by the oppositions in terms that closely suggest Steiner's proportionality model. Alberto Predieri, for example, submits that the Constitution replaced the classical balance over time between majority and opposition, which nobody believed possible, with a "synchronic" balance based on the decentralization of decisional roles in Parliament and other sites.[18] This model called for the participation of all political forces in decisions at different levels and in different alliances, and it broke the traditional contraposition between majority and opposition by giving the latter an opportunity to share in the task of government. Let us see, however, on what

17. On constitution-making see P. Permoli, *La Costituente e i Partiti Politici Italiani* (Bologna: Cappelli, 1966); Carlo Ghisalberti, *Storia Costituzionale d'Italia 1849-1948* (Bari: Laterza, 1974); Giovanni Conti, *La Costituente* (Roma: Edizioni della Voce, 1956); P. Calamandrei and P. Levi, *Commentario Sistematico alla Costituzione Italiana* (Firenze: Barbera, 1950); Meuccio Ruini, *Come Si è Formata la Costituzione* (Milano: Giuffrè, 1961).

18. Alberto Predieri, "Aspetti del Processo Legislativo in Italia," in *Processo allo Stato* (Firenze: Sansoni, 1971; Atti del Convegno sulla Riforma dello Stato, a Cura del Centro di Ricerca e Documentazione "Luigi Einaudi"), pp. 46-55. See a similar interpretation in Giuseppe Guarino, "Intervento," in Leopoldo Piccardi, Norberto Bobbio, and Ferruccio Parri, *La Sinistra Davanti alla Crisi del Parlamento* (Milano: Giuffrè, 1967), pp. 126-135. The "synchronism" of the Italian Constitution is amply debated by various authors contributing to both volumes.

constitutional features this interpretation is based, and how correct it is.

Parliament, to be sure, was recognized as the supreme legislative body, and, as more thoroughly described at the beginning of Chapter II, no restrictions were imposed on the right of parliamentary groups to initiate and transform legislation. While the government shared with Parliament the legislative initiative, no special provisions were made to strengthen this power or to secure in any other way the position of the government vis-à-vis Parliament. Further, Parliament's central role was itself partially curbed by measures of territorial decentralization. Local autonomies were recognized, and regions—some with special status—were constitutionally assigned legislative powers to be exercised by popularly elected regional parliaments. But the dispersion of power did not stop with representative and legislative bodies. Other institutions were to be created, with decisional and control powers, in which the various parties and functional bodies would have a voice. A Constitutional Court, elected in part by Parliament, was empowered to pass final judgment on the constitutionality of existing legislation and on conflicts among organs of the state. A Council of the Judiciary, also partially elected by Parliament, would supervise the organization and the autonomy of judicial services. A National Council for Economy and Labor, composed of representatives of various functional and productive categories, would function as a consultative body and could initiate legislation. Nor were the voters forgotten, for they too could initiate legislation and also call for referenda to abolish existing laws.

To this day, the Communist opposition has no doubts that these provisions, which it had been instrumental in passing, call for and legitimize its active participation, even as opposition, in the formation of the political will.[19] It buttresses its claim by pointing out that the new Constitution, in addition to securing a synchronic distribution of powers, is also filled with norms advocating a radical transformation of society in a more partici-

---

19. The Communist position is illustrated by Communist leaders in Piccardi, Bobbio, Parri, *La Sinistra Italiana*, op. cit. See communications by Giorgio Amendola (pp. 69-78), Pietro Ingrao (pp. 135-148), Renzo Laconi (pp. 190-197). See also Flavio Colonna, "Problemi del Parlamento," in Istituto Antonio Gramsci (a cura di), *La Riforma dello Stato* (Roma: Editori Riuniti, 1968), pp. 113-128.

pant and socially progressive direction. The Constitution sanctioned, to give a few examples, workers' participation in industrial management, the nationalization of "strategic" productive sectors, national health and welfare services, the decentralization of the bureaucracy, free access to education, the autonomy of higher education, and even more grandiose objectives such as the "social use" of private property and the removing of socioeconomic obstacles to personal development.[20] Since these are constitutional provisions, the Communist argument goes, the Constitution also sanctioned the right of the opposition to share in their implementation.[21] To say the least, the provisions committed Parliament to a program of reforms of such momentum that it could not be carried out without the opposition, especially one ideologically attuned to such a program.

But the rational-legal weakness of this "synchronic" interpretation of the Constitution is clear: There is really little in the Constitution that explicitly asserts the model and clearly rules out or is even incompatible with a majority model. Any of the synchronic provisions could be run within a majority system, the more so as none of them goes far in the dispersion of powers it provides. Even regional autonomy, the most synchronic of the provisions, involves parliamentary delegation of powers on potentially limited matters, and is balanced by the executive controls on local autonomy embodied in the survival of the old prefectoral system. Regional autonomy simply recognizes that different majorities may operate at the center and the periphery. It dictates no special role for the opposition in the affairs of government. As to the fact that the opposition may be represented in bodies like the Constitutional Court, the Council of the Judiciary, or the Council for Economy and Labor, it should be pointed out that

20. For the view that the equilibrium of the new constitutional setup centered not only on "synchronism" but also on the transformation of the structure of Italian society, see Alberto Predieri, *Pianificazione e Costituzione* (Milano: Comunità, 1963), pp. 41ff.

21. Renzo Laconi in Piccardi, Bobbio, Parri, op. cit., pp. 194-195, puts it as follows: "The Constitution not only does not presuppose ... [a programmatic contraposition between majority and opposition] ..., but itself indicates, at least in broad lines, the common program committing both the majority and the opposition. This is true not only for economic and social reforms, but also for foreign policy ..., for policies toward the Catholic Church and other religions, for the organization of the armed forces, for issues of law and order, for the press, for school and family issues and so on. This is in other words a true political program which requires a united commitment both of the majority and the opposition and which constitutes the basis of the system. This is our Constitution."

these are bodies of control and proposal, two functions that oppositions normally exercise in majoritarian systems. As to the constitutional norms of social reform, they are only programmatic statements of distant intentions, quite alien to a constitution—that is, to a set of rules of the game. They recognize the generic social intents of the new Italian democracy; they do not dictate how and by whom they shall be implemented.[22] If, on the other hand, the Constitution does not strike as majoritarian either, this is not so much because of a conscious legal choice as because of omission and vagueness. While the Constitution gives the prime minister the right/duty to "direct the general policies of the Government" and to maintain its political unity, thus suggesting the rule of a homogeneous majority, it gives him no special instruments to do so. In reality, the constitutional compromise is very much an open and unfinished one, neither majoritarian nor synchronic. "The emperor wears no clothes," and he cannot be easily outfitted.

The same conclusions on the nature of the constitutional compact can be reached without aid of legal-rational arguments. If the constitutional compromise was meant to avoid the oncoming ideological stalemate, then the fact that the stalemate occurred, and that the compromise made possible only a precarious survival, belies its synchronic quality. An authentic synchronic model, at least in intents, might have taken two forms. The first is almost in the realm of utopia. It would have required a more thorough and more immediately implementable dispersion of powers, not only political but bureaucratic and economic. In it the system would have been left to its own devices, to be operated by the invisible hand of a free political market, and the extreme dispersion of power would have prevented anybody from monopolizing it.[23] Just one point about the utopia is that it required, first and foremost, something inconceivable at the time: breaking and

22. The distinction between *norme programmatiche* and *norme precettive* is commonplace in Italian constitutional doctrine. See, for example, Paolo Barile, *Scritti di Diritto Costituzionale* (Padova: Cedam, 1967), p. 386.

23. Traces of this utopia, mainly inspired by resistance to the growth of a centralized public hand, fear of "partitocracy," and commitment to a liberal economy are found in individual thinkers, such as the liberal economist Luigi Einaudi, first President of the Republic, and Don Luigi Sturzo, the founder of the Popular party after World War I. See also for an impassioned analysis of the ills of "partitocracy," Giuseppe Maranini, *Miti e Realtà della Democrazia* (Milano: Comunità, 1958), esp. Section 2.

dispersing the power of the organized mass parties. Without this, the utopia would have given quite opposite results and could have led to immediate collapse. The second possibility, in the presence of organized parties, was to design an overarching and corporate management of the decisional structure, similar to that adopted by Austria in the same years, in which all parties would have institutionally shared. The task of such structure would have been to form the issue agenda, to negotiate issues, to supervise the operation of the model, and to check the danger of collapse. We have seen how these solutions were politically unacceptable. Instead, the solution was a conventional decisional structure uneasily dividing power between Parliament and government. It was centralized enough to avoid immediate collapse, but not so "managed" to provide for more than wary coexistence through the stalemate. The halfway nature of the compromise left the decisional rules unsettled and made the issue of their legitimacy a central political issue in the country.

In the elections of 1948, following the adoption of the new Constitution, the Christian Democratic party conquered the absolute majority of contested seats for both houses; Communists and Socialists allied in a Popular Front reached their lowest ebb.[24] The pattern for the future seems clear: The DC dominates government coalitions with the smaller parties of the center, Communists and Socialists are frozen in the opposition and monopolize it. The openness of the constitutional compromise and the political victory of the center allow the government to steer the compromise in its favor and to call for a firm "delimitation of the majority."[25] A prominent Catholic leader warns of the Constitution as a potential trap, a Trojan horse in the hands of the opposition. Most of the constitutional provisions go unattended as tools that the opposition may abuse to threaten the power of the majority. No Constitutional Court, no Council for Economy and Labor, no Council of the Judiciary, no referendum provisions, and no regions—except some of those with special status—are created for many years. The norms advocating social reforms and

24. For an analysis of various aggregate aspects of elections from 1946 to 1968, see Celso Ghini, *Le Elezioni in Italia (1946-1968)* (Milano: Edizioni del Calendario, 1968).

25. On the classical period of centrism, see Mammarella, op. cit., chapter 6 and Part III; Kogan, op. cit., chapters 5 and 6; Galli, op. cit., chapter 3; Battaglia et al., op. cit. See also Leo Wollemborg, *Italia al Rallentatore* (Bologna: Il Mulino, 1966), chapter 1.

citizens' participation in various spheres, being only programmatic, are not implemented. But all of this does not amount to a transformation of the model into a strict majoritarian one, since the model does not contain enough "institutional persuasion" to effect a change from the inside. Much of what the majority does to protect itself is to contain the opposition, postpone the creation of those few constitutional channels outside Parliament through which the opposition can act, and squeeze the opposition out of local power by employing its expanding electoral and governmental resources. Though this is the most active period of center rule, this holding posture does not strengthen the majority, except by default. It provides it less with a program of action than with one of reaction. Eventually government and opposition meet in Parliament. And here the stalling force of the compromise operates in force. The majority is short of institutional and political resources to control it; the opposition is gathering enough political if not numerical resources to condition it and to embarrass the majority by questioning the legitimacy of its behavior.

In understanding these developments, the electoral stalemate is just as important as the constitutional compromise. The freezing of the opposition—including, it should be remembered, the smaller extreme right—signals the reproduction within the majority of what Paolo Farneti has called a new "parliamentary microsystem."[26] Within it Christian Democracy monopolizes the center, but considerable space is also left for smaller coalition partners. Some of the partners, and some of the Christian Democrats themselves, are not always available for measures that would further strengthen the executive, are afraid that these may be used against them by dominant factions, and do not always favor extreme containment policies toward the opposition.[27] If the strength of the opposition does not already advise against pushing containment to extreme and hence dangerous consequences, the internal divisions of the majority recommend it. If

26. Paolo Farneti, "Introduzione," in Paolo Farneti (a cura di), *Il Sistema Politico Italiano* (Bologna: Il Mulino, 1973), p. 28. Farneti develops an excellent framework for the analysis of the various periods of Italian political history since the war, centered on the relation between political society, civil society, and state institutions. See pp. 31-40 for his treatment of the 1948-1958 period.

27. On the early development of Left factions within the Christian Democratic Party, see Giorgio Galli and Paolo Facchi, *La Sinistra Democristiana* (Milano: Feltrinelli, 1962).

the weakness of the constitutional compromise does not already make governmental control over policies problematical, the reproduction of ideological divisions within the majority attends to it. In either case, containment and active action founder not just on disagreement about the content of policy packages as on a more basic conflict regarding the type of political coalition formula needed to legitimize them. Indeed, formulas are needed to justify policies that may otherwise be contested under the constitutional compromise. But they still expose each government party to direct constitutional blackmail and do not cement coalitions in a context of slow political attrition. The temptation to be in government is great, but so is the desire to divert the responsibilities that come with it. The uncertainty of the constitutional compromise sets the conditions for this development; the political stalemate seals it. The test of the acceptability of a decision becomes more and more not its content but who sustains it and who opposes it. Similarly, the test of the legitimacy of a coalition does not revolve around its programs but around which parties and factions it includes, and which it leaves out. Coalition negotiators are easily as absorbed by the careful dosage of factions and personalities to be coopted in the coalition as they are by the selection and adjustment of programs. The point of these subtle alchemies is double. They are suggested by the desire to reward friends and put adversaries on probation, a practice common to all democracies, which in Italy goes to extreme lengths. But they are also and more importantly dictated by the knowledge that the wrong mixture would put at stake the survival of the coalition, impeach its credibility, infiltrate it with "snipers" and fair-weather friends. Not surprisingly, this emphasis on so-called "strategies of alliances," while inescapable, is the least likely to bear fruit.

A first major effort to circumvent the problem by legal means, through the adoption in 1953 of an electoral law that would have given 65 percent of the lower-house seats to any electoral alliance of parties winning nationally the absolute majority of the votes, backfired in more than one way. The misplaced hope was that a large numerical majority would provide safer margins for more cohesive and homogeneous legislative coalitions.[28] The center coalition barely missed passing the 50 percent mark, and the law,

---

28. I shall show in Chapter VI why the problem of government coalitions is not one of numerical majorities.

whose adoption had caused perplexities and tensions among members of the coalition, was repealed within a year, amid mutual animosities. The results of the elections marked the end of the De Gasperi leadership and of the golden years of centrism. Despite the DC's absolute majority in Parliament, despite the strong personalized leadership of De Gasperi, and despite his serious efforts to make special room for the smaller secular parties in the coalition, to emarginate the extreme fringes of his party, and thus to build a solid and cohesive basis for government, the experiment had ended poorly. The DC and its secular allies lost considerable electoral support; the Communists fully recovered from the defeat of 1948 and definitely asserted themselves as the major opposition party, far outdistancing the Socialist party. The next opportunity for the government to expand its bases of support and to establish the legitimacy of its action would not come for another ten years. Meanwhile the framework against which the next experiment would be tested had been defined by the constitutional compromise and the political events of the reconstruction years.

While the five years of the first Parliament saw only one prime minister succeeding himself at the head of three coalition governments, the next ten years saw eight different prime ministers trying to steer twelve succeeding governments, some in coalition but some made only of Christian Democratic ministers. The "reasons" for the collapse of so many governments run the whole gamut of disagreements over foreign and domestic affairs, but one should not confuse the immediate occasions with the underlying cause. It is—to borrow from the Italian political jargon—the logic of the "strategies of alliances," the formation of coalitions around "government formulae" and "alignments" rather than programs, that claims so many victims. As stated, behind the conflict about who should govern with whom is not just the competition for who gets what and when, but the unresolved issue of the regime's correct format and the centrifugal impact of the constitutional compromise. The latter has left the center parties enough leeway to be in government alone, but not enough incentives to be the government. The external solicitations of the Communist party mix well if ambivalently with the temptations of permanent power to trigger an unresolved continuity. The opposition, on the other hand, begins to find a political space within this continuity, the more so after the end of the De Gasperi experiment.

The unresolved continuity is also sustained by the fact that the remaining years of the fifties are years of transition and reassessment, in preparation for the portents of the next decade.[29] It is a period during which the parties and national party politics dominate the political scene and pervade all forms of political associationism, political participation, and political debate at all levels and sites. It is a period, also, during which society grows and renovates relatively slowly, giving little indication of the explosion of the sixties. On one side, the major parties retrench and concentrate their main effort in consolidating their positions of power and in expanding their subcultural and organizational control. On the other side, they settle each day more to reap the rewards, such as they are, of the constitutional compromise, and to maneuver within its margins of tolerance. Parliament continues to be the arena for ideological confrontation, but it makes increasing room for the diurnal accommodations which secure for the majority the manipulation of spoils and clienteles and allow the opposition access to the routine affairs of government, and in so doing buttress the opposition's claim to its irreplaceable governing function. While in the previous period the government far outstripped Parliament in initiative and legislation, it now is Parliament that begins to claim its vital space (Table 1, Chapter II).

De Gasperi's failure had been helped, among other things, by the fact that his experiment had been a strictly personal one and relatively little effort had been put, beyond curbing the extreme factions of the party and securing a measure of autonomy from the Church hierarchy, into building the party machinery. The DC had worked as an alliance of mostly prewar Catholic cadres appealing electorally to popular strata controlled and mobilized

29. On the long period of transition from the classical period of centrism to the Center-Left (1953 to the next decade), see Mammarella, op. cit., Part IV; Kogan, op. cit., chapters 7 to 11; Galli, op. cit., chapter 4; Wollemborg, op. cit., chapters 2 and 3; N. Rossi, *Cinque Anni Difficili* (Bologna: Cappelli, 1958). See also in Alberto Spreafico and Joseph LaPalombara (a cura di), *Elezioni e Comportamento Politico in Italia* (Milano: Comunità, 1963) the following essays: Alberto Predieri, "Gli Sviluppi Costituzionali," pp. 5-54; Adolfo Battaglia, "L'Attività Politica," pp. 55-136; Guglielmo Negri and Paolo Ungari, "La Vita dei Partiti," pp. 137-206. See finally Paolo Ungari, "Dal Centro-Destra al Centro-Sinistra," in Mattei Dogan and Orazio Maria Petracca (a cura di), *Partiti Politici e Strutture Sociali in Italia* (Milano: Comunità, 1968), pp. 3-49.

by the organizations of the Catholic subculture.[30] The end of the golden years of centrism induced Fanfani, the party's most resourceful leader after De Gasperi, to concentrate his energies on the internal restructuring of the party, with the objective of making it organizationally self-reliant while at the same time continuing to recruit cadres and monopolize support from the subculture.[31] Of crucial importance in the strategy was the party's skillful use of the innumerable levers to governmental action to attract and organize traditional productive strata of society, often but not always of unquestionable Catholic sentiments. But if the organizational consolidation of the DC compensates for the electoral unsuccess of 1953, and if the habit of government expands every day the resources of the Catholic party, the Communist party is itself busy digging in for the long armistice. As the membership of the Christian Democratic party grows by leaps and bounds, that of the PCI—with a maximum of 2.6 million in the mid-fifties—is hard to match. Nor are the subcultural ramifications of this party, and its capacity to influence and coopt sectors that are not strictly identified with it, less remarkable than those of the DC.[32] The very fact that the PCI can count neither on the equivalent of a ready Catholic subculture and network, nor on the levers of government, and must in some way build its political cadres and its following from scratch, makes its accomplishments the more impressive. And as the party maintains and expands its organizational network, it also expands its electoral

---

30. On the relation between Christian Democracy, the Church, the Catholic subculture, and Catholic organizations, see Agopik Manoukian (a cura di), *La Presenza Sociale del PCI e della DC* (Bologna: Il Mulino, 1968); Francesco Alberoni (a cura di), *L'Attivista di Partito* (Bologna: Il Mulino, 1967); Gianfranco Poggi, *Catholic Action in Italy* (Stanford: Stanford University Press, 1967); Alfonso Prandi, *Chiesa e Politica: La Gerarchia e l'Impegno dei Cattolici in Italia* (Bologna: Il Mulino, 1968).

31. On the organization of Christian Democracy, see Gianfranco Poggi (a cura di), *L'Organizzazione Partitica del PCI e della DC* (Bologna: Il Mulino, 1968); "La Democrazia Cristiana in Italia; Composizione Sociale; Struttura Organizzativa; Distribuzione Geografica delle Correnti," *Tempi Moderni* 4 (1961), pp. 3-22.

32. On the subcultural ramifications of the PCI and its relations with other social movements, see Manoukian, op. cit.; Alberoni, op. cit. On the relative role of subcultures and organizational associations, see Giacomo Sani, "Determinants of Party Preference in Italy: Toward the Integration of Complementary Models," *American Journal of Political Science* 18 (1974), pp. 315-329.

presence in all regions of the country.³³ Already in the fifties the Communists, originally quite weaker in the South, can consider themselves a national party, not inferior to their major adversary in the geographical pervasiveness of their appeal.³⁴

But the consolidation of the parties, and their grip on all aspects of political life, is not all there is to the decade. The consolidation itself has limits. Fanfani's intent to use the reorganization of his party to expand to the left and to capture part of the democratic left bears no fruit, and his excessive activism leads to resentments and to his temporary eclipse within the party toward the closing of the decade. The Communists in turn have expanded in good part at the expense of their Socialist friends and, following the events in Eastern Europe, show signs of organizational stagnation in the second part of the decade. On the whole, the wait-and-see attitude of the parties, entrenched though they are, makes them unprepared for the first signs of change that are beginning to gather. Hence, the eventual refurbishing of the constitutional compromise, designed in part to meet the turning point of the sixties and to legitimize a new and more effective decisional format, will not succeed. The events of Hungary and the XX Congress of the Communist Party of the Soviet Union progressively erode the alliance between Communists and Socialists, of which the former had been the exclusive beneficiaries. The Socialist party, weakened electorally and organizationally, deprived of most of its traditional support by the Communists, initiates in the second part of the decade reunification talks with the Social Democratic party, which had split from the Socialist party in 1947, and begins the slow and uncertain movement toward the area of government.

The stagnation of the political society goes hand in hand with

33. On the organization of the PCI, see Sidney Tarrow, *Peasant Communism in Southern Italy* (New Haven: Yale University Press, 1967), chapters 6 and 8; "Modificazioni Strutturali e Politiche del PCI al suo 9⁰ Congresso," *Tempi Moderni* 2 (1960), pp. 3-43.

34. On the national expansion of the PCI, see Tarrow, op. cit., chapter 7; Giuseppe Di Palma, *Apathy and Participation* (New York: Free Press, 1970), pp. 175-176; Mattei Dogan, "Political Cleavages and Social Stratification in France and Italy," in Seymour M. Lipset and Stein Rokkan, eds., *Party Systems and Voter Alignments* (New York: Free Press, 1967), pp. 129-195, esp. pp. 184-193; Giordano Sivini, "Gli Iscritti alla Democrazia Cristiana e al Partito Comunista Italiano," *Rassegna di Sociologia* 3 (1967), pp. 429-470.

apparent quiet in the larger society, engendered by the type of economic development that is taking place in the country. After a rapid and successful reconstruction, the model of growth envisioned by most analysts was one of steady but relatively slow development within the frame of a comparatively traditional system.[35] And while the government controlled and operated significant sectors of the economy and invested considerably in the expansion of heavy, petrochemical, and natural gas industry, it took an essentially agnostic position on the model of growth and left it in the hands of private initiative and often small operators. In effect, it was exactly this model of development and the low level of expectations accompanying it that allowed the rapid social and economic expansion of the following decade, with its attendant political consequences. The political truce of the fifties, the government's heavy investments in strategic industries, the free hand given private industry, and, equally important, the liberalization of foreign trade since 1951 made possible an intensive industrial accumulation in a context of social immobility. This model of "repressive" development—as a radical economist has recently called it[36]—was characterized by high productive investments, accelerated productivity, a positive foreign trade balance with large export of manufactured goods and limited import of consumers' goods, wage containment, and high rates of savings. Considerable unemployment, income inequality, and the continuing stagnation of some industrial and nonindustrial sectors that had remained marginal in the process of accumulation and rationalization secured relative quiet among the labor forces, undermined the contractual power of their organizations, and, while maintaining the impression of a society far removed from a neocapitalist take-off, made the take-off possible.

The silent changes of the period are sufficient to trigger a rapid take-off by the last year of the decade. The North moves speedily

35. For an excellent general survey of the economic development of Italy and of economic policies, see Augusto Graziani (a cura di), *L'Economia Italiana: 1945-1970* (Bologna: Il Mulino, 1972). The volume contains a vast and up-to-date bibliography on all aspects of the economy and the political economy of Italy since the war. For the period up to the sixties, see especially AA. VV., *Aspetti e Problemi dello Sviluppo Economico in Italia* (Bari: Laterza, 1959); Silvio Pozzani, *L'Economia Italiana: Situazione e Problemi* (Milano: Comunità, 1961).

36. Michele Salvati, "L'Origine della Crisi," *Quaderni Piacentini*, No. 46 (March 1972), pp. 2-30.

toward full employment and causes geographical mobility of unprecedented rate, as laboring masses abandon the South and the farms to move toward the North and the cities. Productive investments take a sharp upturn, especially in sectors oriented toward the internal and consumers' market. And with full if regionally unbalanced employment and the consequent expansion of the consumers' purchasing basis comes the most dramatic social change the country has ever experienced.

The political class is confronted with an unforeseen danger and a challenge. The danger is that the social forces liberated by the change, the sudden mobilization of so many new energies, the uprooting of traditions and economic bonds, may well break that control so skillfully exercised by parties in the previous decade, without which the armistice between parties cannot operate. The challenge, obversely, is whether the political parties will be able to channel these energies and formulate a new model of political society fitting neocapitalist requirements while preserving the parties' role. The danger and the challenge are particularly important for Christian Democracy, a party that had relied heavily on a scenario of moderate social development and social tranquility to sustain its control of traditional masses, its alliance with private capital, and its government monopoly. It now finds itself confronted by contrasting pressures for renovation and for the preservation of positions of privilege acquired during the previous period. The emerging conflict between development and underdevelopment finds a natural arena in a party that defines and maintains itself as an "interclassist" party. But the change is equally important for another party—the PSI—whose role had been ambiguously frozen by the constitutional compromise. For the Socialists the change is an unprecedented occasion to find out their true nature, to emancipate themselves from the Communists, and to establish themselves as a key party in Italian politics. It offers them an opportunity to verify the party's asserted vocation as a marxist party, but also as a Western and democratic party. It invites them to move the country out of the doldrums of the past and to build a political society that best combines the purity of an indigenous socialist tradition with the effectiveness of the laborite democracies of northwestern Europe. Neither Catholics nor Communists should be able to match the Socialists in seizing upon this "historical occasion."

The "Center-Left" was the parties' response to the challenge.[37] It consisted in the movement of the government area to the left, the exit of the more conservative Liberal party from the area, and, in 1963, the final entry of the PSI in the cabinet. But as interesting as the redefinition of the alignments is the climate of expectations that precedes and accompanies the first stages of change. It is a climate that reveals awareness, but also illusions and deceptions. There was a feeling during this period that the mounting social transformation, if intelligently dealt with, would bring about a brand of pragmatic ideologies, and a new way of managing society, more adaptable to the continuously changing shape of issues and demands. Even in the contrast of political interests that supported the change—some of them clearly conservative and manipulative—there was initially an increasing commitment to a "politics of things," to the search for empirical and mutually compatible reforms, away from the logic of alliances and strategic alignments. There was an increasing awareness that only such search could break the deadening spiral of ideological confrontation and everyday logrolling. There was also a feeling, especially among Christian Democratic leaders, that the new formula was an "irreversible" one. It provided a broader and more open basis for decisions, and hence it was the most appropriate one to take the country into the selected club of advanced industrial democracies.

But the season of hopes was short and left a trail of wishful thinking. The formula showed itself quite inferior to the expectations. The only area in which the political response to social change seemed to work was in the containment of potential mass de-alignments in party support. Despite some erosion in the electoral strength of the majority, and the continuation of a slow but steady growth of the PCI, electoral alignments stayed very

37. The best analysis of the formative years of the Center-Left is probably Giuseppe Tamburrano, *Storia e Cronaca del Centro-Sinistra* (Milano: Feltrinelli, 1972). See also Mammarella, op. cit., Part V; Kogan, op. cit., chapters 12 and 13; Wollemborg, op. cit., chapters 4 and 5; Galli, op. cit., chapters 5-8. For an authoritative statement from the Socialist leader who led the party toward the Center-Left, see Pietro Nenni, *Il Socialismo nella Democrazia* (Firenze: Vallecchi, 1966). For a statement by the Catholic leader who headed the first cabinet supported by the PSI, see Amintore Fanfani, *Centro-Sinistra 1962* (Milano: Garzanti, 1963).

stable nationally and locally.[38] At the decisional level, however, the hopes of the Center-Left were of short duration. The best period of the Center-Left was, in fact, the one that preceded its formal sanctioning through the assumption of ministerial responsibilities by the Socialists, and coincided with the first manifestations of rapid social change. It culminated in the 1962-63 Fanfani government, externally supported by the Socialists, and in a series of reforms capped by the nationalization of electric energy. It was, as Giuseppe Tamburrano describes it, the only period of the new experiment seriously oriented toward content and reforms rather than toward alliances and power alchemies.[39] After that, the old logic of the constitutional compromise reasserted itself, in a way in more virulent forms. The Center-Left became a formula with a progressively expressive content. And even as the first years of the Center-Left provided a degree of interparty cohesiveness sufficient to sustain a moderate amount of reform legislation, the new formula failed to alter Parliament's entrenched decisional ways. There are no signs from the legislative outputs we have analyzed that government and Parliament concentrated their skills on the transaction of more substantial legislation. Legislative outputs and transactions remained, by all political accounts of the period, what they typically were before—clientelistic and disaggregated—and agreement on substantial legislation was no more likely now than it was before. The only significant difference with the past was that Parliament's decisional failure combined with the now rapid pace of social change to trigger the emergence of new political forces outside parties and Parliament claiming a central role in the decisional process. The traditional structures of representation had increasing difficulties in containing and monopolizing the articulation and administration of social conflict. In the vacuum of political power, the trend culminated at the end of the sixties in a new upswing of industrial conflict and the emergence of labor unions as new

38. The first signs of a potential change would not appear until 1974, on the occasion of the referendum on repealing the divorce law. On the sociology and ecology of the referendum results, see Alberto Marradi, "Analisi del Referendum sul Divorzio," *Rivista Italiana di Scienza Politica* 4 (1973), pp. 589-644.
39. Tamburrano, op. cit., passim.

potential partners in the decisional process.[40] Meanwhile, the rate of cabinet mortality showed no signs of abatement. Twelve cabinets had fallen in the ten years between the end of De Gasperi's centrism and the formal start of the Center-Left; eleven followed it the next ten years.

But why did the Center-Left fail? At one level there are immediate reasons having to do with the emerging diversity in the motives that led the parties to the new alliance. It is true that all the coalition parties, and in some way even the PCI, saw the "turn to the left" as an opportunity to move from the "repressive" model of development of the fifties to a model of social "integration," which would use "structural reforms," expanding civil liberties, and the "rationalization" of social institutions to build "consensus" out of social change.[41] But the grandiosity of the scenario and the valence-nature of the passwords, although indicative of convergences not to belittle, could not eventually hide substantial differences of interpretation and the essential uncertainty of the model.

In some sectors of Christian Democracy and of the smaller secular partners (Social Democrats and Republicans), the accent was simply on the technical rationalization of social and economic structures as a way to support the economic expansion of the most advanced sectors of the economy and to build the bases of a neocapitalist scenario.[42] These prospective reforms, as aptly pointed out by Michele Salvati, did not require a growth of the public sector, nor were they necessarily democratic.[43] They did not require expanding the powers of workers' organizations and increasing public education, welfare, occupational, and service

40. Alessandro Pizzorno, "I Sindacati nel Sistema Politico Italiano: Aspetti Storici," *Rivista Trimestrale di Diritto Pubblico* 21 (1971), pp. 1510-1559; Gino Giugni, *Il Sindacato tra Contratti e Riforme 1969-1973* (Bari: De Donato, 1973); Alessandro Pizzorno, "Sull'Azione Politica dei Sindacati," *Problemi del Socialismo* 12 (1970), pp. 867-895; U. Romagnoli, "Appunti per una Storia del Movimento Sindacale in Italia (1960-1970)," an appendix to Daniel L. Horowitz, *Storia del Movimento Sindacale in Italia* (Bologna: Il Mulino, 1972). On the relations between unions and parties, see "Sindacato e Partiti," special issue of *Rassegna Sindacale*, Nos. 33-34 (November 1971-February 1972).

41. Expressions in quotation marks here and in many other parts of the book are translations from current Italian political jargon.

42. The position of the Republican party on the Center-Left, its political and economic functions, is well illustrated in various writings by Ugo La Malfa, economist and leader of the party since the early sixties. See Ugo La Malfa, *La Politica Economica in Italia 1946-1962* (Milano: Comunità, 1962); *Polemica Economica a Sinistra* (Roma: Edizioni della Voce, 1971).

43. Salvati, op. cit., p. 20.

opportunities. The social services did not need expansion but streamlining and the application of cost-benefit criteria. And private initiative, if adequately assisted in its rationalization efforts, could provide consumer resources and hence the bases of political consensus. On the other hand, even the rationalization hypothesis had considerable political costs for the DC. It could seriously undermine a number of strategic Christian Democratic clienteles whose ascriptive economic privileges were rooted in the inefficiency of traditional social structures. These clienteles demanded personal benefits, not aggregate reforms, and could be accommodated only by steering the Center-Left toward a politics of expansion of the public sectors—especially sectors concerned with services and welfare—whose enormous resources could best be employed to clientelistic advantages. To some groups of the majority party, therefore, the Center-Left appeared, if properly steered, as an opportunity to legitimize conservative policies under the guise of reform, and thus to consolidate their control of government.

For some Socialists, as well as for other factions of the coalition parties, the Center-Left meant instead an occasion to expand the political bases for a "social-democratic" experiment in which civil and welfare reforms would combine with economic rationalization in a scenario of Scandinavian matrix. But for most Socialists reforms meant more than reformism; they meant a substantial restructuring of economic and political power relations. And because of the special ideological heritage of Italian Socialism—Socialists reasoned—such restructuring could not be conducted without giving the Socialists a privileged position within the coalition. Obtaining such a position should be the test that a redistribution of power was operating, and should represent but a first step toward a Socialist if plural society.[44] As it can be seen, the motivations of the various partners did not mix well. Further, especially in the case of the PSI, their immediate policy applications suffered from a degree of improvisation only compounded by the way events outreached solutions. Technical ignorance,

---

44. On evolutions in the Socialist party and the Socialist movement during this period, see L. Faenza, *La Crisi del Socialismo in Italia* (Bologna: Edizioni Alfa, 1967); Antonio Landolfi, *Il Socialismo Italiano* (Roma: Lerici, 1968); AA. VV., *Classe Operaia, Partiti Politici e Socialismo nella Prospettiva Italiana* (Milano: Feltrinelli, 1966); Roberto Guiducci and Fabrizio Onofri (a cura di), *Costituente Aperta—Le Nuove Frontiere del Socialismo in Italia* (Firenze: Vallecchi, 1966); Roberto Guiducci, *New Deal Socialista* (Firenze: Vallecchi, 1965).

schematic thinking, and lack of habituation to programmatic action combined with conflicting motivations to produce policy proposals that remained unattended or whose outcomes were moot, divisive, or unexpected.[45]

In short, these are the immediate reasons for the new experiment's failure. But, as the reader may surmise, the common cause that triggers and sustains the special reasons for disagreement is again the more basic disagreement on decisional rules. Indeed, though I have loosely presented the Center-Left as an effort to channel abrupt social change and to adapt the political society to the changing circumstances, a more precise reading of the events says that the Center-Left was and could not avoid being—lest it fail—something more important. It was an effort to settle the old issue, which the social mobilization of the sixties was bringing out again, of who participated in power and how. And it is here that the new formula left things unresolved. It managed to refurbish the constitutional compromise threatened by the new decade, but, as with De Gasperi's attempt ten years before, it did not dispel its uncertainty. That the new formula could not hope to cope with social change without coping with the question of decisional rules is almost definitional. A formula that could not be unambiguously acceptable to the Socialists, themselves involved in it, and could neither accommodate nor keep at bay the Communists and the emerging labor organizations, would be very much in question, both on the point of value and on that of effectiveness. Yet this is exactly the nature of the formula. The reason is that the Center-Left was cast within the frame of the old constitutional compromise, and it merely tried to adjust the compromise to the changing times by confiding in a marginal change of government partners and in the good will and mutual trust of the new partners. But whether or not these friendly feelings were genuine, they could not escape deterioration under the spell of the constitutional compromise. The irony of the Center-Left was that, while advocating a "strategy of things" and of pragmatic reforms, it was typically a strategy of alliances. It may be argued that it could not be otherwise, that the formula was imposed by the old constitutional compromise. But this is exactly the point; the impasse could not be broken without a serious effort to alter the compromise. Failing this, the Center-Left revealed itself less a

---

45. Tamburrano, op. cit., esp. pp. 259-272.

choice than a necessity imposed by constitutional circumstances and an evolving social context. It should be remembered that the events of the late fifties and early sixties took the political parties by surprise. They had settled for a long and uneventful armistice and, in preparation for it, had turned their energies inward. The "irreversibility" of the new formula responded to this state of surprise and degenerated into an operation of containment that began to create divisions in the coalition. It was not so much the quality of content and sentiments of commitment that made it eventually irreversible, as the fact that—as the previous center coalitions—it was the only possible one. Which explains why the formula became caught in the same problems of the past. The decisional role of the PCI stayed unresolved. In fact, it became even more central in the political debate and conditioned more heavily the behavior of the majority partners. The alchemies of factions and alliances again dominated the coalition, again became a test for the legitimacy of its decisions, and paralyzed legislative action.

Most telling in understanding the continuity of the unresolved compromise and the increasing centrality of the conflict on decisional rules is the behavior of the new coalition partner. Indeed, the PSI, unlike the smaller partners, has the aspirations of a dominant party, and occupies a delicate position between the government on one side and the PCI and the new labor forces on the other. Its entry into the coalition, despite the claims to common programmatic commitments, introduces an element of diversity, hence instability, not present in the previous coalitions. The diversity is not only in programs and policies but also in the governing vocation of the new partner. There is no doubt that the parties of the old center coalitions were government parties, with no qualms about their vocation. For them the notion of the "delimitation of the majority" made some ideological and utilitarian sense. The disagreement on the constitutional compromise was usually less internal to them than between them and the opposition. It tended to become internal and to thwart decisional action when the delimitation of the majority was used by a faction—most usually Catholic—as a device to "excessively" strengthen the hand of the executive or, something especially resented by the smaller parties, to favor the personal games of that faction. Hence, the opposition's capacity to condition the majority and denounce the ineffectiveness of the decisional rules was usually indirect. The Communists alone did not have the capacity to split and bring down governments; they could only exploit the opportunities offered them when a conflict exploded within the government. And even as the PCI tries to exploit these internal contradictions, it can just as well be said that it was a case of the government's dissenting factions using the PCI to perfect their goals. In sum, under the centrist formula the delimitation of the majority, while failing to secure decisional cohesiveness, postponed the explosion of the tensions in the constitutional compromise.

But the tensions surfaced dramatically with the entry of the Socialists into government. If this event had a merit, it was the double one of fully revealing the weaknesses of the constitutional compromise and the uncertainty of the Socialist vocation. The freezing of the PSI in opposition, together with the PCI, had postponed the test of this vocation. In a way, this period of isolation in the uncomfortable company of the larger Communist ally eventually brought out and emphasized the democratic side of the Socialist party. With the assistance of the post-Stalinist events, it made the party sensitive to a modern and democratic vocation which more than twenty years of alliance with the PCI and the fruitless extremism of the party during the prefascist period had tarnished. But a democratic party is something different from a government party, as it soon appeared when the isolation was broken and the Socialists entered the coalition. The experience brought out in full ambiguities that had been kept untested by years of opposition. The chief unresolved ambiguity concerned the party's role not just as a party in government but as a party of government. Having been the first marxist party in the country in the prefascist period, the party after World War II could not easily reconcile itself to a subordinate role in the opposition, but neither could it easily find a position as ruling party, especially if here too the position was subordinate. Just as in the period of opposition the PCI deprived the Socialists of their political living space, so the period of government placed the PSI within reach of the equally smothering embrace of Christian Democracy. The response of the PSI was two-pronged. On one side it pushed for reunification with the Social Democrats, to build political strength and to present itself as the new labor party of Italy. But unification came only in 1966, after the crisis of the Center-Left had started. As an irresolute rescue operation, it ended within less than three years, after an exeedingly poor showing of the unified party in the 1968 elections.[46] The other response more clearly revealed the way the uncertain compromise still heavily conditioned political developments. It consisted in trying to place the party in a unique role between government and opposition: to make it government and opposition, partner and critic at the same time. Within the context of the constitutional compromise this role could not just mean advocating different types of reform, for all purposes already blocked. It meant reaching for even different and newer alliances, strategically held together by the party itself. The PSI became open advocate within the government of that "synchronic" interpretation of the compromise that the party had also advocated from the opposition. The political formula of the PSI was the achievement of "more advanced equilibria," a new password calling for a greater concurrence of the Communists in decision-making and the eventual entry of a more democratic PCI into the government area. The conflict surrounding the constitutional compromise was now reenacted within the majority; it divided parties and factions, and showed no sign of approaching a solution. The role of the PCI became more than ever a central issue, as did the Communists' claim that the Center-Left had a meaning only insofar as it would seek a new understanding with them. As a result, the Center-Left has been, if possible, an even more uncertain formula than the centrist one. What has sustained it until recently has been the unsettling knowledge that no other formulae were possible and that agreement had run out of space.

Indeed, such is the nature of the unresolved compromise that, after burning formula after formula, the option it now leaves the country is that "historical compromise" of all popular forces—Marxist and Catholic—advocated by the PCI all along. But after thirty years of haggling, this final formula, which ideally resembles a "proportinality" solution, appears more unsettling and

---

46. Cesare Rossi and Fabrizio Achilli, *L'Unificazione Socialista* (Milano: Palazzi, 1969). For a perceptive analysis of the failure of reunification, emphasizing elite, factional, and organizational interests rather than ideological incompatibility, see Felice Rizzi, "Dall'Unificazione alla Scissione Socialista," *Rivista Italiana di Scienza Politica* 3 (1973), pp. 407-424.

divisive than the others. For some it is the only hope left to build effective democracy. For others it would spell its end. For most it is still an uncertain and difficult solution, likely to be imposed by the danger of political collapse rather than by a free and carefully weighted political choice. Even those who sympathize with it—and few if any Socialists do—cannot fail to see behind it the danger of a "conciliar pact" between Communists and Catholics, with sinister implications for democracy itself. And even the Communist party, for all its unflagging commitment to the formula and to the principle of an alliance with the Catholics—both rooted in the history and "Italian" ideology of the party—is less than sanguine about the exact nature of these alliances, the readiness of the party, and the risks they may involve not only for the party but for the country. These uncertainties are not only tactical and partisan, but reflect more importantly the fact that, thirty years after the war, no political force has been able to spell out even to its own satisfaction a viable governing hypothesis. Social and political events are outdistancing political formulae.

But these developments concern more the immediate future than the present, and will be reconsidered in the concluding chapter. For the purpose of our analysis our case rests here.

CONCLUSIONS

The purpose of this chapter was descriptive: to show that decisional ineffectiveness in Italy is not just a case of disagreement on decisional content but also one of disagreement on decisional rules. We have traced the evidence in the constitutional and political events of the last thirty years, and in the conceptions of decisional rules held by members of the political class. We have found disagreement to revolve around the role of government and opposition in decision-making, and to coexist with a constitutional format that is neither clearly majoritarian nor proportionalist. As presented in Chapter I, the Italian case is, in other words, one in which there are no commonly subscribed decisional rules and no agreement on what is constitutionally prescribed. We have also found that disagreement often cuts across parties and factions, across majority and opposition. It is this disagreement that, within Parliament, triggers conflict over "unnatural" legislative alliances, stalls major legislative initiatives, but at the same time leaves parliamentary alliances that include the opposition free to indulge in the transaction of marginal legislation.

In the course of the analysis, however, descriptions of disagreement have implicitly become explanations; historical "hows" have acquired the weight of inescapable "whys." To avoid compelling overdetermination it is now time to sort out and order explanations. This is the task of the next three chapters.

IV

*Politicians in Parliament:
The Political Culture of
Italian Legislators*

I asserted in the previous chapter that the leadership of the Communist party is wrong when it claims that the constitutional compromise explicitly rejected a majority model, and it is also basically wrong when it claims polemically that Christian Democracy has imposed on Parliament a narrow majority system. The truth of the matter, behind the polemics about what should be and what exists, is that the Italian Parliament has rarely operated as a solidly majoritarian one. In contemporary parliamentary democracies majority rule is coequal with the cabinet's strict control over the parliamentary majority, hence over legislative processes. But the notion of a Parliament dominated by a strong executive finds little sympathy among both the Communists and members of the majority. We have indirectly seen this hostility in the respondents' comments on decisional rules; we will see it again as we proceed. In turn, antagonism toward a majority model, far from leaving Parliament with more agreeable solutions, points to a real management problem.

Ideally, and once it is accepted by all parties, a majoritarian Parliament is a relatively smooth body to operate. On one side, the cabinet's strict control of Parliament assigns the latter limited transformative powers and leaves it mostly with the predictable task of legitimizing agreements reached elsewhere. On the other side, the opposition's recognized role of political control and criticism provides a nice and simply identifiable division of labor. On both counts, and making allowance for the discrepancies between the ideal and reality, a majoritarian Parliament is in the position to channel and handle conflict with relative success. If, on the other hand, a strict majoritarian principle does not operate, the roles of majority and opposition are more difficult to define, and executive and parliamentary leadership have a harder time in drawing operative lines. The fact is that, even if the principle is rejected, the distinction between government and opposition cannot be ruled out of existence. It survives as a matter of political reality, and it requires forms of accommodation that are more demanding and less comfortable than those provided by majority rule. Moreover, accommodation must occur within Parliament, which is thus entrusted with a new transformative responsibility. Indeed, at least three sides continue to meet directly within Parliament: a parliamentary majority, an opposition, and the government. And no matter how hamstrung the latter may be, it is by no means the minor side. In Italy, we have seen, the government still maintains preponderant control over legislation. To accommodate these three sides and to negotiate mutually acceptable decisional responsibilities is the task—as we have seen—with which the Italian Parliament has been hopelessly tangled since 1953, when majority rule lost its battle.

The reasons for the failure lie at different levels. Some, as Italians are fond of saying, "lie upstream"; they originate outside of Parliament, and have essentially to do with the fact that both the party system and the inner working of the major parties foster dispersive and irresponsible behavior. Insofar as Parliament "represents," this impact cannot be avoided. But some are internal to Parliament. Insofar as Parliament intends not only to represent and legitimize decisions taken elsewhere but also to negotiate and decide, it needs "negotial" conceptions on the part of its members and organizational resources that fit this role. And here the internal problem lies. Parliament does not have the cultural and institutional premises to carry out the ambitious role it claims. In this sense, it is not a strong institution, and it allows what lies upstream to weigh directly and negatively upon it. In this sense, also, its relations with government rarely manage to assume the form of constructive negotiations and often amount to surreptitious raids in the government area. The image of parliamentary power conveyed by this behavior is illusory. Much has been written in the last two decades about the passing of Parliaments, meaning by this mainly their loss of decisional powers vis-à-vis an expanding government and corporate sector.[1]

But in Italy, the crisis of representative institutions is more complex than a loss of decisional powers in favor of the executive. What strikes above all in the Italian Parliament is not its loss of powers, but its inefficient use: Parliament tries to hold onto powers it cannot administer.[2] And the inefficiency, far from helping the government, enmeshes it too. Government and Parliament confront each other from positions of weakness; and the "natural" predominance of the executive seems more than checked by such countervailing trends.

The task of this chapter is to explore the conceptual and cultural premises needed to run Parliament as a negotial body.[3] The gist of what follows is that Parliament has emerged as a negotial body not by vocation but *faute de mieux*. Parliament has no special predisposition toward negotial roles, no special understanding of the management of conflict through negotiations. Rather, it could not settle for other and more stringent conceptions of its responsibilities. In the light of this impossible predicament, to speak of Parliament as a negotial body is to speak euphemistically.[4]

1. In reality, some parliaments, especially majoritarian, were never meant to have such decisional powers and thus never lost them. They didn't have them before cabinet government developed, when the "king in parliament" formula meant not the power of parliament to legislate with the king, but its power to restrain and control the King's power to legislate *erga omnes*. They didn't acquire them when cabinets absorbed the king's decisional powers, and parliament simply preserved its dual task of political legitimation and control. On these points see Giovanni Sartori, "Dove Va il Parlamento," in S. Somogyi et al., *Il Parlamento Italiano 1946-1963* (Napoli: Edizioni Scientifiche Italiane, 1963), pp. 355-360; Francesco Barbagallo, "Parlamenti: Strutture e Funzioni," *Nord e Sud*, No. 107 (November 1968), pp. 65-85; Alberto Predieri, *Pianificazione e Costituzione* (Milano: Comunità, 1963), pp. 509ff.; K.C. Wheare, *Legislatures* (London: Oxford University Press, 1968), chapter 9. Walter Bagehot ranked law-making fifth of five parliamentary functions, and the choice and legitimation of the executive first: Walter Bagehot, *The English Constitution* (London: Oxford University Press, 1963), p. 117.

2. On the point that the crisis is not one of powers but one of efficiency, see Claudio De Cesare, "Note sulla Fissazione dell'Ordine del Giorno Assembleare," in AA. VV., *Studi per il Ventesimo Anniversario dell'Assemblea Costituente* (Firenze: Vallecchi, 1969), Vol. 5, p. 274. See also, for an acute analysis of the crisis of parliaments in different types of political systems, and for the distinction between powerlessness and inefficiency, Norberto Bobbio, "Le Istituzioni Parlamentari Ieri e Oggi," in Leopoldo Piccardi, Norberto Bobbio, and Ferruccio Parri, *La Sinistra Davanti alla Crisi del Parlamento* (Milano: Giuffrè, 1967), pp. 21-49.

3. The institutional and organizational premises are examined in the next chapter.

4. The theoretical frame for most of the analysis that follows is developed in Giuseppe Di Palma, "The Study of Conflict in Western Society: A Critique of the End of Ideology"

NEGOTIAL ROLES, RECIPROCITY, AND COMPROMISE

The fact that the Italian Parliament does not have the cultural premises to operate as a negotial body began to emerge in the last chapter, when we considered the attitudes of members of Parliament toward majority and proportionality rules. The preference signified by a large majority of the respondents, including Christian Democrats, for mixed or proportionality rules seemed at first to indicate attitudes fitting the operation of a negotial body. However, what also appeared in many of the respondents' comments was a sense of generalized dissatisfaction with the way the rules operated. It variously reflected a belief that other parties had ignored the rules or twisted them to personal advantage and that, in sum, Parliament wasn't working as a trusted negotial body. Coming from a majority of politicians all overtly subscribing to the negotial principle, these views seem to fall into the realm of self-fulfilling prophecies of the least desirable type, those caused by fear of an event. We can understand it as a sort of prisoner's dilemma: Two partners will negotiate not simply because each is separately willing, but only if they "know" that the other is willing. If they don't know, each behaves exactly as he fears the other will. At which point, the lines of reality and expectations become hopelessly tangled, attitudes become truly ambivalent, and it is hard to discern what is projection and what is not.

Transferring this bit of game psychology to the Italian Parliament, I have no reason to question the sincerity of the many deputies and senators of all parties who told us in the interviews that Parliament and the country cannot operate unless a new form of cooperation between majority and opposition is found. It is sufficient, on the other hand, to peruse the newspapers of the last three or four years to recognize that, whatever twist each party gives it, cooperation is the issue of the day for the Italian political class, the issue on which the survival of democracy rests. But good intentions, though indispensable, are not enough. The

---

(Morristown, N.J.: General Learning Press, 1973; a Module in the Political Science Series), esp. pp. 10-16. Of great importance is Eric Nordlinger, *Conflict Regulation in Divided Societies* (Cambridge, Mass.: Harvard University, Center for International Affairs, Occasional Papers in International Affairs, No. 29, January 1972), chapter 3. Similar insights, but formulated in a more legalistic frame, on the cultural requirements of a negotial body are found in Mario Pacelli, "Intervento," in *Processo allo Stato* (Firenze: Sansoni, 1971, Atti del Convegno sulla Riforma dello Stato, a Cura del Centro di Ricerca e Documentazione "Luigi Einaudi"), pp. 121-138.

point is aptly made in Robert Putnam's recent study of the political attitudes of British and Italian members of Parliament.[5] In comparing their attitudes toward compromise, Putnam reports that as many Italian as British parliamentarians (respectively 68 and 67 percent) said that in a sharp political controversy they would "seek a solution acceptable to both sides" rather than "stick to their guns." Putnam notes, however, that, despite this endorsement of compromise, Italians are clearly less likely than Britons actually to compose their differences. What they lack is not good intentions, but the belief that compromise is politically possible and attainable. On the latter point, I would argue that the crux of the matter lies in the fact that a negotial body needs usually, and on most important matters, trust of reciprocal intentions among its members. To say that a partner will not negotiate, despite his good intentions, unless he knows that the others will do likewise, is to say that none trusts the others to play by the same code, none is sure that the others will reserve for him the same treatment he would personally apply. In other words, none is sure that "rules of reciprocity" shall be applied.[6] But reciprocity, if fully intended, also says that charity begins at home. Since mechanisms of projection operate here, reciprocity can be judged not only by the treatment each partner expects to receive, but also by that which he is ready and willing to extend to the other side.

It is this posture that is by and large poorly represented in the Italian Parliament. Once again, as we have already begun to sense, the limits show up simultaneously with affirmation of support in principle for a negotial system. In each party, we asked *half* of the members of Parliament in the sample a question very similar to Putnam's: What did they think of a situation in which "the parties in Parliament have substantially different views on an important piece of legislation, one involving an important social or political reform? Should parties favor a compromise, or remain firm in their positions?" We further insisted that the respondents make, as much as possible, a firm choice, even if it did not completely reflect their sentiments. Few

---

5. Robert Putnam, *The Beliefs of Politicians* (New Haven: Yale University Press, 1973), p. 153.

6. On "reciprocity," see Richard Fenno, "The House Appropriations Committee as a Political System: The Problem of Integration," *American Political Science Review* 56 (1962), pp. 310-324.

of the respondents, at least among those I interviewed personally, felt uncomfortable about the choice, and only one in four indicated he would rather see the parties stand firm on their views (Table 30).[7] There was some difference between parties, with the Communists more favorable to compromise than Socialists and Christian Democrats by 6 and 11 percent margins, respectively. But the difference is less impressive than the substantial agreement in favor of compromise between and within parties. Also, in commenting on the reason for their choice, the most frequent statements made among all parties were that compromise was important to avoid stalling the reform suggested in the question or having it passed in the "wrong form," and that too often these things had happened in the past because of the ideological "narrowness" of many parties.

It superficially seems, were we to stop at this point, that the principle of reciprocity is established. But, in order to become an active operative code, reciprocity demands more than a general acceptance of the idea of compromise, an idea which, in any case, appears almost imposed in a Parliament numerically controlled by no single party. It demands seeking compromise actively, taking upon oneself the responsibility, indeed involving the other partners in the same logic. In this regard, the other half of the respondents, after having been presented with the same case of legislative disagreement among parties, were confronted with different alternatives. "Do you think," they were asked, "that the main responsibility of *your party* in this situation should be to *seek* a compromise *actively,* or should it be to stand firm on its positions, or should its behavior depend on the particular circumstances of

TABLE 30. Percentage Preferring and Opposing Compromise by Parties on Important Legislation[1]

	DC (26)	PSI (24)	PCI (30)	Total (80)
Compromise	65.4 (17)	70.8 (17)	76.7 (23)	71.25 (57)
Remain firm	34.6 (9)	29.2 (7)	23.3 (7)	28.75 (23)

[1]The question was asked of only half the respondents.

7. Summary percentages are used here and in other tables for ready reference, in view of the limited differences among parties. The reader should remember, however, that the samples are stratified by party and therefore summary percentages are, strictly speaking, unwarranted.

the case?" The differences from the first wording are three. First, the reference is not to parties in general, but to the respondent's party. Second, what is at issue is not just favoring compromise, but actively and responsibly seeking it. Third, the respondents may opt for a qualified answer.

The answers provide a striking contrast with those of the first question (Table 31). It may not be surprising and it reveals nothing peculiar about Italian parliamentarians to find that 74 percent of the respondents "seized" upon the last alternative and indicated that their peferences depended on the specifics of the case. This compares with only 15 percent who declared that the party should seek compromise under all circumstances, and 11 percent who opposed the idea just as unconditionally. Party affiliation made no significant difference in the choice of the qualified alternative. But more interesting results emerged when we asked the respondents who chose this alternative to indicate which, in a set of four, was the most important factor on which the compromising behavior of their own party should depend: should it depend mainly on "whether the other parties are equally well pedisposed toward compromise"; on "how important the legislation is"; on "how likely it is that the legislation would otherwise not pass"; or on "how seriously compromise might jeopardize the unity of your party"? Sixty-eight percent (40 respondents) indicated that they were mainly concerned with the attitudes of the other parties. This means that, altogether, 61 percent of this half of the sample (49 respondents) either opposed outright the idea that their party should be responsible for seeking compromise, or made the idea rest on the other parties' equal disposition. The finding may seem unimpressive. Numerically, the majority is large but not overwhelming. Logically, one may

TABLE 31. Percentage Preferring and Opposing Their Party Seeking Compromise on Important Legislation[1]

	DC (26)	PSI (24)	PCI (30)	Total (80)
Compromise	19.2 (5)	16.7 (4)	10.0 (3)	15.0 (12)
Remain firm	7.7 (2)	12.5 (3)	13.3 (4)	11.25 (9)
Depends	73.1 (19)	70.8 (17)	76.7 (23)	73.75 (59)

[1] Question asked of respondents who were not asked the question in Table 30.

feel, it only stands to reason that, in matters of give-and-take, each partner be alert and expect equal treatment. It should be noticed, however, that the respondents were offered a choice among four equally reasonable and important factors. That two out of three respondents concentrated their attention on just one of them is remarkable, the more so since, at closer scrutiny, there is really no inescapable reason why a party should make the pursuit of compromise rest mainly on what the other parties are ready to do. The logic is only in the eyes of the beholder, and I cannot more fully agree with the words of a Socialist deputy who caught the fault in the reasoning:

In a way it may seem rational to choose the first . . . [factor]. Tactically every party, in seeking compromise, should be advised to take a wait-and-see attitude. It should make sure that the other parties behave similarly. It is a matter of protecting one's interests, and of securing the best results for oneself out of the situation . . . But strategically it can be quite a disastrous way of behaving. If each party waits for the other parties to make the first move . . . you can say goodbye to compromise. Compromise is not a factual given, it is something—a way of looking at things—which is created and demonstrated through action, through good will. Every party—it is a natural disposition—tries to bring grist to its own mill. This is not the problem, the problem is when we don't trust each other, when we prejudge our motives. (PSI 40)

If this politician is right, the amount of concern with the behavior of other parties that we have found speaks poorly for reciprocity. Beneath this overt concern is the punctilious and painful awareness, exhibited by most politicians, of the narrowly defined boundaries within which Parliament operates and which constrain compromise. References to this immediate reality—marked more often by bickering than by comfortable accommodation—surface as soon as we move from generalities to qualifications and applications. Most illuminating in this context are the comments of two members of Parliament, a Christian Democrat and a Communist. If these politicians differ from their colleagues, it is not on their feelings, but on the fact that they expanded on them at great length. The Christian Democrat actually favored compromises unconditionally; the Communist made it depend on the need to save the legislation. Yet their explanations of the choice have a common ring; they speak to each other. Both men are alert to interparty issues; both are tangled in their complexity. Hence, their comments have a searching quality that most persuasively reveals the difficulties of reciprocity. In particular, the Christian Democrat is a member of a leftist faction of the party, traditionally rather open to the opposition and to the notion of a dialogue between government and PCI. Yet his answer was a rather strong and eloquent critique of the Communist party's attitudes toward the dialogue.

It is natural that, in a situation like the one you present, it is in the interest of every party to look for a basis of agreement with the others. With a party like ours, I would even say that it is our duty to seek such understandings. First of all, we are a party ... with great government responsibilities. .... And then also, we are a composite party, a party that is based on the same popular strata to which also our adversary appeals. It is natural therefore that ... the Communists and we must move in parallel directions. ... But we must be careful here .... If you allow me, yours is a leading question, a trap. Let's look at reality as it is concretely, and here it is clear that you want to know if we are ready for a dialogue not only with our government allies but also with the Communists. And we [his faction] certainly are, and we show our good will ... also through our action within our party. ... This, however, cannot be and must not be a one-sided relation, and the Communists delude themselves if they still think ..., but I don't think many of them do any more, if they hope to use the dialogue to break the unity of our party. In sum, I don't think that the Communists have yet demonstrated genuine sentiments toward an agreement. Maybe there is good will, I don't deny it, but what is still missing is the democratic method. In may cases their invitations to a dialogue are nothing but requests for one-sided concessions, if not outright blackmail. ... And then there are things on which compromises are not allowed, because here is where the Communists remain outside the democratic area, that is to say on the questions of freedom, pluralism, the protection of private initiative, and even on the autonomy of unions from political parties. We are well disposed ... toward a dialogue, toward agreements ... but the Communists must demonstrate this capacity with facts, not with words. (DC 17)

To which came the Communist's tailored answer:

I would say that, if it is a matter of saving a reform, we are certainly always open to a constructive understanding, provided, that is to say, that the purpose of the reform is not betrayed. For example, on the question of divorce, it has been above all the open action of our party that has made an agreement possible with the Catholics, while at the same time preserving the principle. These, however, are atypical situations. ... We are the opposition, and as such we are still subject to the legislative initiative of the government. ... On the theme of reforms ... it is not a question of compromises, the question is to make them or not to make them, and here it is the duty of the DC and its government allies to introduce in Parliament those reforms requested by the country. Our task is that of stimulating [the government] and of pushing [the reforms] forward, and ... it is not because the Communists want impossible reforms that they are not made. It is because there is no political will on the part of the government, and it is because of this that Parliament does not function. ... Parliament should be the clearinghouse of the system, the center where reform agreements among the great popular forces in the country are consolidated. But the DC does not want to ... initiate and discuss them. And then also, we must understand each other on the meaning of this word, because certainly when one says "compromise" it is not a word that scares us. ... But this doesn't mean to give in at any price, so that we can obtain access to the levers of power. For example, we do not make deals on the Constitution. The regions, the Constitutional Court, the Council of the Judiciary, the abolition of the fascist codes, bureaucratic reform, all of ... these are not things to obtain by bartering. When we have obtained them, that is not us but the country ... , it is because the democratic forces have compelled the DC government to be faithful to the constitutional pact. (PCI 8)

With such firm institutional memories of conflict, it is hard to fathom how reciprocity, even as it is advocated, can fully operate. The point is not which party is right and which is wrong. In a sense, the Communists are correct in claiming that on matters of social and political reform it is the lack of political will and initiative on the part of the government that stalemates legislation. The defect is recognized by sectors of informed public opinion that go well beyond the PCI.[8] But such a critical posture toward the government, expressed at the same time as a negotial system is advocated, is not likely to bring out a government already stuck in the morass of a highly volatile and heterogeneous coalition. As stated, reciprocity needs two to play, and if reciprocity is not extended by one partner it is most likely obtained by neither.

Such sentiments of suspicion are confirmed in a question similar to the one above, but asked much later in the interview and designed to see how the respondents perceived and evaluated the role of the major parties *other than theirs* in matters of compromise. "At times," the question read, "the various parties in Parliament employ compromises and agreements to pass legislation on which their interests do not coincide. How do you consider the behavior of the (PCI and PSI) ... (PCI and DC) ...

---

8. See, for instance, Nicola Greco, "Carenza di Coordinamento, Policentrismo e Contrattualismo nell'Attività di Governo," *Studi Parlamentari e di Politica Costituzionale*, Vol. 2, No. 4 (1969), pp. 23-42.

(PSI and DC) in these circumstances?" The pattern of answers is straightforward and, in some ways, anticlimatic (Table 32). Because the question, by asking about other parties, is the reciprocal of the previous one, it ends up by touching very similar chords. Although the respondents were not expressly asked to do so, few missed the opportunity to comment on the behavior of their own party. And the interesting side is not that practically all such comments were laudatory—even from Christian Democrats, who may have good reasons to disagree internally, but who seemed to be thinking more in terms of the behavior of their own faction. Rather, it is the fact that, in commenting on their own group, the respondents took compromise to be a natural or unavoidable aspect of the political game, which their party tries to channel and orient rather than resist. Some of them—like a very prominent Communist politician, usually identified as the leader of the "soft" wing of his party—used the occasion to restate their commitment to compromise as a general method.

As I said, our party considers these practices [of compromise] an important aspect of parliamentary life, from which the party cannot shy away. In a Parliament like the Italian, in which the very majority is the product of a coalition, and in which there are strong oppositions like ours, every legislative solution implies a compromise. This is not what constitutes reason for criticism. It is the nature of the compromise, which must be evaluated as it is from time to time. The practice of seeking a legislative compromise in a pluralistic Parliament with several political forces, is a necessity. (PCI 35)

But, as the comments moved to the details of how the other parties behaved, most answers revealed again a serious and paralyzing concern with the limits and dangers of compromise, and with questions of mutual trust. The idea of compromise as a

TABLE 32. Percentage Disapproving the Behavior of Other Parties in Matters of Compromise

	DC (52)	*PSI (48)*	*PCI (60)*
Disapprove DC	—	47.9 (23)	78.3 (47)
Disapprove PSI	46.2 (24)	—	61.7 (37)
Disapprove PCI	67.3 (35)	45.8 (22)	—

reciprocal method lost impact, and strict partisan considerations took the center stage, which made the legitimacy of compromise mainly rest on the particular coalition of parties that had engendered it. As a consequence, comments from members of one party turned out to be very predictable mirror images of the comments from the opposite party, and showed once more basic disagreement on decisional rules. Communist comments amounted to an overwhelming condemnation of the kind of compromises practiced by the other major parties as deleterious and confusing, insofar as they usually excluded the PCI and involved "unprincipled" deals between members of the coalition exclusively. They resented in particular that their former Socialist allies often lacked "vigilance" in these matters and failed to appreciate that "without Communist participation, the country cannot be governed." They concluded that the position of the PCI is for a "dialogue among all the parties of the constitutional spectrum," a code that leaves out only the extreme right. Christian Democratic respondents were predictably more divided than the Communists. Members of the left factions of the party showed, in more or less guarded tones, sympathy for the position of Communists on compromise, and welcomed a progressive opening of the practice. Members of other factions were more suspicious of compromises reaching beyond the coalition, and more disturbed at the ambiguous behavior of the Socialist allies toward the rest of the coalition and toward the PCI. In fact, they were in many cases more tolerant of the PCI which, as opposition, had no commitment to the coalition and was somehow entitled to try to expand it, than of their Socialist partners in government who, with their alleged openings toward the PCI, threatened the coalition. The Socialist respondents reciprocated the treatment by the other parties and defended their uncomfortable middle position by attacking both sides in more or less evenhanded fashion. While on the whole their perception of the other parties seemed the most favorable, perhaps since they saw themselves as the linchpin in interparty negotiations, they also berated the PCI for "crowding in" on them and the DC for strong-arm tactics in trying to twist coalition compromises to its own clientelistic interests.

A summary description of the way each party evaluates the

other's behavior in matters of compromise is reported in Table 32.[9] Again, what emerges from these answers, as from the previous ones, is that the question of compromise is a very central and nagging one in the minds of Italian politicians, and it elicits some of the most involved and "felt" answers. Comparatively few politicians have found firm and definitive personal solutions. Few are comfortbly rigid on an uncompromising, zero-sum game. Few, on the other hand, perceive compromise and its behavioral and attitudinal requisites without qualms and personal doubts, as a permanent and fairly well-oiled method of bringing parties together. The largest single group is made of politicians who, while unwilling to reject compromise, are still unable to articulate and internalize it into a full-fledged operational code of reciprocity. The full articulation of these mixed sentiments is often better appreciated through the respondents' comments and through open-ended questions than through forced-choice answers.

We may appropriately pause here and detail our theoretical map before proceeding. Our discussion of reciprocity and of the empirical evidence bearing on it allows us better to understand why, as seen in the first part of the previous chapter, Parliament has no firmly accepted decisional rule. Reciprocity, by the meaning of the word, implies that each partner shall adopt in his behavior toward the others a set of norms recognizing and trusting the others' role in the exchange situation. These norms are mirror-identical when the roles in the exchange situation are the same; they are special to each partner when the roles are distinctive. In this regard, a point made at the beginning of the chapter was that no Parliament, even if negotial, bases itself on perfectly interchangeable roles, such as those involved in the barter of similarly valued services and goods. Whatever the decisional format of Parliament, reciprocity means recognizing and protecting, though in different forms, the distinctive roles of majority and minority. More precisely, in an era of organized parties and active government, it means recognizing the respec-

---

9. The coding of the answers was done independently by four judges. Agreement by a majority of three was required. In cases of disagreement, the disagreement was solved in conference with the main investigator. A similar panel was used for coding other questions examined in this chapter. Disagreement occurred in 10 to 20 percent of the cases, depending on the questions to be coded.

tive roles of government and opposition parties. In British-style parliamentary systems, the formal adoption of majority rule and the firm definition of decisional responsibilities do not mean, as we have learned, the absence of reciprocity. On the contrary, such systems cannot authentically operate without the presence of community and elite norms restraining what John Calhoun called "absolute government," that is, the rule of an unchecked majority. Nor can they operate without unwritten norms enforcing the opposition's political control on the government and securing alternance in government. In systems that have resisted strict majority rule, on the other hand, reciprocity should not be coequal with the obliteration of the distinction between government and opposition, but must be considered as merely a new way of warding off the undesirable effects of the distinction, while preserving it. Irrespective of normative considerations, the fact is, at any rate, that the distinction remains and cannot be dealt with by ignoring it. As our interviews show, government and opposition are very much an immediate reality in the Italian Parliament, a reality which, even within the efforts to accommodate it in a negotial system, points consistently to different roles. In this sense, the task of reciprocity is to combine and balance norms requiring special behaviors from each partner.

Two such norms have appeared, implicitly or explicitly, in this and the preceding chapter. The first norm, to be applied and respected by the opposition and by parliamentary groups in general, is the recognition of *the government's duty/right to govern*, to act upon issue conflicts, and to take responsibilities for its actions. Insofar as the norm points to the protection of a duty, its special importance lies in the fact that, if correctly applied, it takes the government to task. That is, it makes it difficult for the government to hide stagnation behind the alibi of an unruly Parliament. If the norm fails, the alternative—in the presence of many parties—is a *régime d'assemblée*, where all parties are in government and nobody governs, where all issues and interests weigh directly on the government but none are aggregated, and where unanimity is the principle but the tyranny of minorities temporarily allied with each other is the reality. As to the second norm, reciprocity means also balancing governing needs with the interest of the opposition to share in the legislative initiative and to negotiate government decisions.[10] There is no better term to refer to this norm than *concurrent majority*. However, both terms—the government's duty/right to govern and concurrent majority—restate immediately Parliament's impossible predicament: It is required to combine the best of the two ideal norms *because* the balance of political forces does not allow a choice for either.

I shall close the analysis of reciprocity with some observations and evidence on concurrent majority, the government's duty/right to govern, and how they relate to each other. What is needed is simply retracing some of the empirical and theoretical claims already made at several points and backing them with some final evidence.

CONCURRENT MAJORITY, AND THE GOVERNMENT'S DUTY/RIGHT TO GOVERN

I first referred to concurrent majority when examining legislative outputs. There we noticed that legislation was "concurrent" in many ways. Most legislation is approved by large majorities going beyond the coalition and including the PCI; parliamentary initiative, even by the PCI, preserves an importance unparalleled in other Parliaments; and Communist amendments to government legislation are more successful than those of the opposition in other parliaments. But there I also observed that the use of the term *concurrence* was inappropriate and misleading, since the legislative behavior it intended to classify, far from resting on an improved method for coexistence, pointed to its failure. The observed behavior is not the result of a shared norm of concurrent majority, balancing and tempering the equally recognized prerogatives of the government. It is rather the consequence of a highly dispersive mix of orientations toward the two norms, which denies the balance, undercuts both norms, but parcels out to each party a share of the legislative action. There is, as noticed, considerable division within Parliament on the issue of whether and how the opposition should participate in legislative decisions. But, as shown below, there is wide support among all parliamentary groups for the notion that Parliament is the supreme repository of legislative prerogatives and should not

---

10. Let me make clear that I do not advocate the negotial model. I am simply showing what it takes to operate it, if this is the model Parliament is saddled with.

abdicate them in favor of the government. This attitudinal mix leaves the opposition a back-door entrance to legislative process, often through alliances of convenience with other groups jealous of their parliamentary prerogatives. But it also leaves the issue of concurrent majority unresolved; it is insufficient to support a negotiated legislative program; and it seriously undermines all the while the government's decisional perogatives. The presence of the attitudinal mix emerges from the analysis of two sets of questions in the interviews.

Attitudes toward the role of the Communist opposition in the legislative process are directly expressed in a double question having to do with whether the respondent and his party approved of two different behaviors of the PCI: One in which the party supports *important* government legislation, either in the final vote or during debate, *thus making passage possible;* one in which it votes against, despite the fact that the legislation contains elements which the party saw with positive eye. The results are predictably partisan (Table 33). Aside from the unanimous approval by the Communists, the behavior received divided support among the other parties. The Socialists approved a positive vote from the PCI by a limited margin, but were more critical of negative votes on good legislation, which they tended to regard as an unnecessary show of partisanship. Christian Democrats were more opposed. Close to one out of three approved a concurrent vote from the PCI; fewer approved a negative one. One interesting aspect of the two sets of attitudes is, incidentally, that politicians who condemned a concurrent vote (but not those who approved) also tended almost always to condemn a negative one. That is, for respondents who welcomed concurrence, a negative vote was in some cases an understandable posture, in others a matter of disappointment at the party's partisan calculations. For those who opposed concurrence, a negative vote was always

TABLE 33. Percentage Approving Voting Behavior by the PCI on Important Government Legislation

	DC (52)	*PSI (48)*	*PCI (60)*
Decisive positive vote	30.8 (16)	52.1 (25)	100.0 (60)
Negative vote	23.1 (12)	37.5 (18)	100.0 (60)

further proof of the Communists' fundamentally untrustworthy and alien nature.[11] Christian Democrats were also divided along factional lines, at least for what concerns approval of concurrence, with members of leftist factions on the approving side and others more strongly opposed.

Most of the Christian Democrats and the Socialists who opposed concurrence explicitly stressed the distinction raised by the question between cases in which the Communist votes were "additional," that is, the government bill had enough coalition votes to succeed without external support, and cases where the votes were decisive. In the latter case, the PCI vote was taken as an indication that the Communists had taken hold of the government bill and, through amendments and deals with sectors of the coalition, made it into their own bill. References were made to present and past occasions in which this had happened, and these were condemned as examples of Communist tactics to embarrass and disrupt the majority. Members of the majority who approved Communist concurrence took a clearly different view. They agreed with Communist respondents that a decisive vote by the opposition is not only perfectly constitutional, but serves often to rescue government legislation from being buried in cases in which government itself lacks enough will and commitment to see it through.[12] Occasions for decisive concurrence on important legislation, it should be pointed out, are in fact objectively rare, as most alliances stretching outside the coalition are alliances of convenience involving minor legislation. What counts, however, is

11. Cross-tabulation of the two questions gives the following percentages (DC and PSI combined; raw figures in parentheses):

		NEGATIVE VOTE	
		Approve	*Disapprove*
POSITIVE VOTE	Approve	58.5 (24)	41.5 (17)
	Disapprove	10.7 (6)	89.3 (53)

12. Cross-tabulation with Table 28 in Chapter III reveals that, given their similarity, attitudes toward the PCI's voting behavior are closely related to attitudes toward majority and proportionality rules, with politicians favoring proportionality also approving a positive vote by the PCI. What is more interesting, however, is that politicians are more likely to favor the principle of proportionality than an actual positive vote by the PCI. The difference is understandable, since concurrence in the first case does not touch the unity of the parliamentary majority; in the second it substitutes in part the majority.

not the incidence of the phenomenon but its political importance, the political stir it creates, the way it divides the majority.

But what is more interesting about attitudes toward Communist concurrence is the way they relate empirically to attitudes toward the government's duty/right to govern and toward the prerogatives of government and Parliament in legislative matters. I will examine the relation in a few paragraphs. Let us first examine attitudes toward the government. A question that touches closely on the issue asked the respondents what they thought of occasions when the parliamentary majority substantially amends government legislation against the government's desires. The question drew some of the sharpest and most self-assured answers in the interview, the content of which would have made it difficult to guess, had one not known, which party the respondent belonged to. Even among Christian Democrats, who were the least sympathetic to the practice, more than six out of ten respondents defended it as politically appropriate (Table 34). In essence, all the answers in support of the practice pointed to Parliament as more diversified and closer to the electorate than the government, hence more capable of responding to and

TABLE 34. Percentage Approving Substantial Amendments of Government Legislation by the Parliamentary Majority

DC (52)	PSI (48)	PCI (60)
61.5 (32)	81.25 (39)	85.0 (51)

mediating social demands, and entitled to the right of final decision. One of the more moderate answers came from a young and ambitious DC deputy, an intellectual who is usually identified as an articulate defender of strict majority discipline and a staunch supporter of government leadership, and who displayed majoritarian sentiments in many of his answers.

Parliament has at times objectively improved government proposals. I think the government should think through its projects more carefully, so as to improve their quality. The government . . . that is, should discuss its projects more extensively with its political parties, its groups in Parliament, the sectors directly affected by legislation. Only when the government can behave in this way can the government ask for complete support from Parliament. And I personally would welcome this type of arrangement. But, as of now, it doesn't seem to me that the government has always been able to mediate in a conclusive way within itself the demands of the various constituencies. And that is why I am compelled to say that this task must fall to Parliament. (DC 50)

Stronger answers were given by the Socialists, of whom four out of five found the practice of amending essentially correct, and by the Communists, who overwhelmingly defended it, although recognizing at times the needs of the government.[13] A rather restrained PCI deputy, not unlike his DC colleague, blamed the government for being unable to hold a majority together, and at the same time advocated Parliament's duty to seek and create such majorities.

It is clear that this [Parliament's amending of government bills] may break precarious balances, achieved by the government at a high cost. But this means that the agreement within government isn't strong enough to pass the test of the parliamentary majority. It is therefore right that it be modified.... When the government coalition is in crisis ... at a certain point Parliament becomes decisive and it can rescue legislation bogged down in the government. When in the fifties the DC had a strong majority and a strong center in De Gasperi, then these problems didn't exist. But today the legislative difficulties derive from the fact that there is no government, there is no majority to preserve. And then I must say I don't see why we should defer to this government that doesn't exist. First, ... the laws are already the result of a coalition compromise, then the compromise isn't definitive enough, and therefore it is broken and it has to be readjusted in Parliament, etc. Anyway, Parliament has the duty to act like this. I think that a government can mediate problems if it has a strong majority behind it; otherwise there wouldn't be any crisis. (PCI 21)

Both the Communist and the Christian Democratic respondent justified parliamentary prerogatives as a way to shore up and sustain the job of the government, when the latter fails to achieve a stable understanding on a piece of legislation. Both expanded their remarks to link them to the existing crisis of the government coalition. There is, however, an irony in these statements—especially the Communist's—and by no means an intended one. In a way the intervention of Parliament, which these politicians claim should remedy the incapacity of government to act, is in

---

13. The few Communists who condemned the practice interpreted it as a sign of the generalized irresponsibility and lack of political will of the government parties. They condemned what was for most Communists the consequence rather than the cause.

part its symptom, in part its cause. Indeed, for most other respondents parliamentary intervention in government matters was not so much a question of assisting in the business of government as one of protecting parliamentary prerogatives from government interference. And one key aspect of the findings is that these attitudes are by no means confined to back-benchers and opposition. We discovered that they are just as frequent among a group of twenty-four respondents who, belonging to the majority, occupy or have occupied positions of leadership in government, in the parties, or in Parliament (present and former vice-presidents of the chambers, committee chairmen, presidents and vice-presidents of the parliamentary groups, ministers and undersecretaries, members of party executive bureaus). That is, one would expect that a member of the majority with an experience as parliamentary officer would be more sensitive to the needs of the government and would reveal more "governmental" attitudes, the more so if now or in the past he has also occupied a position of leadership in his party. But we found no evidence of this. Even former cabinet members (undersecretaries and ministers) showed limited governmental attitudes. Sixteen of the twenty-four respondents, or 66.7 percent, approved the amending behavior of the majority; five of the nine in the group with a cabinet experience did likewise.[14] One interpretation of the latter finding is that, since all cabinet officers are recruited from Parliament and remain in it long afterwards, they do not change attitudes very easily as a result of cabinet experience.

The extent to which attachment to parliamentary prerogatives and suspicion of government power are rooted is also revealed by the way members of Parliament perceived Parliament's chief functions. In one question the respondents were asked what they thought of what Italian constitutionalists call "delegificazione," that is, the transfer of decision-making powers on special matters from Parliament to executive bodies. In another, they were asked how they would rank law-making compared to "Parliament's other functions." In both cases, overwhelming majorities confirmed the legislators' attachment to their legislative prerogatives and to the preeminence of Parliament vis-à-vis governments.

14. Nine respondents is too small a number for conclusive claims about cabinet officers. Nevertheless, present and former cabinet members are not that many, and the group was made up of rather influential politicians, with rather long records of government service.

Only a small fraction of the respondents said they did not consider law-making the supreme function of Parliament (Table 35). They were mostly Socialists and Christian Democrats, and they all pointed to political control over the executive as the chief function. All other respondents saw the matter otherwise. Whether out of lack of legal sophistication, a different reading of constitutional deontology, or political considerations, Parliament was for them synonymous with legislature. There were repeated references to the importance of political control and the need to strengthen it but, when the chips were down, it was law-making that took precedence. As a Communist senator put it:

> It is all nice and beautiful to say that Parliament should exercise a greater political control. In the end, what guarantees . . . [political control] is above all an efficient and careful use of the legislative instrument on the part of Parliament. (PCI 51)

With such views, *delegificazione* found a rather unsympathetic audience among the respondents. Among those who drew the distinction, there was near unanimity on the need to delegate legislation on minor matters to other representative or bureaucratic institutions, and proud reference to the legisative powers of the newly created regional councils. But opposition to the delegation of more substantive legislative powers was equally adamant. Since the principle involved transferring legislative powers to the executive and curbing private initiative in this regard, it was supported by no Communists and, in predictable fashion, by approximately one out of every four Socialists and Christian Democrats (Table 36).

In sum, a Parliament that staunchly defends its right to alter government legislation significantly, that considers making laws its chief occupation, and that fears major *delegificazione* does not

TABLE 35. Percentage Choosing Law-Making as Most Important Function of Parliament

	DC (52)	PSI (48)	PCI (60)
Law-making	76.9 (40)	70.8 (34)	88.3 (53)
Other functions	23.1 (12)	29.2 (14)	11.7 (7)

seem in the best position to seek a balance of powers with government. The notion of parliamentary supremacy is ill-suited to such balance and seriously imperils the government's duty/right to govern. The notion that law-making is the main and exclusive function of Parliament strikes a jarring note in a system that, by being parliamentary, does not recognize and institutionalize a strict separation of powers.

It may be thought at this point that there is a close tie between these attitudes toward government-Parliament relations and attitudes toward concurrence by the PCI. It makes some sense, for example, to speculate that politicians who defend the prerogatives of Parliament vis-à-vis the government are arguing in effect against strict majority rule enforced by a strong government, and will hence accept and be more open toward a more central role of the PCI in the decisional process. It makes even more sense to argue that, vice versa, politicians who defend the special role of the government may consequently advocate a more clear division in the roles of majority and opposition. If support for these hypotheses is found, it could then be said that, though there is no agreement on the place of government, opposition, and parliamentary majority in the legislative process, there are at least clear battle lines drawn between supporters of opposite decisional conceptions, with each of the two sides taking congruent positions on the matters at issue. If support is not found, the presence of a vast majority asserting the prerogatives of Parliament helps in no way the solution of the Communist role: That majority remains divided on the latter. To buttress the hypotheses it should be pointed out that parties do make the connection in their public pronouncements: they do justify their attitudes toward the PCI in terms of their conceptions of what government-Parliament relations should be. However, empirical support for the connection is of a special and revealing kind (Table 37).

Table 36. Percentage Approving *Delegificazione* on Important Matters[1]

DC (36)	PSI (39)	PCI (52)
30.6 (11)	25.6 (10)	—

[1]Only respondents who drew the distinction between minor and important matters

TABLE 37. Attitudes toward Decisive Vote by the PCI in Favor of Government Legislation, by Attitudes toward Majority Amendments to Government Legislation, in Percentage

	DC (52)	
	Disapprove PCI vote (36)	Approve PCI vote (16)
Disapprove amendments (20)	75.0 (15)	25.0 (5)
Approve amendments (20)	65.6 (21)	34.4 (11)

	PSI (48)	
	Disapprove PCI vote (23)	Approve PCI vote (25)
Disapprove amendments (9)	66.7 (6)	33.3 (3)
Approve amendments (39)	43.6 (17)	56.4 (22)

Leaving aside the Communists, for whom the two sets of attitudes are invariant, we do find that the few politicians who oppose as politically ill-advised majority amendments to government legislation extend this attitude of support for government action to a closure toward the PCI. A very large majority of Socialists and Christian Democrats in this group judge negatively the fact that legislation initiated by the government may succeed because of the decisive support of the PCI. But, on the other side, the many politicians who defend the legislative prerogatives of Parliament do not easily extend them to the PCI. It is true that they are *relatively* more tolerant of the Communists' legislative behavior, but—more important—a large number of them still resent it (almost half of the Socialists, two out of three Christian Democrats). One revealing aspect here is the attitudes of the various factions within the DC. We have seen that the left of this party is strongly supportive of Communist concurrence, while the other factions tend to oppose it. But there are no discernible differences among the factions on the issue of Parliament's amending powers: The left factions are no more pro-Parliament than the other factions. This means that the left's greater openness to the PCI cannot be explained by its conceptions of government-Parliament relations. Nor does the greater inclination of the other factions to keep the PCI at bay convince them of the need for a more assertive government leadership.

No matter how we try to argue the logical and psychological connections between the two sets of attitudes, they seem in fact to be rather extraneous to most politicians. For a minority advocating government leadership, the connection is there. But for a larger group the two dimensions are distant. Just as attitudes toward the PCI divided the parties internally, so they now cut across conceptions of Parliament and government. And here is the political importance of these findings. Although strong sentiments of attachment to parliamentary prerogatives are widespread among the majority, they do not extend to including a new formula regulating relations between majority and opposition. In fact, by asserting the preeminence of Parliament and the dispersion of decisional powers on one side, and by dividing on the Communist issue, on the other, the majority makes relations with the opposition that much more ambiguous. But, without providing a solution, these mixed sentiments provide the PCI with a convenient entry in the legislative process. For one thing, it is objectively difficult to prevent a party of the size and resources of the PCI from taking advantage of a situation in which Parliament asserts its primacy. For another thing, a parliamentary majority attached to its prerogatives is not alien to marriages of convenience with the opposition.

In sum, the government's duty/right to govern and concurrence by the opposition have found no clear acceptance *and no way to coexist in an effective operational code*. Neither has imposed itself upon the other. Both are very much at issue, both live at a stand–off, and in so doing they are one immediate cause of legislative indecisiveness.

PARTISANSHIP, ELITE AUTONOMY, AND CONCEPTIONS OF REPRESENTATION

We may pause again at this point and detail our theoretical map one step further. I have said that Parliament lacks the cultural conditions for operating as a negotial body; specifically, it lacks reciprocity. I now intend to go one step back in the chain of causality and examine what cultural factors are in turn important for the operation of reciprocity. The factors can be derived rather intuitively if we stress one particular aspect of the notion of reciprocity. Logical derivation should avoid the danger of "misplaced concreteness" in claiming their importance in the Italian context.

It is clear from much of the discussion in the previous pages that reciprocity, in a Parliament where many parties with a distinctive political base meet, means concretely moderating partisan demands in favor of accords among parties. It means, in other words, what John Manley, referring to the operation of the committee system in the American Congress, calls "restrained partisanship."[15] Cast in such terms, the norm states that legislators must see themselves as more than partisans pursuing their party demands. They are to assume responsibility for achieving mutually satisfactory solutions and they must be ready, if necessary, to yield on some of their demands and trade on others. In principle, the norm is not an impossible one to meet. Restrained partisanship does not require that the contestants renounce their partisanship, adopt any common purpose beyond the achievement of a tolerable solution, or show any special convergence of interests. Aside from the fact that partisanship is in the democratic interest of an open articulation of issues, bending reciprocal demands does not signify renouncing respective goals. It does not mean pursuing extremely demanding positive-sum games in which contestants strive for a basic transformation of images and goals and are even ready to lose to increase the utilities of others. Restrained partisanship does not even have to operate all the time. What is simply required is, when necessary, an adjustive posture, a posture that assumes partisanship and can be manifested through a variety of methods and behaviors.[16] Nevertheless, as we have amply seen from attitudes toward compromise, restrained partisanship, while frequently and genuinely advocated in principle, is substantially extraneous to most Italian legislators.

One set of reasons can be logically derived from the notion of

---

15. John Manley, "The House Committee on Ways and Means: Conflict Management in a Congressional Committee," *American Political Science Review* 59 (1965), pp. 927-939. See also Fenno, op. cit., for a similar concept of "minimal partisanship."

16. For the notion of partisan adjustment, see Charles Lindblom, *The Intelligence of Democracy* (New York: Free Press, 1965), esp. chapters 2 and 20. Partisan adjustment does not deny partisan disagreement; it is a disjointed method for accommodating it.

restrained partisanship itself. Indeed, the notion dictates relations not only between elites of different parties, but also between elites and the partisan base they represent. The point of the latter relations is that legislators are most unlikely to subscribe to restrained partisanship unless at the same time they also embrace a norm of "elite autonomy" from their political base. Elite autonomy, in other words, comes close to being a necessary condition for the operation of restrained partisanship and reciprocity. It demands that legislators see themselves free of constraints from partisan and constituency demands, that they define their role as going beyond that of a mere party delegate, that they feel competent to commit their rank and file to their legislative choices, even when these may involve partisan dissatisfaction.[17] Legislators who construe their role as strictly bound by the partisan interests they represent are most unlikely to risk their political position by compromising on such interests. For one thing, they may fear losing status with their party following by betraying their trust; for another, they may fear losing credibility with legislators of other parties by being unable to commit their following.[18]

---

17. It may be objected that there is a substantial difference between partisan constraints and constraints coming from the electorate at large. The former, coming from party organization and cadres, are intuitively likely to curb elite accommodation. The latter, coming from voters who are often uninvolved in party activities, may or may not curb elites, depending on the nature of the voters' demands. It is possible that the voters demand elite accommodation and an end to conflict. My answer to the objection is double. First, as I make clear in the next text paragraph, what counts is the way legislators see the electorate and envision constraints. The chapter will show that legislators see party and electoral constraints as one and the same thing. They are constrained because they embrace a populist-partisan creed, which sees parties and voters closely linked by a two-way network of communication and ideology. Second, it is doubtful that Italian voters are more appreciative and understanding of compromise and what it takes to enforce it than political leaders. We should remember here the relatively high level of partisan hostility among Italian voters reported in 1963 by Almond and Verba in their comparative study of political culture. These findings are confirmed by very recent research by Giacomo Sani reporting widespread opposition among voters to elite proposals for a governing agreement between Communists and the majority. As Sani well argues, thirty years of fierce electoral competition among parties, designed to delegitimize each other, have left their deep mark on the Italian voters. See Gabriel Almond and Sidney Verba, *The Civic Culture* (Princeton: Princeton University Press, 1963), esp. chapter 5; Giacomo Sani, "Mass Perceptions of 'Anti-System' Parties: The Case of Italy" (paper delivered at the American Political Science Association meeting, Chicago, September 1974). Additional evidence on a possible thawing of popular attitudes toward the PCI will be considered in the last chapter.

18. Nordlinger, op. cit., pp. 74-87.

One clarification is in order, before moving to evidence, concerning the meaning of elite autonomy. The term refers to what legislators think about their role, not to any actual state of affairs as to their real degree of autonomy. It is possible, in other words, that partisan constraints, while perceived or self-imposed, have no structural basis. In fact, even after making allowance for significant national differences in the matter, there is still ample evidence that political elites are by profession often more likely than their followers to evaluate issues in a partisan perspective.[19] And what they may present as partisan constraints are often projections of their own partisan orientations and role definitions.[20] At the same time, political elites, at least those interacting across group lines, also have, by virtue of their role as decision-makers, a greater professional stimulus to mediate issues.[21] Whether they will give priority to the latter, however, depends on their notions of elite autonomy, in regard to which the presence of actual constraints need not concern us here. In sum, we are not preoccupied now with whether the political base of parties is more or less supportive of mediations and accommodations than its leadership, nor with where constraints within parties originate.[22] What counts per se is how legislators conceive these mat-

19. See the classical statement in Herbert McClosky et al., "Issue Conflict and Consensus among Party Leaders and Followers," *American Political Science Review* 54 (1960), pp. 406-427. See also Samuel Barnes, "Ideology and the Organization of Conflict: On the Relationship between Political Thought and Behavior," *Journal of Politics* 28 (1966), pp. 513-530. On partisanship as an elite attribute in other countries, see Duncan MacRae, *Parliament, Parties, and Society in France 1946-1958* (New York: St. Martin's Press, 1967), esp. pp. 326ff.; Philip Converse and Georges Dupeux, "Politicization of the Electorate in France and the United States," *Public Opinion Quarterly* 26 (1962), pp. 1-23. For an analysis of this and other points raised in this paragraph, see Di Palma, op. cit., pp. 7-10 and 15-16; Rodney Stiefbold, "Segmented Pluralism and Consociational Democracy in Austria: Problems of Political Stability and Change," in Martin O. Heisler, ed., *Politics in Europe* (New York: McKay, 1974), esp. pp. 147-155.

20. Richard Hamilton, "Party Systems, Party Organizations, and the Politics of New Masses," in *Proceedings of the Third International Conference on Comparative Political Sociology* (Berlin: Freien Universität Berlin, 1968), p. 132; Murray Edelman, "Myths, Metaphors and Political Conformity," *Psychiatry* 30 (1967), pp. 217-228.

21. Herbert McClosky, "Consensus and Ideology in American Politics," *American Political Science Review*, 58 (1964), pp. 361-382; Almond and Verba, op. cit., pp. 486-487.

22. As we shall see in Chapter VI, these constraints derive from the multiparty system, the organizational and electoral strategies of parties, and the type of partisan electorate they have managed to create. Constraints go so far that we find little difference in images of party and elite roles between legislators and party cadres. The term *constraints* is in a way inappropriate, as Italian legislators are true creatures of their parties. For two classical statements on party constraints upon members of Parliament, see Roberto Michels, *Political Parties* (Glencoe: Free Press, 1949), Part II; Maurice Duverger, *Les Partis Politiques* (Paris: Armand Colin, 1951), pp. 211-235.

ters, on the assumption that decision-making falls directly upon them, and that therefore their conceptions often have real and immediate consequences for their decisional style.

We asked several question of our respondents, touching more or less directly upon conceptions of elite autonomy. Some have to do with legislators' relations with the electorate and the basis of their parties, others with their conceptions of the role and functions of a representative.[23] The general and strong impression that emerges from the answers is that it makes little sense to speak of legislators' autonomy in the Italian parliamentary context. Not only is there acute awareness among the respondents of the partisan roles in which legislators are cast and of the negotial constraints which these impose—something which we have learned already from other answers—but there is also an apparent acceptance of such roles as proper and required of a legislator. The latter image may be somewhat surprising. It does not square with conventional views of legislators as a rather independent breed, resentful of narrow party and constituency directives, and striving to assert their special prerogatives and their exclusive political insights. Within a European context, it seems at odds with the notion that legislators, because of their special role and their exposure to colleagues of other parties, escape the discipline of organized mass parties and are often in conflict with the internal party leadership. However, for reasons to be discussed in this chapter and in the chapter on the party system, such views of conflict between legislators and their parties are, at least in Italy, misplaced. There is, first of all, a strong populist component to the political style of most Italian parliamentarians. It is reflected in their sentiments toward parliamentary supremacy, since supremacy is closely associated with the belief that Parliament is the political body closest to the country and the most genuine expression of the voters' needs and demands. Within Parliament, in

---

23. The classical collaborative study on legislative roles is John Wahlke et al., *The Legislative System* (New York: Wiley, 1962). See also John Wahlke and Heinz Eulau, eds., *Legislative Behavior* (New York: Wiley, 1959); Allan Kornberg, "The Rules of the Game in the Canadian House of Commons," *Journal of Politics* 26 (1964), pp. 336-363, and *Canadian Legislative Behavior* (New York: Holt, Rinehart and Winston, 1967), chapter 6; Malcolm Jewell, "Attitudinal Determinants of Legislative Behavior: The Utility of Role Analysis," in Allan Kornberg and Lloyd Musolf, eds., *Legislatures in Developmental Perspective* (Durham: Duke University Press, 1970), pp. 460-500; Samuel Patterson and John Wahlke, eds., *Comparative Legislative Behavior* (New York: Wiley, 1972), Part III; Fréderic Debuyst, *La Fonction Parlementaire en Belgique: Mécanismes d'Accès et Images* (Bruxelles: CRISP, 1967), Part II, chapter 3.

turn, the presence of political parties is inescapable; indeed, because parties are the main interpreters of popular sentiments, they give structure to Parliament and legitimacy to its members.

To put it in other words, the concept of elite autonomy struck many legislators as odd and alien to the "Italian experience." Although nothing in the questions suggested such reading, elite autonomy evoked among many respondents an image of the legislator as an unattached entrepreneur, a sort of stereotype "American senator" strong on personal resources and heedless of partisan and popular responsibilities. It also evoked an unattached and nonpartisan electorate, indifferent to group appeals, depoliticized, and hence easily manipulated by legislators. For most respondents elite autonomy made no sense in a country where neither legislators nor voters can (and should) be separated from the party label they carry. One aspect that impresses in practically all interviews is the fact that politicians continuously describe beliefs, events, experiences, not as personal ones, but as something they share with other members of their parties. Questions couched in personal terms, as most of them were, elicited "collective" answers, in which the whole party speaks through the respondent. In only two cases, a Socialist and a Christian Democratic deputy, both from the North, were we clearly confronted with politicians who seemed to construe politics as a personal game and showed in the content and style of their answers all the trappings of the political entrepreneur. This is not to say that their answers were more genuine than those of their colleagues. The latter did not "hide" their personal feelings behind orthodox smokescreens; they just projected them in a partisan role. I have, for instance, no reason to disbelieve the sentiments of the Communist senator who, speaking implicitly for many of her colleagues in all parties, sharply commented on our questions on legislators' roles and relations with the electorate in the following terms:

You keep talking about parliamentarians and the electorate as if they were some sort of undifferentiated and disembodied entities floating in mid-air. But behind them there is a precise reality, which is made of parties, organizations, ideologies, historical commitments, and divisions, which is the Italian reality. I don't know any such thing as the electorate in general. I know that there are electorates of each party, each with its own ... demands and aspirations, and this is the reality which we recognize.... You ask each member of Parliament about his ideas, what he does, as if there existed such thing as a "model parliamentarian." But these questions don't have any sense if you ignore the parties and the social classes to which we belong. . . . One reads a lot today about the Italian political class, about its defects, its lack of preparation. But this so-called political class is a readymade sociological category, a polemical invention, because the political class is very diverse both objectively and subjectively. . . . It's understood that each member of Parliament feels that he has precise responsibilities toward his base and his party, because after all we are a country with strong party organizations. But each party has its own way of adhering to this responsibility, and I wouldn't feel comfortable in placing DC and PCI quite on the same level. (PCI 1)

To be sure, the senator has a point: The questions were often couched in nonpartisan terms, and references to the electorate were often generic. It was up to the respondents to give them a partisan content, which they often and eloquently did. One first question designed to explore attitudes toward elite autonomy asked, for instance, what the respondents thought the relation should be between legislators and the electorate: "Should legislators operate in Parliament according to their conscience and their best political knowledge, even if this may contrast with the expectations of the electorate, or should they strive to adhere to the expectations of the latter?" Only about 20 percent of the respondents—divided roughly equally among parties—were ready to make a normative choice, and almost all opted for the autonomy of the legislator. The rest rejected the alternative as artificial and offered in their answers an often dazzling and impassioned display of dialectics, designed to compose what they considered a false antinomy. The result is a type of answer that basically rejects the logic of elite autonomy in favor of a closer symbiosis between legislators, parties, and electorate. It shows that members of the Italian Parliament think at times in very similar ways about their roles, even across party lines.

Many respondents in all parties did point out that divergences between legislators and the voters are, of course, not uncommon, especially since at times the electorate may have narrower views of legislation than legislators, and may seek immediate and personal benefits. In such cases, they argued, a mutual understanding should be sought, and legislators may eventually have to proceed according to their better judgment. But, in a fashion observed already in other answers, most of them went on from these preliminary observations to comments that revealed their discomfort with the normative choice. In essence, they found the choice extraneous to the Italian parliamentary context. Some resolved the discomfort by cutting short their answer; many more became involved in elaborate explanations. In all cases, however, the argument amounted at least to the following: In the Italian Parliament there are no individual legislators but organized parties, which should provide the link between legislators and the country; therefore there shouldn't be and there usually isn't any divergence between legislators and voters, because the parties provide both with the same ideology. If divergences exist, it means that the legislator—or his very party—has failed in his function. This is another way of saying that legislators should have little special status on account of their decisional functions, the more so as this status is not obtained vis-à-vis an undifferentiated electorate, but in respect to organized parties of which the legislators are direct expression.

One DC deputy put these sentiments more explicitly than others:

I would be tempted to say that I prefer the first choice, but it really seems to me that this would avoid what is the real problem. . . . That is, the responsibility of a member of Parliament is a responsibility that concerns neither his individual conscience nor a so-called electorate, but is first of all toward his own party, and by doing this . . . toward the electorate that the party represents. And it is only in this sense that we can say that the duty of a deputy is to follow his own conscience, but it is clear that this conscience involves a pact with his own party. It is a conscience that he has developed in his party life, and for which he is responsible not only to himself but also to his party colleagues. With this I am not saying that he must obey the party *perinde ac cadaver* . . . we are not the Church after all. But I say that *we* are the party and we have a collective responsibility. To finish, I would like to add that in this relation we also find a solution for the role of the electorate, in the sense that the electorate is represented by the party, and therefore . . . a member of Parliament who acts according to his political conscience acts also—if you forgive the Hegelian touch—according to the desires of his voters. (DC 39)

We had suggested to our respondents a choice between two traditional Burkeian roles—that of a trustee and that of a voters' delegate. What most of them opted for, even though this was not suggested, was the role of what may be called a party delegate, where responsibility to a party has much greater persuasiveness, and more seriously limits autonomy, than responsibility toward a more distant and not always present electorate. To be more precise, the coding of the answers yielded the results reported in Table 38. Almost irrespective of their party, members of Parliament rejected the role of "voters' delegate," gave little support to the role of "trustee," and chose by a good majority the role of "party delegate." The remaining minority opted for a role, most often shortly and perfunctorily articulated, that could be called "compromiser," insofar as respondents pointed to the need to balance electoral demands with a representative's convictions. Fifty to 65 percent of the respondents—depending on the party—choosing the role of party delegate may not seem an impressive majority. The role, however, was not suggested and was the most difficult to articulate. And even if the two roles offered by the question were not acceptable—as for most they were not—a generic statement to the effect that the two should be balanced would have offered the easiest way out. The fact that only a minority "got away" with such statement is witness to the centrality of the party in the relation between representatives and the electorate. As the party takes the center stage, the term *electorate* loses its undifferentiated features, and becomes progressively identified, as in the comments of the Communist senator, with the base, the rank and file, the organized and active membership of each party. In the extreme, the term is a synonym for the party organization and apparatus, as distinguished from the party's parliamentary contingent. Hence, for many legislators the question of elite autonomy becomes simply a question of whether legislators should enjoy special independence with respect to the party; and the answer is most often negative. Responsibility to the electorate makes sense to an Italian politician and becomes legitimate only when the electorate is conceived of as a set of separate and organized entities.

TABLE 38. Conceptions of the Role of the Parliamentarian Vis-à-Vis the Electorate, in Percentage

	DC (52)	PSI (48)	PCI (60)
Voters' delegate	5.8 (3)	4.2 (2)	3.3 (2)
Trustee	19.2 (10)	14.6 (7)	13.3 (8)
Party delegate	50.0 (26)	62.5 (30)	65.0 (39)
Compromiser	25.0 (13)	18.75 (9)	18.3 (11)

These views of the electorate as recognizable political families, closely interwoven with parties and legislators, show up in a number of other questions, also having to do with representation and relations with the electorate. One question asked the respondents which groups they thought their representative mandate referred to: the whole country, all the voters of their party, all the voters of their constituency, the voters who had voted for them, or some other category. A first interesting result of the question is that very few respondents—approximately 10 percent, half of them Christian Democrats—considered local constituencies and local party voters as the source of their mandate (Table 39). The rest of the legislators thought of themselves as having a national mandate, and they were approximately equally divided between those who construed their mandate as referring to all voters in the country and those who construed it in strictly partisan terms. The large number of politicians who think of their mandate as involving all voters seems to conflict with the previous finding that most legislators think of the electorate in terms of separate party families. But it should be kept in mind that the principle that every legislator represents all citizens is enshrined in the Constitution. It was difficult for many legislators to ignore this fact. Quite a few made explicit reference to it and, interestingly enough, all respondents with a law degree, irrespective of their party affiliation, defined their mandate in constitutional terms. But, despite its legal weight on opinions, the constitutional norm does not seem to have much consequence as an operative concept, informing other facets of elite opinion and behavior. No matter what category the respondents thought they represented—whether country, party, or constituency—a series of

TABLE 39. Which Group a Member of Parliament Thinks He Represents, in Percentage

	DC (52)	*PSI (48)*	*PCI (60)*
Local constituency	7.7 (4)	4.2 (2)	6.6 (4)
Local party voters	5.8 (3)	4.2 (2)	—
National party voters	38.5 (20)	47.9 (23)	50.0 (30)
Whole country	48.1 (25)	43.75 (21)	43.3 (26)

follow-up questions reveals that, as a matter of concrete operational codes, representation almost always involved the idea of translating and absorbing popular demands in a partisan ideology.

This transformation is rather intuitive in the case of those members of Parliament who claimed at the start that they represented only a partisan electorate. These respondents were asked two follow-up questions. They were first asked how they saw the group they had said they represented. Did they see it as "rather homogeneous in its social composition and in its political attitudes, and how, or rather diversified, and how?" Almost all respondents made it a point that their group was rather diversified and included individuals and categories from all paths of life (Table 40). Communists were particularly careful in trying to dispel the view that theirs was an electorate predominantly made up of workers and lower-status categories. As one of them, a prominent Southern senator, explained it:

> Ideally, we are a party of the working class. But around the ideology of the working class we organize the most different social strata—peasants, students, tradesmen, intellectuals, employees, businessmen. . . . Otherwise we would fail our mission as a national party, that is as a party capable of forming around itself Gramsci's "historical bloc." (PCI 9)

Not unlike him, however, a large majority of the respondents combined social diversity with political homogeneity, and variously explained that what held together the many groups they represented was a common political ideology. Only 20 percent of the respondents—half of them Christian Democrats—found the groups they represented to be also politically diversified, or specified that political homogeneity did not mean that their supporters possessed precise, articulate, and perfectly identical beliefs.

TABLE 40. Percentage Who See Their Party Electorate as Socially and Politically Homogeneous[1]

	DC (23)	PSI (25)	PCI (30)
Socially homogeneous	17.4 (4)	40.0 (10)	26.7 (8)
Politically homogeneous	65.2 (15)	88.0 (22)	83.3 (25)

[1] Only respondents who said they represent local or national party voters

Given the prevalent perceptions of the political make-up of represented groups, the following question drew a similarly modal response. "According to you," we asked, "what does your representative mandate consist of? How do you interpret it? That is, what does it mean to represent the groups you referred to?" "To represent" was taken in general to mean interpreting popular demands, acting in their behalf, giving them legislative expression. The finding is per se not shattering, except that, once again, the party appeared as the linchpin in the relation. As shown in Table 41, two out of three respondents, with little differences among parties, introduced the party in their answer without any probing on our part. It was the party organization that gave structure and unity to the demands of the electorate and, at the same time, provided the representative with a directive for action. By comparison with the party, representatives appeared to have little personal initiative in reconciling and channeling popular demands, except as agents of the party. A Socialist senator offered a rather precise and succinct version of his colleagues' sentiments in this regard:

I sit in Parliament because my party and I are committed to a program which the Socialist electorate has chosen as its own. And therefore we must do everything to remain as faithful as possible to it. That's what is called "to represent." (PSI 32)

The remaining one-third used, as it is likely to happen with open-ended questions, more generic and evasive formulas, such as "acting in the interests of the voters," "trying to interpret the voters' sentiments as best as one can," "learning to be a serious and informed legislator." In such cases a probing question was employed, asking the respondent to expand on the statement. As a result, slightly less than one-third of these elusive respondents ended up by making reference to the party as the essential guide in performing their representative job.

TABLE 41. Percentage Mentioning Adherence to Their Party as the Way to Carry Out the Representative Mandate[1]

DC (23)	PSI (25)	PCI (30)
60.9 (14)	64.0 (16)	73.3 (22)

[1] Only respondents who said they represent local or national party voters

But the respondents analyzed here are those who had said they represented only a part of the electorate: their view of representation as a partisan role was to be expected. What is more interesting is that those who saw themselves as representing the whole national community came also, when their attitudes were probed, to the same partisan conclusions. These respondents were confronted with the following dilemma: "You have been elected with the votes of only a part of the electorate. So have all other members of Parliament. But your mandate refers to the whole national community and other legislators feel the same way about their mandate. How do you reconcile the nature of the mandate with the facts of electoral support?" A few of the respondents must have taken the question as impertinent or legally and philosophically naive, as their answers, even after probing, never went beyond assertions to the effect that representing the national community is a constitutional duty, that the Constitution expressly forbids a party mandate, that electoral support and representation should not be confused, that the conflict does not exist in their minds, or that in any case it is most often resolved by giving primacy to the constitutional dictate (Table 42). Some others took a pluralist posture on the matter, arguing that no representative and no party is a repository of absolute truth. Hence, they either suggested that the interests of the community are best served by free competition among parties and interests, or indicated that each party should do its best not to be confined

TABLE 42. How Members of Parliament Reconcile Limited Electoral Support with a National Constitutional Mandate, in Percentage[1]

	DC (25)	PSI (21)	PCI (26)
By restating the constitutional mandate	28.0 (7)	14.3 (3)	7.7 (2)
By recognizing the diversity of parties and interests	16.0 (4)	23.8 (5)	7.7 (2)
By adhering to party interpretations of national interest	56.0 (14)	61.9 (13)	84.6 (22)

[1] Only respondents who said they represent the national community.

by the facts of electoral support and should try to diversify its appeals and the interests it serves.

As a Socialist parliamentarian, who combined both sentiments, put it:

> In a multiparty system like ours we can't escape the inevitable fact that electorally each one of us is the expression of only a sector of the country, and at times a very small one. This is how democracies work; otherwise they wouldn't be democracies. The interests of the community are not served by any single party, but by all the parties together, through a system of free competition of programs and ideas. When there are many parties . . . this requires that each party go beyond itself and try to "listen-in" to other parties, to all the groups. (PSI 14)

The connection with restrained partisanship is stated herein in rather simple and direct fashion, and it offers one solution to the dilemma of representation presented in the question. But this type of statement was definitely a minority one. Together with statements that simply insisted on the constitutional dictate, it accounts for only 32 percent of the answers.

The remaining respondents—especially the Communists, but also a majority of Christian Democrats—took a somewhat more elaborate and complex tack on the question. In a way, their type of answer offered a more concerted effort to rescue the constitutional dictate and to reconcile it with their partisan commitments. But they could do this only by claiming that, of all parties, theirs was the one that best interpreted the generalized interests of the country. They had to take an exclusive position that recognized little space for similar claims by other parties: Each respondent, as member of *his* party, felt that he served the national community by serving *that* party. But what happens to parliamentary relations when so many legislators anoint their party and their partisan ideology with a superior national mission? Far from suggesting negotial predispositions, these attitudes suggest partisan exclusiveness in the extreme, and little decisional autonomy for legislators. An excellent illustration of this thinking is provided by a Christian Democrat who, like the last respondent I quoted, began by acknowledging the reality of a multiparty system, but gave the dilemma a different solution.

> The reconciliation [referred to in the question] exists, at least in our party. . . . The principle expressed by the Constitution is an ideal principle, with which all parties should inspire themselves. Our party con-

siders itself as a national force, and we work on the basis of the opinion that our program corresponds to the general interests of the country; it doesn't simply represent the interests of narrow categories. When therefore we act in keeping with our party program we don't betray the concept of representation. On the contrary, this is the best way to be faithful to it and to the Constitution. This cannot always be said of other parties.... We believe that exactly insofar as we act as a united party and as representatives of our own voters, we at the same time act not ... in a narrow way ..., [but] we adhere ... to a general function vis-à-vis all the voters. (DC 29)

As the answer indicates, respondents who had started by describing themselves as representatives of the whole community eventually converged with those respondents who had started with a partisan view of representation. Indeed, the former respondents, like the latter, were finally asked what it meant to them to represent. Their answer can be surmised (Table 43). After probing, most of them answered in a way whose synthesis is best expressed by a Communist politician:

[To represent] ... means to give legislative expression to the political demands of the wider possible strata of the electorate, in the light of my party's political platforms. (PCI 55)

We may close this section on elite autonomy and partisanship[24] by clinching a last matter of relevance for legislative behavior. We have found so far that legislative roles tend to be strongly defined by party commitments, indeed by commitments to party organizations more than to party electorates. Many interviews also consistently referred to the parties as agents that structure the electorate. That is, legislators seem to view their parties as leaders vis-

TABLE 43. Percentage Mentioning Adherence to Their Party as the Way to Carry Out the Representative Mandate[1]

DC (25)	PSI (21)	PCI (26)
56.0 (14)	71.4 (15)	65.4 (17)

[1] Only respondents who said they represent the national community

24. As it can be surmised, correlations between answers to the various questions analyzed in this section are, within each of the two groups, very high. They confirm that in each party there is a majority, at times very substantial, that—no matter how questioned—thinks consistently of its role in strictly partisan terms. A halo effect may in part account for the results; but in the case of political elites such a halo may also be the natural result of their very role and their everyday experiences.

à-vis their social and political base, not as passive carriers of its interests and opinions. Final confirmation of this view emerges from a question asked in another section of the interview. Here members of Parliament were asked to choose between three conceptions of their party and their electorate:

1. The party is a rather faithful objective expression of the historical interests of the groups that support it. Within it the cadres and the more active part have a very important, yet substantially secondary function with respect to those groups. It is these that basically give the party platforms an ideology. The party refines, articulates, strengthens, and enacts them, as well as adapts them to current needs and events, if necessary. But it remains a necessary expression of its base.

2. The electorate and its party are inseparable and essential elements in the elaboration of platforms and ideology. The party forms and educates the electorate and transforms its interests into platforms and ideologies. Without the party there couldn't be any informed and politicized electorate. But the electorate participates directly in this transformation through a continuous political exchange. Without the participation of the electorate, and without such exchange, the party would have no direction.

3. The party electorate has a function which, we must recognize, is rather secondary with respect to the party organization. It limits itself to showing support for or withdrawing support from the platforms and ideology of the party. But these are basically elaborated by the cadres and the more organized part of the party. The cadres, if necessary, adapt platforms and ideology to current popular sentiments and to social change, so as to strengthen the party politically and electorally.

If the reader is already able to guess the modal answer to these alternatives (Table 44), I would hope it is because I have led him

TABLE 44. Conceptions of Ideological Flow between One's Party and Its Electorate, in Percentage

	DC (52)	PSI (48)	PCI (60)
Objective model	5.8 (3)	10.4 (5)	11.7 (7)
Elitist model	34.6 (18)	27.1 (13)	6.7 (4)
Organizational model	59.6 (31)	62.5 (30)	81.7 (49)

to the conclusion. After some coaxing and probing, given the respondents' habitual dislike for forced choices, only 22 percent showed any appreciation of the third, or "elitist" model, despite our efforts to present it in the most reasonable light. Even fewer—9 percent—opted for the "objective" model, which was introduced more for completeness than because we thought that members of the Parliament—Italian or not—would buy it. Preferences went largely to the second, or "organizational" model, which from the viewpoint of autonomy and restrained partisanship is most likely the least appropriate. Its inappropriateness lies in its legitimizing party positions in the light of an asserted constant feedback from and to the electorate. The "blackmailing" power of this conception, in which the party gives and receives ideology from the electorate, the ultimate respository of democratic legitimacy, is unavoidable. An ideology of popular participation combines with exclusive partisan-organizational roles in a mixture that leaves little room for trade-offs among parties. Platforms and ideologies acquire an untouchable quality from a double source: insofar as they symbolize popular sentiments, and insofar as they are concretely elaborated by party professionals who see themselves as the ultimate guardians of popular orthodoxy. It is the assignment of the guardian role to party and party elites that makes this model in a way even less compatible than the "objective" one with ideas of partisan restraint.

This interpretation acquires substance from the comments accompanying close to half the answers. There were a few, among the respondents who opted for the "elitist" model, who came at it from a strictly authoritarian perspective. They read the question as an occasion to launch a little tirade about the perils of mass democracy, the ignorance of the electorate, and the need for parties, especially their own, to guide the electorate and introduce a degree of sanity and restraint in popular democracy. Incidentally, all these respondents were Christian Democrats. The other "elitist" respondents took a more relaxed and adaptive view of the matter. For them, lack of active involvement by the electorate was a fact of life, which the parties were called upon to remedy by acting in behalf of the voters. Tied to this was the notion that reality changes, that the expectations of voters change, and therefore parties should always anticipate these changes, renew themselves, and offer the voters new and more attractive alternatives. Such comments suggest a "Downsian" model of party competition, in which parties should seek new and marginal electorates, if necessary by shaping and realigning them.

As a Socialist respondent expressed it, perhaps in a vein of polemical exaggeration and wish-fulfillment:

People today are not interested in party ideologies, and have no time to get involved [in them]. It is the parties that are left with these tasks. There is a warning, an alarm signal in all this, for my party and all parties. The voters want parties with fresh ideas, not the old ideological parties, and our party must look for new electors and new ideas. Hence we must not be afraid to discard our old party conceptions, as if we were bound to them forever. If we move in the right direction, our electorate will understand and follow us. (PSI 23)

Respondents who chose the "objective" model were much less verbal about their choice. To them the choice was obvious, comments were rarely offered, and they amount to a restatement of the model. But comments from the majority who chose the "organizational" model were again abundant and articulate, and unity of sentiments was remarkable in view of the large number of respondents involved. Their comments singularly contrasted with the pragmatic and adaptive views reported in the quote above. Relations between parties and the electorate were not a matter of discrete exchanges, in which parties and voters interact as need be and do not always converge, but were essential, as in the following comment, to maintaining the unity and political power of each party.

Well, it would be nonsensical to say that the leadership of a party must limit itself to passively receiving the indications of its base. . . . It must transform them in a general vision by using elements of political doctrine and of economic and scientific knowledge; it must transform them in a political line which orients and educates. We attach extreme importance to the educational function of the party—as Gramsci conceived of it—because the party is also a school which trains and gives conscience, hence it is not a passive administrator of each voter's wishes. . . . But we must not forget the other aspect of this relation, which requires the active presence of the electorate with its contributions, and here is the important difference with . . . [the third model] which to me looks like an elitist and "electoralist" one, alienated from reality.

Other comments contrasted their choice even more closely with the "elitist" model, by emphasizing that the strength of a party cannot be maintained without preserving a close relation with traditional party constituencies, and without providing them with reasons for political unity. One respondent put it as follows:

Ideologies are not invented, and they are not "sold" to the voters. A party that doesn't maintain a constant dialogue with its own base doesn't last very long; it will eventually lose ground and will disperse its electorate. Even from a narrow electoral viewpoint, a party without a precise ideology, rooted in the reality of its following, doesn't travel very far. Maybe it has some temporary successes, as it has happened to . . . [some small Italian parties], but it cannot last. In substance, it is a party of adventurers, ready to exploit temporary moods.

The reader may have guessed that the two quotations—especially the first one, with its reference to Gramsci—are from Communist respondents. The "organizational" model seems more attractive to Communists and Socialists, the "elitist" to Christian Democrats. In fact, both quotes are from Christian Democrats[25] and, while Christian Democrats were indeed less likely to prefer the "organizational" model than members of other parties, a majority of them did prefer it. There may be some intellectual pretentiousness in the choice of such a model in a party as loose as Christian Democracy. Yet, as the following analysis suggests, underneath it all there is also a populist-partisan view of elite-mass relations as congenial to a Catholic as it is to a Marxist.

The question analyzed above was preceded much earlier in the interview by a series of four "channeling" questions asking the respondents what importance they attached, from the viewpoint of their work, to the opinions of the electorate; whether there were other special opinions, interests, and information to which they attached as much or more importance; how difficult they thought it was to know the opinions of the electorate; and what sources they employed to know them. Most respondents seemed surprised that we should even raise such pseudo-issues. In answer to the first question, they pointed out that public opinion was naturally "extremely important," "essential for a member of Parliament," "irreplaceable as a guide to action." Few used lesser adjectives, and very few took a more searching attitude toward the question. Whether these were automatic responses to heavily sanctioned norms or corresponded to personal operational codes,

---

25. DC 6 and DC 14.

they were asserted with the conviction of the obvious. As to the second question, many granted that other opinions and information were also important, but very few gave them status greater than or even equal to public opinion, and these were mostly respondents who pointed to the primacy of their party's positions. As to the third question, a majority of 55 percent saw no essential difficulty in knowing the opinions of the electorate, and those who perceived difficulties tended overwhelmingly to see them as merely technical ones. They very rarely had to do with the intrinsic nature and status of public opinion, but more often with a legislator's inability, because of *surmenage*, to keep in touch with the voters.

But the most important question for our purposes, and the one that revealed what the term *electorate* meant to the respondents, was the last one: How did legislators verify the opinions of the electorate? The question referred to the electorate in general, with no party labels attached. But answers indicated that the respondents preferred to think of it—as the Communist senator who made a firm point of it in the first quotation in this section—as the active membership of their party. The question offered a choice of various sources through which to verify opinions: direct contact with the electorate; the national press; the party press; the local press; local contact with the party organization and allied political organizations; contact with corporate and interest group organizations in general; contact with corporate and interest groups closer to the legislator. The respondents were asked to choose the two most frequent and the two least frequent sources. More than 90 percent, with few party differences, indicated that one of the two most frequent sources was direct contact with formal organizations of the party, its allied political movements, their members and activists. Direct contact with the electorate, mentioned by more than 60 percent of the respondents, was the second most popular choice, and 80 percent of *these* respondents also mentioned contact with party organizations. Upon probing, we found no significant differences in the meaning of the two choices. All other choices followed at a much greater distance. Here, as in answers to other questions, elite-mass relations are mostly relations within the same political family, and within its most active part. Elites assign great importance to public opinion, and have confidence that they are in touch with it, but what elites verify and dialogue with most of the time is not so much public opinion at large as the opinion of their parties.

I will no longer belabor the point.[26]

CULTURE, GENERATIONS, INSTITUTIONAL LEARNING

The thrust of the chapter, with its insistence on cultural conditions for legislative performance, may suggest a rather dim future for the Italian Parliament, one in which the perpetuation of the same orientations in the present generation of politicians will further degrade performance. But as I shall demonstrate in a while, and contrary to some theories, there is apparently little intrinsically generational about elite orientations, at least in Italy. If they don't change, it is not so much because of the weight of generational learning; it is rather because of politico-institutional arrangements—internal and external to Parliament—which require and sustain them. I shall argue in the last two chapters on the Italian party system that such arrangements are indeed likely to endure for the near future. But this does not alter the fact that institutional arrangements do change, can change abruptly, do not require a previous change in elite culture, and can in turn reform institutional culture and/or behavior.

According to one important theory concerning the sources of political orientations, elite cultural orientations are rather permanent, they are learned early in life—in young adulthood or even before—in response to the dominant political climate of the formative years, and they leave a firm though not indelible mark later in life.[27] It follows that, in the Italian case, given the preva-

26. In view of the theoretical claims continuously made in this section, the reader may rest assured that populist-partisan sentiments do in fact undermine acceptance of reciprocity and compromise. We find, for example, that politicians who see their role as that of a party delegate are less likely to favor compromise among parties, especially if compromise must be initiated by their own party, less likely to look favorably on the behavior of other parties in matters of compromise, and, if they are Christian Democrats, less likely to approve of concurrent votes by the Communists. The same suspicious attitudes toward reciprocity and compromise hold true if we look at politicians who perceive their constituency in majoritarian terms, or who embrace the "organizational" model of voters-party flow. The relations are not always very clean because Italian politicians are skewed toward the populist-partisan extreme. In a way, to show this skewness is more important to our argument than to show the relations.

27. On generational theories, see Karl Mannheim, "The Problem of Generations," in Karl Mannheim, *Essays on the Sociology of Knowledge* (New York: Oxford University Press,

lent orientations of members of Parliament today, a significant change could not occur at best until a new generation of politicians, entering politics now, sits in Parliament. This line of reasoning cannot be easily dismissed. No observer of the Italian scene can fail to realize how much memories of the political past, attachments to traditional allegiances, and self-fulfilling fears of historical cleavages dominate the political debate in the country. The force of such "historical" images is tremendous and inescapable. Also, theory and research on political socialization amply buttress the importance of generational experiences in cultural learning. The last contribution to this line of analysis comes from Robert Putnam's study of Italian and British politicians. It clearly shows, for instance, that perceptions of politics as conflict-ridden steadily grow with the age of Italian politicians, and it persuasively argues, by comparing this pattern with that of Britons, that the growth is not due to "aging" but to generational differences, whereby older politicians reflect in their present views the greater conflict in Italian history they experienced in their formative years.[28]

But there are other ways of explaining elite culture. Elites may learn within institutions, and in response to their role requirements, organizational arrangements, and structural inducements (institutional socialization).[29] Alternatively, elites may be chosen by institutions if they demonstrate special capacities for institutional roles and possess the approved orientations (selective

---

1952), pp. 276-322. A classical essay on political socialization, emphasizing learning and cognition, is Herbert Hyman, *Political Socialization* (Glencoe: Free Press, 1959), esp. chapters 3 and 6. On the problems involved in distinguishing between age and generational effects, see Angus Campbell et al., *The American Voter* (New York: Wiley, 1960), pp. 161-167; Donald Stokes and David Butler, *Political Change in Britain* (New York: St. Martin's Press, 1969), pp. 248-274. On the effects of generation on political elites, see Robert Putnam, "The Political Attitudes of Senior Civil Servants in Western Europe: A Preliminary Report," *British Journal of Political Science* 3 (1973), pp. 257-290; Robert Dahl, *Polyarchy* (New Haven: Yale University Press, 1971), pp. 167-169.

28. Putnam, *The Beliefs of Politicians*, op. cit., pp. 139-149. See also, for the role of generation in the formation of partisan hostility, ibid., pp. 64-68.

29. Fenno, op. cit., pp. 320-323; Lewis Edinger and Donald Searing, "Social Background in Elite Analysis: A Methodological Inquiry," *American Political Science Review* 61 (1967), pp. 428-455; Donald Searing, "The Comparative Study of Elite Socialization," *Comparative Political Studies* 1 (1969), pp. 471-500; Allen Barton, "Determinants of Leadership Attitudes in a Socialist Society," in Allen Barton et al., eds., *Opinion-Making Elites in Yugoslavia* (New York: Praeger, 1973), pp. 220-262; Giuseppe Di Palma, *Apathy and Participation* (New York: Free Press, 1970), pp. 104-110.

recruitment).[30] Or aspiring elites may learn roles and orientations in anticipation of successful entry (anticipatory socialization).[31] The corollary common to the three alternatives is that institutional culture should change as institutions are changed. All these interpretations are plausible in our case because most of the elite orientations discussed in this chapter refer to one specific institution. They very closely concern legislative roles, elite relations, and perceptions of mass politics that are central to the operation of Parliament and to the expected behavior of its members. It follows that the orientations of Italian legislators may reflect not only diffuse life experiences and "ancestral" memories, but also the more immediate and specific institutional requirements and incentives of Parliament and parties. In fact, whatever generational differences exist originally between old and new or prospective elites may be considerably reduced by the equalizing effects of institutional expectations.

In keeping with generational theories and with Putnam's findings, we have looked to see if in fact younger legislators reveal less partisan attitudes, are more sensitive to reciprocity norms, more attuned to elite autonomy, less bound by electoral demands and partisan roles.[32] But we have also looked for institutional effects, as they can be revealed by seniority in Parliament and in active politics and by different career patterns. We have found a beguiling and somewhat frustrating mix. Only in two cases have we discovered clear relations between age and orientation. Irrespective of parties, members of Parliament who in principle favor compromise among parties tend to be younger than those who oppose it (Table 45). So are Christian Democrats

30. Kenneth Prewitt, "Political Socialization and Leadership Selection," *The Annals of the American Academy of Political and Social Science* 361 (1965), pp. 96-111; Dwaine Marvick, "Political Recruitment and Careers," *International Encyclopedia of the Social Sciences* (New York: Crowell-Collier and Macmillan, 1968), Vol. 12, pp. 273-282; Di Palma, *Apathy and Participation*, op. cit., pp. 104-110.

31. Prewitt, op. cit.; Marvick, op. cit.; John Rex, "Capitalism, Elites, and the Ruling Class," in Philip Stanworth and Anthony Giddens, eds., *Elites and Power in British Society* (London: Cambridge University Press, 1974), pp. 208-219. For an excellent general review of various theories of elite socialization, see Robert Putnam, *The Comparative Study of Political Elites* (Englewood Cliffs, N.J.: Prentice-Hall, 1976), chapter 4.

32. Expectations of decline in populist-partisan feelings rest not only on the greater conflict experienced in their formative years by older Italian politicians who grew up under and immediately after Fascism, but also on general theories about the "end of ideology." See, however, for a critique of the "end of ideology" literature Di Palma, "The Study of Conflict in Western Society," op. cit., esp. pp. 1-5.

TABLE 45. Average Age and Age Range by Attitudes toward Compromise[1]

	DC (26)		PSI (24)		PCI (30)	
	Age	Range	Age	Range	Age	Range
Compromise	46	33-51	44	39-47	47	35-65
Remain firm	61	45-68	56	41-67	55	47-63

[1] See Table 30 in this chapter. The question about compromise was asked of only half the respondents.

(but neither Socialists nor Communists) who favor mixed and proportionality rule over majority rule (Table 46). We also find that such age differences basically hold even after introducing suitable statistical adjustment for the effects of seniority in Parliament and in active politics, two factors closely associated with age. But we find no differences in seniority independent of age. Also, seniority shows no relation with other orientations. Party by party, legislators who disapprove of a decisive vote by the PCI in favor of government legislation, who distrust the behavior of other parties in matters of compromise, who see themselves as party delegates rather than voters' trustees or compromisers, or who interpret their mandate in partisan terms are not more politically seasoned than their colleagues who take opposite positions.[33] But the revealing discovery is that in consequence *neither are they older than their colleagues.* Apparently, young or old, seniors or back-benchers, Italian legislators show in these cases distinctive similarities in political orientations.

I shall dispense with presenting in table format this series of

TABLE 46. Average Age and Age Range by Preference toward Different Decisional Rules[1]

	DC (52)		PSI (48)		PCI (60)	
	Age	Range	Age	Range	Age	Range
Majority	63	51-68	43	39-67	55	54-65
Proportionality	41	33-49	51	36-69	47	38-63
Mixed	46	39-52	48	41-52	49	41-67

[1] See Table 28, Chapter III.

33. See Tables 32, 33, 38, 41, and 43 in this chapter for these variables.

"non-findings" and move to the interpretation of the mix. What it tells us is that generational change, as similarly shown by Putnam, may favor generalized predispositions toward compromise, as older cohorts of legislators, grown politically under Fascism and in the tense postwar era, slowly retire.[34] Among Christian Democrats generational change may also favor a lessening of strict majoritarian principles.[35] But with these two orientations younger politicians are already part of the majority. Let us not forget that compromise is already accepted in principle by more than two out of three respondents, and that majority rule is far from being firmly shared by members of the governing parties, even Christian Democrats. That is possibly why seniority in politics and Parliament makes no difference here, over and above age: a lengthy career in parties and Parliament does not undo generational learning because in a way it does not conflict with it. Yet we have already seen in the course of the chapter that acceptance in principle of a more open and negotial Parliament has limited consequences when we examine concrete applications and more specific orientations, and is curbed by partisan images and roles. It is exactly when we move to these orientations and roles, showing partisan distrust and strict partisanship by great majorities, that younger members of Parliament, *despite their greater predisposition toward compromise*, join their elders. To be sure, since tenure in Parliament makes no difference either, this convergence of old and young is not the result of indoctrination within Parliament. But the fact that Parliament does not indoctrinate does not rule out the effects of institutional expectations. It is still plausible that orientations of distrust and partisanship are hardened in prospective legislators as they are recruited in active politics and before they enter Parliament. The point is difficult to prove without a comparison with potential elites who never entered politics, or who abandoned it early and before entering

---

34. Alternatively, differences on compromise may be the result of aging and would therefore disappear as younger legislators age. There is no way to test the hypothesis directly. But since aging takes place in Parliament, so that parliamentary experience is an important component of the experience of aging, yet tenure in Parliament does not affect feelings toward compromise, the hypothesis does not seem very plausible.

35. The reason why generation and preferences for decisional rules are not related among Communists and Socialists is rather intuitive. There is no reason why even older Socialists, let alone Communists, having been in the opposition for most of their lives, should particularly defend majority rule.

Parliament. That is, the number of years that members of Parliament have spent in politics may still not show up in their orientations, exactly because they *have* made it to Parliament, presumably after youthful induction in politics and/or a largely successful and prolonged training. Indeed, even respondents who are in Parliament for the first time report they have been already active in politics for an average of eighteen years. And almost all respondents who came of age after Fascism reported becoming involved in active politics in their teens.

Some evidence in support of institutional socialization comes, however, from a special and deviant minority of members of Parliament: a group of fourteen respondents—six of them Christian Democrats—made up of all respondents with no more than six years in active politics. They differ from all other respondents in that by large majorities they reported trust in the behavior of other parties in matters of compromise, saw themselves as voters' trustees or compromisers, and construed their representative mandate in nonpartisan terms.[36] Further analysis also reveals that the political and professional career of the group is in more than one way different from that of the large majority of legislators. They were all in Parliament for the first time, and most of them (1) had entered politics not because of party merits but because of their status in the community or the profession; (2) devoted limited time to party work; (3) drew their livelihood from outside politics; and (4) did not envision politics as their future profession.[37] They were, however, not among the youngest legislators, as they were mostly established professionals and community leaders in their mid-forties.

In conclusion, given its small size, this group explains only in part why some members of Parliament deviate from the normal orientations of partisanship and distrust. But the nature of the group suggests the significant impact of politico-institutional socialization upon cultural orientations, one that a minority of

---

36. The smallness of the group accounts for the earlier finding that, in the aggregate, political seniority does not change with changes in orientations.

37. However, when all respondents are compared, neither tenure in Parliament, as already seen, nor the other four factors taken alone are associated with orientations. When an Index of Political Professionalism is built, using seniority in Parliament and politics and the four factors above, it relates to orientations, but mainly because the low end of the index is almost exclusively made of our fourteen respondents.

outside beginners, who side-enter Parliament because of unique and possibly expendable nonpartisan merits, is better equipped to avoid. For most legislators socialization occurs before election to Parliament, as they enter active party politics. For the generations that came of age after Fascism, who typically joined their parties in their teens, when most generational learning occurs, generational and politico-institutional experiences are in fact inseparable. And only a few years of exposure to organized politics seem necessary to adopt the approved orientations and otherwise to abandon politics or to be rejected. This is so because the orientations to be learned strictly concern the performance of institutionally defined roles. This leaves in principle the possibility that successful institutional change—initiated independently of cultural change—triggers a redefinition of roles and short-circuits the longer effects of generational factors on orientations and behavior.

CONCLUSIONS

Many of the sentiments expressed by Italian politicians and explored in this chapter—whether values, beliefs, or perceptions of reality—may strike at times as being at odds with the way Italian politics operates and Parliament behaves. The very consensus surrounding many of the expressed sentiments and bringing together members of various parties may leave the reader with an uncomfortable sense of disbelief. How can we square, for instance, lack of support for the cultural norm of reciprocity with a recurrent theme in this book: the constant parliamentary practice of trade-offs even across majority-opposition lines? If members of Parliament find it so difficult to trust party opponents when seeking accommodation, why do political analysts find the practice of compromise one of the salient features of parliamentary and committee behavior? How can insistence by Christian Democratic respondents on partisanship and party duty be reconciled with the fact that their party is essentially a federation of allied factions whose attitudes toward each other are, at best, those of friendly enemies? And what to make of their asserted ideological attachments in a party that is more known for its attachment to power than to principles of action? Most parliamentarians have also described ideological relations between parties and voters as a close two-way flow of communication and influence. We have above raised doubts that this perception corresponds to how the Christian Democratic party—with its loose organization and clientelistic orientations—operates. But the doubts can be extended to the PCI, on the grounds that its organizational ideology—with its stress on "democratic centralism" and the cohesiveness of party cadres—makes the inner core of the party more equal than the voters.

Lest the reader be carried away by these assorted doubts and throw the baby away with the bath, let me again describe the ground on which we stood at the beginning of the chapter. The purpose of the chapter was to verify whether in the Italian Parliament there existed the cultural premises—both in terms of norms and of perceptions of reality—for its operation as a negotial body. In essence, ours was a negative exercise: We tried to deduce logically the cultural conditions for the operation of a negotial body, and then found them wanting. We looked for reciprocity, restrained partisanship, elite autonomy, trustee roles; and we found mutual distrust, strong partisanship, populist values, and delegate roles. This does not mean that the latter cultural package causes and comfortably fits analogous parliamentary practices. I have not described Italian parliamentary behavior as strictly partisan, alien to accommodations, and adamant on zero-sum games. My claim is more modest: Such cultural premises, even if "betrayed" in practice, and whatever else they may sustain, cannot comfortably sustain and justify negotial behavior. Abstract notions of partisan duty, electoral responsibility, ideological purity, poorly combine with the reality of many parties bound to live together within the same household. It is not so much that they are philosophically or logically at odds with mutual coexistence as that they cannot provide any pragmatic guide to such coexistence. They are too remote from problems of coexistence, and too concerned with the preservation of abstract images and general principles, to allow for the more relaxed and possibilistic standards required for the performance of a multipartisan decisional body. Legislators are not insensitive to the need for coexistence and may seek to adapt behavior accordingly. But as long as these adaptive efforts are not maintained by an overt and appropriate operational code, their motives are often muted, their life is uncertain, and their results are trivial.

On the point of motives, very few respondents have elevated adaptation to the dignity of a public code of behavior. Partisan values and perceptions of a partisan reality feed into each other to prevent this. Yet there is nothing intrinsically less correct, and less "democratic," about such a code, except in the minds of the respondents. There is, in other words, no reason in my opinion why our respondents should continue to perceive and extol a partisan reality unless they believe it to be either factually accurate or normatively superior or both. But the belief has paradoxical consequences for legislative behavior. Since adaptation cannot be sustained by higher motives, practical ones step in. Convergences between parties become instruments of everyday power. They are sought by members of the majority to protect factional interests, to maintain lines of legislative input open to parliamentary coteries, to exchange legislation designed to establish credit with electoral clienteles. On the side of the opposition, they offer a valuable opportunity to keep a foot in the doorway of government. Simply said, the political culture of Parliament does not prevent compromise, it displaces it to smaller matters, where it appears less dangerous to each partner and more feasible. In this sense, it is basically incorrect to discount partisan-populist sentiments expressed by members of Parliament as inconsequential mouthings of socially desirable roles. With all due regard to any existing slack between culture and behavior, the fact remains that these sentiments cannot support the operation of a negotial body on the matters that count. In fact, neither can they alone support a majoritarian Parliament, on the ground that it too, as stated in the opening pages of the chapter, needs principles of reciprocity and mutual confidence.

On the other hand, elite culture is not all there is to the operation of Parliament. Legislative orientations alone are neither strategic nor, to go one step further, sufficient causes of legislative performance. There are other causes on whose persistence the future of legislative behavior may more closely hinge. They are structural causes which—in keeping with the claims made in the previous section—in part explain and in part buttress cultural ones. On the point of strategic importance, as already discussed, what explains orientations and what lies at the root of poor performance is an objective fact of Italian politics into which professional politicians are socialized: a lack of alternance in government and the uncertain equilibrium between numerous political forces. On the point of sufficiency, the prevailing cultural orientations of legislators, with their emphasis on partisanship and distrust, may satisfactorily explain why legislation of major importance is unlikely to be approved. But—to amend a statement made in these conclusions—orientations alone don't go as far in explaining the other side of legislative performance: the spread of logrolling legislation. Logrolling, to be sure, avoids mutual interference, makes possible the exchange of favors even among groups which cannot otherwise see eye to eye, and can therefore displace more important legislation. What makes logrolling not only a possible but also a dominant practice, however, are the formal and informal rules of Parliament, which allow and in a way sustain it. Let me recall in this regard that in the postwar constitutional compromise Parliament and its rules were designed with the intent of protecting partisan differences while making for a degree of constructive coexistence. But the compromise had a quite different and dispersive effect, mainly because it relied on expressive instruments—proportional representation and free legislative initiative—and provided no channeling of cohesive decisional behavior, either in a corporate-negotial or majoritarian direction. Designed as an open and unstructured forum, Parliament offers today a convenient arena for the unrestrained expression of partisan sentiments, but its rules also leave convenient escape routes open for everyday transactions. The rules constitute significant incentives for legislators to put aside divisive and unmanageable issues and to concentrate on ordinary administration; they facilitate irresponsible and centrifugal tendencies.

To explore these rules and their effect on legislative outputs is the task of the next chapter, which will continue the analysis conducted in Chapter II. There, as it will be recalled, we stopped at the door of Parliament: We looked at the types of legislative proposals that are submitted to Parliament but paid limited attention to how Parliament treats incoming legislation.

V

Parliamentary Procedures and Legislative Outputs

In a recent theoretical essay on legislative behavior, Maurizio Cotta, a young Italian scholar, reminds us that an exclusive emphasis on the individual characteristics of legislators—social, career, or attitudinal—does a disservice to the study of legislative behavior. Such characteristics have a limited capacity to predict performance, unless we know how they are distributed among the various institutional "sites" and unless legislators are studied within the structural context in which they operate. "Ignorance of the structural dimension is the more serious, the more complex and structured is the institution to be studied."[1]

THE *INTERNA CORPORIS* OF PARLIAMENTS

It may be objected that the distinction between individual and institutional levels is not always possible, especially when individual roles of institutional import are involved. But such difficulties do not deny the distinction; they rather suggest that individuals operating within an institution often learn and adapt in response to institutional requirements and inducements. I may add that even in the case of Italian legislators, who often define their roles and relations in similar fashion, what counts for their performance is not only the modality of their individual orientations, but also the support these obtain from parliament's organizational and procedural features. On the point of how institutional and individual factors relate causally to each other, it cannot be ruled out that the former often inform the latter. And

---

1. Maurizio Cotta, "Il Problema del Bicameralismo-Monocameralismo nel Quadro di una Analisi Struttural-Funzionale del Parlamento," *Rivista Italiana di Scienza Politica* 1 (1971), p. 554.

on the point of institutional effects, they are not to be confused with individual ones.

Cotta suggests a few institutional dimensions of particular importance for performance.[2] A first dimension is imported into parliament from outside. Insofar as parliament is an elected body, it is an "arena" replicating within itself the political divisions that exist in the larger political society and reflecting in its internal structuring the principal political groupings that compete for popular support. Today, these groupings are mainly the political parties; hence typologies of party systems can be used within this dimension to capture the way parliament is internally articulated and structured around organized interests. Parliaments can thus be compared in terms of party fragmentation, party cohesiveness, success of coalition behavior, and the degree to which they are numerically balanced, dominated by a majority, or minority-oriented.[3] Since this composite dimension touches upon parliament as an arena, and deals with effects that are external, we will examine it in the next chapter.

There are, however, other and more clearly internal dimensions that deserve immediate analysis. One dimension, which we may call organizational, has to do with the way decisional responsibilities relative to the various phases of the legislative process are allocated to various units within parliament. The criteria of allocation bear on the autonomy of parliament vis-à-vis other bodies. A key aspect is the way parliament is articulated in committees. We may ideally go from one extreme where the committee system is evanescent, parliament tends to operate as an undifferentiated whole, and the floor is the crucial decisional site, to one where committees are the key to performance and parliament is in effect little more than the sum-total of several smaller parliaments.[4] The place of a specific legislature along this continuum depends on whether its committees are permanent or ad hoc, and whether they are specialized by subject

2. Ibid., pp. 552-562.
3. See Fred Riggs, "Legislative Structures: Some Thoughts on Elective National Assemblies" (mimeographed, 1970), for the distinction between balanced, majority-oriented, and minority-oriented legislatures.
4. A recent discussion of legislative committees, their relations to the whole legislature, and the effects on committee systems of parties, constitutional structure, and political culture is found in Malcolm Shaw and John Lees, "Commissioni Legislative e Sistema Politico," *Rivista Italiana di Scienza Politica* 4 (1974), pp. 165-195.

matter or are simply a convenient device for speeding up incoming legislation. Not least, it also depends on whether committees are—in Nelson Polsby's term—"institutionalized" by reason of their continuity in membership and leadership, their control on committee seniority and career, their capacity to socialize members in their internal norms and to create internal cohesiveness in the face of partisan diversity.[5] Other things being equal, a legislature with a strongly institutionalized committee system and a high level of decentralization tends to correspond to what Polsby calls a transformative legislature—one, that is to say, that does not limit itself to replicating, arena-like, the contrasting demands and interests that impinge on it from outside, but employs its remarkable institutional resources to mold legislative demands and autonomously create its own legislation.[6] Its style of operation is negotial and balanced rather than majoritarian, and legislative roles are defined more by the institution's *interna corporis* than by the bodies from which legislators are recruited.

This organizational dimension is in turn closely tied to a procedural one; indeed, it can be considered a salient extension of it. Parliaments follow different procedures and practices in handling legislative inputs, which significantly impinge upon outputs. A listing of parliamentary procedures and practices could never be exhaustive. They are by no means limited to the written rules of the house or to the legal customs defined by constitutionalists and enforced by jurisprudence. A few procedures, of special importance for legislative performance, need mentioning, however. Some parliaments are minority- and individually-centered and take the single legislator as the unit whose activities and rights need protection and support. They tend to combine, if not all, at least a number of the following features. They attribute ample and essentially unrestrained powers of initiative and amendment to individual legislators. They impose no cloture and no lesser restrictions on debate. They recognize limited powers of direction and control to bodies external to parliament—such as the government and, insofar as

---

5. Nelson Polsby, "The Institutionalization of the U.S. House of Representatives," *American Political Science Review* 58 (1968), pp. 144-168.

6. Nelson Polsby, "Legislatures" (mimeographed, 1974), pp. 32-33 (for the distinction between "arenas" and "transformative legislatures"), pp. 33-37 (for the place of committees in both).

they are expression of externally organized parties, the parliamentary groups themselves. They attribute, however, notable powers to bodies internal to parliament—such as committees, their chairmen, and presidents of the assembly—in fixing the legislative agenda and otherwise supervising the legislative process. These powers are designed to protect parliament from external interference, and individual legislators from partisan and group pressure. Hence these parliaments also tend to apply unanimity or composite majority rules to procedural decisions, or to trust such decisions to impartial officers.

Parliaments that are group-oriented, on the other hand, focus upon organized parties as the significant unit for decisional inputs and processing. Hence parliamentary groups and party whips assume a very important role in the various phases of the legislative process. Parliamentary initiative and amending powers, if still recognized, are the objects of strict group discipline and are removed from the whims of individual legislators. Debate is equally the object of strict planning, with stringent rules on length and manner of debate, the allocation of speaking time to each group, and cloture. Above all, serious restrictions are imposed upon the power of committee chairmen to control legislation by controlling their own agenda and the manner of reporting to the assembly. The site of decision is not the committee but the more partisan floor. But to say that comprehensive legislative planning takes precedence over checks and balances, and that organized groups overshadow individual legislators, is close to saying that a stable majority sets and controls legislative procedures. Indeed, the development of strong parliamentary groups with significant procedural powers is especially visible in legislatures characterized by a clear division of decisional responsibilities between majority and opposition.[7] And within these legislatures a conference of parliamentary-group presidents usually makes procedural and agenda decisions by simple majority. Or, when these powers are assigned to a single officer, such as the Leader of the House in Great Britain, his role is not that of an impartial presiding officer but that of a majority leader strictly bound by government instructions. In sum, as with the organizational dimension observed before, parliamentary practices and

---

7. Herman Van Impe, *Le Rôle de la Majorité Parlementaire dans la Vie Politique Belge* (Bruxelles: Etablissements Emile Bruylant, 1966), chapter 2.

procedures suggest an ideal distinction between parliaments that are majority-oriented and parliaments that favor and implement in their internal rules individual and minority prerogatives.

There is likely to be a degree of empirical fit between the three institutional dimensions just described. As Cotta suggests, it is, for instance, unlikely that a parliament with highly cohesive parties will decentralize decisional powers to its committees or leave much room for individual and minority initiative. It is unlikely that a parliament with strong committees will assign much control over the legislative agenda to parties and parliamentary groups.[8] Hence, it is possible to rank parliaments along an empirically plausible gradient, from those solidly dominated in their organization and procedures by the initiative of one cohesive party to those with a weak structure of parties and organized around the initiative of individuals and shifting groups.

The Italian Parliament, however, escapes easy classification. In terms of its organizational and procedural dimensions, it belongs in many ways to the latter group of parliaments.[9] The power of its committees to enact legislation, the importance of private initiative, the few restrictions on debate, the limited governmental and majority control over the legislative process, the consistent use of the secret vote, and other features we have observed through this book, are all typical of parliaments jealous of their rights and possibly endowed with considerable transformative resources.[10] But the organizational and procedural dimensions of the Italian Parliament do not fit its partisan structure. While the former suggest balanced and transformative roles, the latter point to an arena-like Parliament, dominated by the presence of a number of

8. Cotta, op. cit., p. 560.

9. An interesting commentary on the Italian Parliament's standing rules is that they are essentially the same as those of the *trasformista* Parliament of the prefascist period, when alliances of notables rather than organized parties dominated the assembly. The Senate formally voted new standing rules in 1948. But these were heavily inspired by the previous Parliament. The Chamber of Deputies simply adopted, without a formal deliberation and with few changes, the old standing rules. See Antonio Maccanico, "Aspetti Costituzionali della Riforma dei Regolamenti Parlamentari," in AA. VV. *Studi per il Ventesimo Anniversario dell'Assemblea Costituente* (Firenze: Vallecchi, 1969), Vol. 5, pp. 455-467.

10. In terms of the strength of its committee system, Shaw and Lees rank the Italian Parliament second only to the American Congress and, in order, ahead of the legislatures of Chile, West Germany, the Philippines, Canada, Great Britain, India, and Japan. Shaw and Lees, op cit., pp. 169-170.

highly organized, mostly cohesive political parties, which transfer to Parliament the political divisions they incarnate in the larger society. These parties provide the main structure around which conflict expresses itself in Parliament, and check Parliament's transformative potentials. As it will be remembered, this combination of a fragmented but mostly stable and internally cohesive structure of parliamentary groups with parliamentary rules protecting individual and minority prerogatives resulted from the constitutional compromise after the war, and had negative consequences for legislative effectiveness. On one side, parliamentary rules offered one incentive for even smaller parties to maintain their identity and remain politically active. On the other, they offered no incentives, when combined with strong partisan distinctions, for decisional agreement on important issues, but rather contributed to the proliferation and disaggregation of legislation.

We began an empirical analysis of these legislative effects in Chapter II. However, in assessing the level of disaggregation of proposed and enacted legislation, we paid little formal attention to how the rules and processes internal to Parliament actually contribute to such disaggregation. That is the purpose of the present chapter, and since government legislation should in principle be more capable than private legislation of resisting parliamentary manipulation, our attention will be on the former and more difficult case.

GOVERNMENT LEGISLATION AND PARLIAMENTARY TRANSFORMATION

Let us begin by recalling the type of legislation that government usually submits to Parliament (see treatment in Chapter II). Government legislation has natural advantages over private: it enjoys a broader basis of consensus among the members of the coalition, which goes a long way in explaining its high rate of approval. But the consensus is reached at a cost. Government legislation is hardly less disaggregated than private: it deals largely with microsectional interests, it invests heavily in the marginal upkeep of special sectors of the civil service, it distributes narrow benefits to its immediate subjects, it avoids negative redistributive consequences. What the government introduces in Parliament has little to do with the legislative programs that coalition partners agree upon at the outset of every new coalition. Progressive disagreements within the coalition, changing attitudes toward the opposition, and the emergence of new political and social situations cause continuous shifting and renegotiations of the programs or the shelving of substantial parts of them, and lead eventually to the collapse of the coalition. A necessarily rough estimate from newspaper accounts of the period, comparing original coalition agreements with final legislative action, indicates that approximately 10 percent of the original legislative programs of the six Center-Left cabinets during the Fifth Parliament (1968-1972) ever arrived, in one form or another, in Parliament. And it should be kept in mind that in most instances a cabinet adopts large parts of the unfinished program of a previous one.

The bulk of proposed government legislation is made of provisions not always so important as to be sanctioned in the coalition program, yet necessary to keep the machinery of government and private interests going and sufficiently narrow to obtain coalition support within the cabinet. An important place in this legislation is occupied by projects initiated by single ministers and their bureaucracy, with which the rest of the cabinet does not interfere, and more recently by emergency provisions dealing with urgent issues. In both instances the projects tend to be of the disaggregated type. When single ministers and their bureaucracies press their own legislation, they are typically "maintenance" or pet projects designed to benefit special clienteles—often the bureaucracy itself. It is not unusual that the cabinet approves these projects—on the principle of "senatorial" courtesy—even before they are formally drafted, and with limited knowledge of their exact nature.[11] As to emergency legislation, it may likely deal with important issues. In fact, it has often been used to cope with demands for significant reforms which could no longer be postponed. But, to secure swift parliamentary approval, such legislation must often deal with such demands in the tamest way. It must avoid hurting established interests and upsetting the equilibria of the coalition.

One aspect that bears on this point is the way emergency

11. Nicola Greco, "Carenza di Coordinamento, Policentrismo e Contrattualismo nell'Attività del Governo," *Studi Parlamentari e di Politica Costituzionale*, Vol. 2, No. 4 (1969), pp. 23-42.

legislation is usually drafted and presented to Parliament. Much of it is put together through so-called *stralcio* laws, that is, literally, by "extracting" single provisions from a broader and inactive legislative project while indefinitely shelving the rest of it. It is a more than fair guess that what is shelved is not necessarily what is less urgent, but what is politically least costly. Under exceptional circumstances, emergency legislation can also, by constitutional norm, take the form of government decree-laws, whose effects, however, cease if Parliament does not convert them into law within sixty days. The procedure cuts both ways. It gives the government special powers of initiative and enforcement, but the need for immediate conversion by Parliament, and the risk that a filibustering minority can block it, also advise against controversial provisions.[12] Communist critics have pointed to the increasing use of decree-laws (85 during the Fourth Parliament, against 119 during the first three) as evidence of the expanding power of government.[13] The increase may just as well indicate the crowding-in of issues unresolved over the years, as governments remained inactive.

This, in sum, is the type of legislation that the government can afford to agree upon. Conversely, much of its legislative program fails even before entering Parliament. The constrictions of coalitions and of shifting consensus impose this behavior. There is no ready, formal way of proving the point, but it is one on which politicians and political analysts insist. The most difficult parts of the government program are killed by the government itself; the rest enjoys a degree of coalition commitment that is often patched up at the expense of programmatic relevance.

In view of this, the Communists have a point when arguing that much of the blame for legislative ineffectiveness does not belong

12. One classical case in point is university reform. Preparatory work began with great fanfare in the early sixties; but after the failure of various and more ambitious projects in two previous legislatures, the Sixth Parliament settled in 1973 for a *mini-riforma* adopted by urgent decree-law. Its only significant features are a plan for the appointment of 7,500 new tenured professors in the next three years (thus tripling tenured positions), and student representation in university governance, two provisions which, aside from their urgency, have attractive benefits for the parties that support them. University reform is postponed sine die.

13. Flavio Colonna, "Problemi del Parlamento," in Istituto Antonio Gramsci (a cura di), *La Riforma dello Stato* (Roma: Editori Riuniti, 1968), pp. 113-128.

with Parliament and its dispersive mechanisms, but with the government. However, this is not the whole story. To say the least, responsibilities cannot be easily separated. The displacement of government programs does not stop at the door of Parliament. Not all government legislation enters Parliament with the same amount of cabinet support and the same chances of success. Emergency legislation is usually on a better footing, especially if it relies on *stralcio* procedure and on decree-laws. Legislation that is formally the government's but actually the child of a single ministry and its bureaucracy can count on the cabinet's senatorial courtesy, but it also has to move by its own devices, and its success is in good part a function of the influence of its proponents and the clientele it serves. It is not completely unusual, on the other hand, for the government to introduce legislation on which negotiations have been less than successful and which does not therefore rely on a preestablished consensus. Pressures from individual coalition partners or from influential sectors of public opinion may induce the government to proceed nevertheless, to save face, to maintain credibility, or to change the site of negotiation. This happens at times with "qualifying" legislation, dealing with broad social and economic issues, on which agreement is more difficult but which the government cannot always afford to postpone. The decision of the government is to let this legislation float and find its agreement within Parliament.

The obvious expectation in regard to Parliament's response to government proposals is that Parliament will end up by enacting those proposals that arrive with more solid cabinet support. If support is uncertain within the cabinet, it is even less attainable in the more heterogeneous parliamentary environment. But there is more to parliamentary behavior than this. What is most interesting is that parliamentary mechanisms contribute to continuing that screening process initiated by the government by which special room is made for feasible legislation to the detriment of more difficult programmatic commitments. This is done especially through the use Parliament makes of the standing committees' decisional powers and through the fixing of the floor and committee agenda.

THE STANDING COMMITTEES AND
THE DECENTRALIZED PROCEDURE

The most interesting aspect of the standing committees in the Italian Parliament, it will be recalled, is their authority to pass laws. According to Article 72 of the Constitution, Parliament may, with a few exceptions, give such authority to its committees.[14] Specifically, according to the standing rules of each house, it is the president of each house who, upon assigning a legislative proposal to a committee competent by reason of subject matter, decides at his complete discretion whether the committee shall be empowered to enact it into law or whether it shall report to the floor for final action.[15] In practice, as we shall see below (Tables 47 and 48), most private and especially government legislation is enacted through the former or "decentralized" procedure, which thus lends organizational support to the high legislative output typical of the Italian Parliament. But this procedure is only one characteristic that marks the standing committees as important decisional centers within Parliament.[16] Another characteristic is that, when the committees act under "ordinary" procedure, the legislation they report to the floor, even if it comes from the government, may bear little resemblance to the original draft. Aside from the amending powers of each committee member, committees usually employ drafting subcommittees which include the opposition, collect government and other proposals

14. The exceptions concern the budget, the ratification of international treaties, laws on constitutional and electoral matters, and the delegation of law-making powers to the government.

15. This means that a law may follow a different procedure in each house. References to Parliament's standing rules in this chapter are based on the standing rules before the reform of 1971. Some comments on the reform are found in the conclusions of the chapter. My analysis of parliamentary rules has been especially helped by interviews with the permanent secretaries of seven of the fourteen standing committees of the Chamber of Deputies. The committees closely duplicate the major government departments.

16. On the standing committees in the Italian Parliament, see Elio Rogati Valentini, "Le Commissioni Permanenti della Camera dei Deputati," *Il Politico* 35 (1970), pp. 511-537; Leopoldo Elia, "Commissioni Parlamentari," *Enciclopedia del Diritto* 7 (1960), pp. 895-910; V. Longi and M. Stramacci, *Le Commissioni Legislative nel Parlamento Italiano* (Roma, 1953); Rocco Garruto, "Le Commissioni Parlamentari," *La Funzione Amministrativa* 14 (1965), pp. 744-768, 796-819. An ample legal analysis of the committee system and all other aspects of parliamentary work and an ample bibliography are found in a collective volume published by the Segretariato Generale of the Chamber of Deputies. See V. Longi and M. Stramacci (a cura di), *Il Regolamento della Camera dei Deputati—Storia, Istituti, Procedure* (Roma: Camera dei Deputati, 1968).

relative to the same subject matter, and prepare new drafts for committee discussion. The new draft reflects in various degrees a negotiated balance of the various proposals. The government has little means of preventing this procedure, aside from voicing its dissent and using its political clout.

Also important among committee features is the fact that committee chairmen are formally the only masters of their agenda and the only ones who have the power to convene the committees. No deadlines can be imposed by the house or its president on legislation assigned to the committees under the decentralized procedure. Deadlines *can* be imposed on legislation that follows the ordinary procedure, but they are in fact rarely enforced and committees easily obtain a postponement from a majority of the house. In this way, committees and especially their chairmen exercise, directly or indirectly, a considerable amount of control on the working of the floor itself, and represent veritable checkpoints in the legislative process.

The importance of the committees' procedural powers, and their special consequences for legislative outputs, will become more apparent when we look at the way the agenda is set. Suffice it to say that, together with the decentralized procedure, the powers point to a degree of pluralism and dispersion in the sites of parliamentary decisions. If we add to this the fact that committee meetings are not open to the public, that committees often arrive at decisions without formal votes, and that, given their size, their general style of operation is more informal and collegial than the floor's, we can also say that the committees, especially when they are called to enact laws, tend to adopt more balanced roles and to relax partisan and ideological distinctions. These factors may explain in part why legislation is more likely to be approved if assigned to the decentralized procedure (Table 48) and why approval is swifter (Table 51). They may also help explain why such legislation is more likely to pass with the vote of the Communist party than legislation following the ordinary procedure (Tables 6 and 8, Chapter II).

But there is another side to the committees' organization and operation, one which undercuts their capacity for cross-partisan legislative accomplishments. Despite their special status, the committees do not by any means approach the institutional capacities and the independent prestige most typically associated with the committees of the American Congress. It is sufficient to pay a visit to the crammed offices of any committee to "feel" this physically. These offices are usually composed of one or two impressive halls, stuffed with good-old solid furniture but short on office equipment, which must serve at the same time as conference rooms for an average of forty committee members (twenty-five in the Senate) and as offices for the committee's small staff (one permanent secretary, one or two typists, and possibly one librarian in charge of a small archive). These quarters seem more to befit an aging Victorian club than a bustling center of power.

But the power of committees can also and more reliably be measured by the resources, the power, and the political independence of their chairmen. Italian chairmen—let alone plain members, who are not even entitled to an office—have no personal staff, no special budget to allocate freely, no other organizational resources. More important, they have nothing approaching the political resources—subpoena, hearing, and investigative—attributed to their American colleagues.[17] In short, chairmanships are not among the most coveted offices and are not therefore achieved through a highly ritualized and inflexible seniority system. I compared committee chairmen in our sample (four in all) with ordinary members of their respective committees, to see if the former had been in the same committee longer than the latter; I found no significant difference. Chairmanships are usually considered stepping-stones to much more desirable ministerial positions, or consolation prizes for former ministers and undersecretaries. Formally, chairmen are elected by a majority of their committee. In fact, chairmanships are allocated among members of the coalition parties according to criteria of

17. Before the reform of 1971, committees in the Chamber of Deputies were not allowed to hear persons extraneous to Parliament, except for members of the cabinet, and had limited formal inspective powers. Since the reform they can summon civil servants, with the "agreement" of the president of the Chamber and of the government, and can investigate the application of laws and other acts of Parliament by the government. If a formal hearing is approved by the president of the Chamber, a committee can also hear private witnesses. But subpoena powers are still uncertain, hearings are still rare, and their political consequences are limited. Longi and Stramacci, *Le Commissioni Legislative nel Parlamento Italiano*, op cit., p. 47; Mario Pacelli, "L'Inchiesta Parlamentare come Strumento di Controllo Politico," *Nuova Rassegna di Legislazione, Dottrina e Giurisprudenza* 21 (1965), pp. 2893-2914; Gaetano Silvestri, "Considerazioni sui Poteri e i Limiti delle Commissioni Parlamentari d'Inchiesta," *Il Politico* 35 (1970), pp. 538-588.

partisan equilibrium and are relinquished whenever the party to which a chairman belongs leaves the coalition or a new Parliament is elected. Also, though most chairmen are confirmed in their posts, the rules of the house require that committees, and hence chairmanships, be reconstituted every two years (one year, before 1965). Because of all these facts, committees are almost never dominated over time by a single and powerful chairman, and tend to underplay criteria of personal competence and legislative specialization. Even to the informed public, committee chairmen are either obscure personalities who occupy no space in the news, or personalities whose notoriety does not rest on their chairmanship.

Since prestige is not attached to committee service and seniority does not determine committee career, turnover in committee membership is also frequent. Forty-five percent of the sampled members of Parliament with more than one term of office had belonged to a different committee in the previous Parliament. There is no special incentive, aside from personal preference, to stay in a committee, to learn its ropes, and to develop habits peculiar to a committee. Nor is there pressure in this sense from the parties. Members of Parliament indicate their choice of committee to their parliamentary group, but it is the leadership of the group which, in the words of the standing rules, "designates its delegates" by dividing its membership equally among the committees. With such a criterion of equal allocation, and with many committees to be staffed (fourteen in the Chamber of Deputies, eleven in the Senate), it is inevitable that criteria of competence and personal interest fall by the wayside. This is especially true of the smaller parties, whose members, since committees must reflect as much as possible the party composition of the assembly, have to double in several committees. But even members of the larger parties know that they serve in the committees not so much by the strength of their special skills as by virtue of party assignment.

Thus the committees, for all their decisional powers, are short on the institutional means, the special mores, and the capacity for socialization typical of committee-centered legislatures, and are still designed around parties, partisan alignments, and partisan roles. They are in a way decisional microcosms, but they are also microcosms of a larger partisan reality which interferes with their full institutionalization. The presence of parties is too vivid, and the committees' transformative and institutional resources are too limited for the committees to improve legislative performance.

The ambiguous position occupied by the committees in the legislative process is well reflected in the views of politicians and political analysts. We asked members of Parliament as well as the committees' permanent secretaries what they thought of the power attributed to the committee to pass legislation: Did they see advantages or disadvantages, and which? Most respondents expressed typically ambivalent views, quite similar to those also expressed by students of the committee system. They began by praising the informality surrounding committee work, which makes the public demagoguery characteristic of floor debates unnecessary or out of place. They found that the relative privacy of the committees allowed their members to put aside, for once, general principles and to search for agreement. They appreciated the fact that committee work puts a premium on solving issues and making decisions, as against eloquence, ideology, and partisan pressure.

But, at least among non-Communists (we will look at the position of the PCI in the conclusions), the advantages turned, *in the same respondents* and in the same breath, into disadvantages, two of which are paramount. The first is that the adoption of decentralized procedure has produced the opposite effect from that for which it was originally designed: instead of improving the workload capacity of Parliament and thus giving its members more time for careful consideration of legislative proposals, it has swamped Parliament with legislative demands that would otherwise have been addressed to other representative and bureaucratic bodies. The quality of legislation has suffered, both because the work load has outstripped organizational capacities and because the relative independence the committees enjoy from each other and from the floor has fragmented legislation and left it without coordination.[18] Attention has been shifted from salient legislation and important political issues to routine tasks. And the very powers enjoyed by the committees, as well as the informality

---

18. Giovanni Sartori, "Dove Va il Parlamento?" in S. Somogyi et al., *Il Parlamento Italiano 1946-1963* (Napoli: Edizione Scientifiche Italiane, 1963), pp. 377-378; Costantino Mortati, "Intervento," in Leopoldo Piccardi, Norberto Bobbio, and Ferruccio Parri (a cura di), *La Sinistra Davanti alla Crisi del Parlamento* (Milano: Giuffrè, 1967), esp. pp. 108-109.

of their operation, have made them a ready target of private and civil-service groups, which have become their main clients and supporters. Thus, stifling ideological concerns have been replaced not so much by technical competence as by narrow clientelistic concerns, or by a mixture of subjection and generalized suspicion toward the latter.

The second disadvantage of the decentralized procedure to be mentioned, closely linked to the first, is that it further confuses relations between government and opposition. Some respondents objected to the fact that the procedure weakens the government's legislative program by giving precedence to minor legislation, by leaving the opposition a good margin of initiative and influence within the committees, and by shielding the committees from the government. About the latter effect, these respondents remarked at times that the inclusion of the procedure in the Constitution responded not only to misplaced purposes of legislative effectiveness, but also to an unfortunate desire to check strong government and to control its legislative powers.[19] But doubts as to the effect of the procedure on government and opposition are not limited to respondents who favor strong majority rule. Respondents who are less than sympathetic toward the notion also shared such doubts, on the ground that the procedure, aside from disaggregating government legislation and hence failing the needs of the country, has not succeeded in providing government by dialogue. Though the opposition finds in the committees some way of communicating with the majority, this has not helped legislative accomplishments at all. On the contrary, the opposition has been captured, like the government, by the same logic of everyday survival. It can safely influence only marginal matters and low-quality legislation, whose political effects it has, however, no time and resources to control, busy as it is in producing laws.

Typical of these ambivalent feelings is the statement of a Socialist deputy:

19. A similar point is made by Mortati, ibid., and by Elia, op. cit., p. 896. A defense of the Italian committee system as providing greater efficiency, greater power for Parliament, and a better understanding between government and opposition can be found in Sondra Koff, "Innovative Procedure in Law-Making: The Legislative Function of Italian Parliamentary Commissions" (mimeographed, undated; to appear in *Parliamentary Affairs*). Koff's is a useful review of the salient features in the organization and functioning of the Italian committee system. It is also the only one in English that I am aware of.

Well, the advantages [of the decentralized procedure] are there. To put it in simple words, the procedure is much simpler, more attentive to questions of content, more productive. Also in the committees we come to know each other much better, to understand each other better, despite our party differences. There is a more open dialogue. The majority shows itself to be less close, and the Communist opposition shows comprehension for the needs of the government majority.

[As to] disadvantages, well those are there too. Despite the good will, it doesn't seem to me that [the procedure] helps much in improving the quality of our legislation. Our committees are literally afloat in a sea of legislative proposals in which they move without a compass, and which serve nobody, neither the interests of a responsible government, even less the opposition. The method is there, but the results are not on the level. . . . In my view the reasons are many, starting with very important constitutional and political questions of a very general order. But without going too far, there is a very immediate cause; that is, in our Parliament there still is absolutely no planning of legislative activities, and therefore the committees end up by occupying themselves with the most trivial things, which after all are the things that surround and obsess us every day. (PSI 14)

This answer contains probably the best explanation for the ambivalent feelings expressed by the respondents. What most politicians see in the committees' law-making authority is an intention gone wrong, a device which, poorly used, erodes legislative programs while supplying limited side benefits. This does not mean that choices are not made as to how to use this authority. It means that the authority is granted and employed to process and speed up minute legislation, while the most important and controversial legislation is often left behind. We can begin to document this by looking first at the type of legislation assigned to the decentralized and the ordinary procedures. The analysis relies on the sample of four hundred legislative proposals and their classifications first employed in Chapter II.

As Table 47 shows, two criteria of assignment are of great importance, each at work independently of the other. The first criterion has to do with the type of proponent. Here, to be sure, the decentralized procedure is most often used for government projects. The next and slightly less important criterion is the level of aggregation of legislation. With both government and especially private projects, the procedure is most often used for what we classified in Chapter II as microsectional legislation. The committees are, as commonly claimed, the typical site for pro-

TABLE 47. Type of Parliamentary Procedure Adopted for Legislative Proposals, by Type of Proponent and Level of Aggregation of Proposals, in Percentage

	Government Proposals		
	National/Sectional	Microsectional	Total
Ordinary procedure	33.0 (35)	14.8 (12)	25.1 (47)
Decentralized procedure[1]	67.0 (71)	85.2 (69)	74.9 (140)
Total	100.0 (106)	100.0 (81)	100.0 (187)
	Private Proposals		
	National/Sectional	Microsectional	Total
Ordinary procedure	62.5 (45)	39.2 (40)	48.9 (85)
Decentralized Procedure[1]	37.5 (27)	60.8 (62)	51.1 (89)
Total	100.0 (72)	100.0 (102)	100.0 (174)
	All Proposals[2]		
	National/Sectional	Microsectional	Total
Ordinary Procedure	44.9 (80)	28.4 (52)	36.6 (132)
Decentralized Procedure[1]	55.1 (98)	71.6 (131)	63.4 (229)
Total	100.0 (178)	100.0 (183)	100.0 (361)

[1] Includes proposals, 30 in all, assigned to the procedure in only one house.
[2] Since the sample is stratified by proponent, these figures do not reflect the universe.

ducing *leggine* that is, the type of legislation most likely to find easy support in the committees, even if it is introduced by single individuals and has not been prenegotiated. National and sectional legislation, on the other hand, is assigned to the ordinary procedure more often than legislation of lesser aggregation. In a way, this criterion of assignment has one ready explanation. The ordinary procedure, because of its formal and public character, is considered most appropriate for legislation of greater scope. In fact, the procedure is expressly required, as mentioned, for some especially important legislation.

But not all national and sectional legislation is assigned to the ordinary procedure. In fact, if we concentrate on government legislation, which is what interests us here, only one-third of it follows the procedure. What other selection criteria, if any, inform the choice? A tempting hypothesis is that national and sectional legislation initiated by the government contains obviously most of whatever proposals with uncertain coalition support still manage to reach Parliament, and that this is one reason why, at parity of importance, some of that legislation is assigned to the ordinary procedure. In short, when important government legislation is controversial, it tends to be assigned to the ordinary procedure. In part, it is a way of expediting the most feasible legislation, by reserving it for the swifter decentralized procedure; in part, it is again a recognition that the more controversial legislation is, the more it cannot avoid a public debate. In turn, a formal and publicized procedure is least likely to provide for accommodation where the preconditions did not exist. Admittedly, this is a theoretically long-winded set of claims, and empirically there is no direct way of knowing about the extent of existing support for each proposal. Further, the reader who is tempted, as I was, to tease an answer by comparing the rates of success of the two procedures, on the assumption that the ordinary one should be the least propitious for the government, will be rather disappointed. The results (Table 48) are in the expected direction, but they are not very impressive. More impressive is that, whatever the procedure and the level of aggregation, rates of approval of government projects are rather uniformly high. It is only with private legislation that procedure makes a substantial difference. Could it be that level of support does not determine assignment or that, contrary to the claim, legislation with least support goes to the easier decentralized procedure? Or could it be that this procedure is not especially easier for the government, and that the government has enough resources to find agreement for the most difficult legislation even on the floor of Parliament? Could it be that, since the most difficult government programs usually do not even arrive in Parliament, their impact is too limited to show up through indirect data? Are our claims wrong?

Evidence suggesting that we may not be wrong after all comes if we look more closely at the content of national and sectional

TABLE 48. Rates of Approval of Legislative Proposals, by Type of Parliamentary Procedure, Type of Proponent, and Level of Aggregation of Proposals, in Percentage[1]

	Government Proposals		
	National/ Sectional	Microsectional	Total
Ordindary procedure	68.6 (24)	83.3 (10)	72.3 (34)
Decentralized Procedure	77.5 (55)	87.0 (60)	82.1 (115)
Total	74.5 (79)	86.4 (70)	79.7 (149)

	Private Proposals		
	National/ Sectional	Microsectional	Total
Ordinary procedure	0.0 (–)	22.5 (9)	10.6 (9)
Decentralized Procedure	33.3 (9)	29.0 (18)	30.3 (27)
Total	12.5 (9)	26.5 (27)	20.7 (36)

	All Proposals[2]		
	National/ Sectional	Microsectional	Total
Ordinary procedure	30.0 (24)	36.5 (19)	32.6 (43)
Decentralized Procedure	65.3 (64)	59.5 (78)	62.0 (142)
Total	49.4 (88)	53.0 (97)	51.2 (185)

[1] Percentages are based on absolute figures in Table 47.
[2] Since the sample is stratified by proponent, these figures do not reflect the universe.

legislation. We have already seen in Chapter II (see especially Table 17) that this legislation contains most of what we classified as proposals having mixed or depriving effects on subjects other than those to which they are directly addressed. We now find (Table 49) that almost half of the national and sectional legislation originating from the government and assigned to the ordinary procedure contains proposals with mixed and depriving effects, half of which fail to become law (Table 50), *thus accounting for almost all failures in the former and larger class* (8 out of 11). We find, on the other hand, that only 22.5 percent of the national and sectional legislation assigned to the decentralized procedure is made of mixed or depriving proposals, less than one-third of which fail, accounting for less than one-third of all failures in the former and larger class (5 out of 16).

This evidence, while still inferential, is at least congruent with our previous claims. It is the very clarity of the pattern, despite the limited number of cases, that makes the claims credible. National and sectional legislation is likely to be especially controversial when its external effects, instead of being generally beneficial or of little import, deprive some or all groups of their benefits. This is especially so when political institutions, as in Italy, enjoy little trust and support. It is exactly this legislation that is most likely to fail, *especially if assigned to the ordinary procedure*, and the most economical interpretation is that failure in this case is due at least in good part to the difficulty of the procedure. The interpretation is not foolproof, as we cannot definitely rule out that even within this more homogenous class of legislation it is still quality of legislation that accounts for failure. Not all legislation with mixed and depriving consequences is of equal difficulty and controversiality, and the most

TABLE 49. External Effects of National and Sectional Legislation Initiated by the Government, within Procedure of Approval, in Percentage

		Procedure	
		Decentralized	Ordinary
EFFECTS	Mixed-Depriving	22.5 (16)	45.7 (16)
	Neutral-Beneficial	77.5 (55)	54.3 (19)
	Total	100.0 (71)	100.0 (35)

TABLE 50. Percentage of Failure of National and Sectional Legislation Initiated by the Government, within Procedure of Approval and by External Effects[1]

		Procedure	
		Decentralized	Ordinary
EFFECTS	Mixed-Depriving	31.25 (5)	50.0 (8)
	Neutral-Beneficial	20.0 (11)	15.8 (3)
	Total	22.5 (16)	31.4 (11)

[1] Percentages are calculated on absolute figures in Table 49.

difficult and controversial—while assigned to the ordinary procedure—may fail only because of these two qualities. We have no direct measure of the two qualities allowing us to discard the counterinterpretation; but after what we have seen about the different style of operation of the committees and the floor, a degree of disbelief on its plausibility seems appropriate. When legislation is apparently controversial to begin with, and the bases for agreement do not clearly exist, a procedure that rewards open partisanship does not seem likely to favor agreement.[20]

I have suggested that controversial legislation is assigned to the ordinary procedure because the nature of the legislation makes it politically appropriate that a more publicized, more formal, and more complex treatment be used. But I have also suggested that the procedure is used in order to shelve such legislation and to avoid having to cope with it.[21] In support of this claim, let me anticipate that legislation fails almost exclusively because it never comes up on the agenda, and that this type of failure is more likely to occur when the ordinary procedure is used. This means that the decision to assign controversial legislation to the floor is not only a decision to give the debate the proper publicity, it is also a decision that much of that legislation shall never come up for discussion at all. Since controversial legislation may lack a clear initial commitment to begin with, there is no special incentive to make room for it, but there is one to take the path of least resistance. In this sense, the mechanisms of Parliament function actively, Gresham-like, to displace conflictual legislation, whose enactment is more uncertain, more costly, or less desirable, in favor of more palatable but more marginal legislation.

We can appreciate these points better if we remember that the choice between the two procedures is made by the president of the assembly. The president is elected by a majority of the assembly[22] and is therefore, needless to say, a Christian Democrat

---

20. Others may want to argue that the ordinary procedure completely accounts for failure. We will see, however, in discussing the setting of the agenda, that this legislation finds difficulties also when assigned to the decentralized procedure.

21. This is not to advocate that difficult legislation should be assigned to the decentralized procedure. It is simply to pinpoint what things Parliament is set up to accommodate and what it is not.

22. With the reform of 1971, the majority required to elect the president of the Chamber of Deputies has been brought to two-thirds of the assembly in the first ballot, two-thirds of the voters in the second, and the absolute majority of the voters in the third.

or a member of one of the more important coalition parties. In addition to his powers of assignment, he enjoys other considerable prerogatives in organizing, supervising, and directing the activities of Parliament (chief among them the setting of the agenda), and he is empowered to interpret rules and to give legal sanctions to customs and precedents.[23] But he does not use such powers for the exclusive benefit of the parties that elect him. Whatever his formal powers, he cannot reasonably exercise them without the support or at least the tolerance of most of the parliamentary groups. On this score, his is a nonpartisan office and is interpreted as such by most political observers and in most constitutional doctrine.[24] This is probably one reason why, incidentally, presidents are consistently senior party statesmen or middle-of-the-roaders.[25] In a way, the very cumulation of prerogatives and resources in a single man, in a Parliament where many parties operate, makes him a guarantor of constitutional equilibria, not a party agent.

The fact that presidents are faithful to or, if you wish, hemmed in by their delicate role most likely explains why nobody usually interferes with their decision to assign legislation to the decentralized procedure. Although their decision can be constitutionally reversed by the government, one-fifth of the competent committee, or one-tenth of the assembly, rarely have either the government or the opposition made use of the prerogative. The president in fact rarely troubles to consult the government or the parliamentary leadership, and the latter two in turn rarely press their preferences.[26] Why such lack of conflict on such matter?

---

23. On the powers of the president in interpreting rules and establishing precedents, see Maccanico, op. cit. On the prerogatives of the president in general, see G. Ferrara, *Il Presidente di Assemblea Parlamentare* (Roma, 1965); Ettore Terzi, "Presidente d'Assemblea, Governo e Gruppi Politici nell'Organizzazione del Lavoro Parlamentare," *Studi Parlamentari e di Politica Costituzionale*, Vol. 1, No. 1 (1968), pp. 35-60; Federico Mohrhoff, "L'Evoluzione dell'Istituto Presidenziale del Parlamento Italiano (1848-1958)," *Montecitorio*, Vol. 13, No. 1 (1959), pp. 3-13; Nicola Greco, "Funzione di Rappresentanza ed Autonomia Politica dei Presidenti di Assemblee Parlamentari," *Montecitorio*, Vol. 21 (1967), No. 1-2, pp. 5-29; No. 3-6, pp. 5-18.

24. Greco, ibid.; Ferrara, op cit., esp. p. 14.

25. The only significant exception is Amintore Fanfani, the recognized leader of the Christian Democratic Party and several times party secretary and prime minister, who chaired the Senate during the Fifth Parliament.

26. What seems more likely is the opposite type of disagreement: When a piece of legislation has been assigned to the ordinary procedure, the committee handling it may ask for the simpler procedure. The president (and the assembly) usually accede to the request.

Because, to put it in the blunt words of the committees' permanent secretaries and of other observers, neither the government nor the opposition has a vested interest. Given the importance of assignment matters, this can only mean that both government and opposition have reason to trust the chair to do a satisfactory job by a balanced use of its assignment prerogatives. And the simplest rule of thumb for a president who wants to preserve the trust of a divided Parliament is to take decisions which, without necessarily pleasing, least offend the competing forces.[27] In different words, the president finds it difficult, assuming that he so wants to act, to use his general trust to give the parliamentary process his personal political imprint. His criteria of action are criteria of balancing and avoidance, used disjointedly and not always consciously, in which political and technical considerations shade into each other. It is easy to see how they can produce the kind of displacement of controversial legislation documented above. In fact, the government may have introduced such legislation without a clear intent to further press it and face a divisive debate, and therefore may not find it convenient to question the president's decision. The opposition, on the other hand, may find the decision equally agreeable, at least insofar as it leaves the committees open for legislation on which its influence is likely greater.

But procedural assignment is not the only tool the parliamentary leadership uses to affect displacement. Whatever procedure is chosen, the parliamentary leadership can also rely on its control of the floor and committee agenda to achieve similar results.

THE AGENDA

There is some disagreement among constitutional analysts about who in the Italian Parliament is the ultimate master of the floor agenda. The disagreement revolves around the relative powers

---

27. As pointed out in Chapter II, if the Communist party were displeased with the way the president uses his prerogatives, it could easily bring Parliament to a standstill by dumping committee legislation on the floor. That it does no do so means that the party has no interest in an extreme tactic which, aside from value considerations, may backfire. It also means that the party finds the use made of the assignment procedure basically acceptable.

of the president and the assembly, and is helped by the fact that parliamentary rules regulate the matter only scantily and indirectly.[28] For some analysts it is always the assembly that ultimately decides the order of its activities, while the president and other parliamentary bodies have only powers of initiative and proposal. For others, it is the president who not only prepares but has the right to decide the agenda autonomously and discretionally. More important than this legal disagreement, however, are the practices which Parliament early evolved. Whatever the legal significance of the practice, it is the president who actually sets the agenda and transmits it to the house, but the house rarely challenges it. If somebody curbs the president's power, it is not the assembly but the committee chairmen, who, by controlling their own committees, indirectly control the floor agenda.

The president decides the floor agenda in a manner similar to the way he decides on approval procedures. Consultations with the government and with parliamentary leadership on long-range planning seldom occur and are seldom asked for, yet habitually no conflict arises. The government usually indicates its preference about the order in which its proposals should be discussed, but it does not further pursue the matter. The unique role the president is called upon to play emerges more convincingly if we consider how an early attempt to reallocate agenda powers came to fail. In 1950 reform of the standing rules of the Chamber of Deputies created the Conference of Presidents, a body designed to work with the president of the chamber in fixing and supervising the agenda.[29] The Conference is made up of the president and his office (vice-presidents and secretaries representing most of the parties), the committee chairmen, and the presidents of the parliamentary groups, and is called at the discretion of the president to discuss and reach agreements on the agenda. Originally, the Communists saw in it an invaluable opportunity to participate directly in legislative planning. According to them, the agenda should be jointly adopted by all

---

28. See, for contrasting interpretations, Ferrara, op. cit., pp. 253-260; V. Longi, "Convocazione della Camera," *Rassegna Parlamentare* 1 (1959), No. 8-8, p. 51. General up-to-date discussions of the agenda and the role of the various parliamentary bodies are found in Claudio De Cesare, "Note sulla Fissazione dell'Ordine del Giorno Assembleare," in AA. VV., *Studi per il Ventesimo Anniversario dell'Assemblea Costituente* (Firenze: Vallecchi, 1969), Vol. 5, pp. 257-352; Terzi, op. cit.

29. A similar body has also evolved, by custom, in the Senate.

parties represented in the Conference and should include items submitted by the minorities. Also, agreements should be comprehensive and long-range rather than limited to single cases. They would obviously require reciprocal concessions, within which the Communist party would be ready to curb its freedom of action and accept strict order in the ways and tempos of debate in exchange for greater minority inputs. Despite Communist aspirations, the Conference never became such a planning agency, and the Communists have rarely pressed its primacy. Although it is convened frequently (at least in a rump group composed only of the presidents of the parliamentary groups), the very fact that its decisions must be unanimous has confined its activities to matters of maintenance and ordinary administration or to urgent matters, and has prevented it from giving a new political direction to parliamentary works.[30]

The diversity of the group interests represented in the Conference makes unanimity difficult to achieve and reasserts the importance of the president. The concentration of the agenda powers in the hands of a single president, despite the existence of the Conference, is a recognition by the parliamentary groups that the heterogeneity of their political positions makes collegial work particularly unfruitful, and that the ensuing procedural conflict could lead to risky solutions and would further impair the day-to-day functioning of Parliament.[31] Conflicts would have to be resolved by the assembly, which could act under its power to approve or reject the calendar of the following day by simple majority of the voters. The uncertainty of the solution is clear to both government and opposition. For the government it presents the risk of a coup by an occasional majority. For the opposition the risk is an attractive possibility, but one it cannot plan. In either case, the end results may not be worth the acrimony they create, especially since the floor is better equipped to reject a proposed agenda than to formulate a new one.

But the power to influence legislative outputs that by exclusion is recognized as the president's is quite considerable and requires

---

30. The story of the Conference of Presidents is told in De Cesare, op. cit., pp. 288-295. See also Aristide Savignano, *I Gruppi Parlamentari* (Napoli: Morano Editore, 1965), pp. 172-181.

31. On parliamentary groups, see Savignano, ibid.; Terzi, op. cit.; Gian Franco Ciaurro, "Gli Organi della Camera," in Longi and Stramacci, op. cit., pp. 240-251.

the greatest care and restraint in its use. As Arthur Bentley put it seventy years ago, "Most bills that become laws do so after a fight with other bills for space in the calendar, rather than after a fight with an opposition of a more direct kind."[32] It is a most fitting description of the Italian case. To anticipate the evidence in Table 52, practically all legislation that fails to be enacted never comes to a final negative vote; that is, it dies because elections are called and Parliament is dissolved before debate is completed.[33] It might be parsimonious to argue that this type of failure is merely the necessary consequence of a weighty schedule which does not allow Parliament enough time for all legislation. But such interpretation, according to which failure would best be explained by a first-come-first-served principle, is belied by a few facts which, taken together, eventually suggest that the president (and the committee chairmen) operate priority choices.

One fact is that, as we already know, the decision to assign to one or the other of the two approval procedures, itself not a random decision, affects the chances of success of legislation because, for one thing, it affects the speed with which it is approved. On the average, the ordinary procedure more than doubles the time of approval of private legislation and increases by approximately 50 percent that of government legislation (Table 51). A second fact is that, except for legislation presented in the fifth and last year of each Parliament, which lacks objectively the time to come up for consideration, the time at which

TABLE 51. Days Passed between a Proposal's Introduction in Parliament and Its Approval by Both Houses, by Proponent and Procedure[1]

Government (149)		Private (36)	
Decentralized (115)	Ordinary (34)	Decentralized (27)	Ordinary (9)
164	239	379	778

[1]Vittorio Mortara, *L'Analisi Quantitativa del Processo Legislativo* (Bologna: Il Mulino, 1970), p. 189, reports respectively 148.1, 182.6, 337.2, and 601.0 days. These, however, are working days, not including summer and winter recesses. Ours are real days.

32. Arthur Bentley, *The Process of Government* (Bloomington, Indiana: Principia Press, 1949; first published, 1908), p. 493.

33. I am indebted to Professor Vittorio Mortara for the analysis that follows. He brought to my attention the importance of the agenda and discussed with me some of his early analyses, which I have in part replicated.

legislation is presented in relation to the life span of a Parliament makes no difference in its ability to complete (successfully or unsuccessfully) debate. This is reported by Vittorio Mortara, working with the "Predieri-Mortara" sample, and is confirmed by our sample.[34] It is a finding that one would not expect under the first-come-first-served hypothesis. If only time objectively at disposal were what counts, legislation presented earlier should most likely complete debate more often. A third fact is that government as well as private legislation do not fail of completion at just any point during the legislative process; they fail almost in their entirety *even before coming to a vote* in the *first* house in which they have been presented (see Table 52 below). This, too, does not square with the notion of failure for lack of time which, if correct, should cause failures to be more equally distributed throughout the legislative process, and legislation introduced earlier to fail at a more advanced stage. It squares better with the obvious fact that legislation fails of completion not because Parliament is overworked but because some legislation is slowed down and left behind. And, fourth, the decisive point here is that early blockage is no so much the natural result of long-drawn and inconclusive debates on the floor and in the committees, as it is the consequence of leadership decisions that delay debate.

To prove the last point, consider first that there are three crucial junctures at which agenda decisions are taken. The first is when the president assigns incoming legislation to a committee. Here what counts is not what the decision is, but how long it takes to make it. By holding back on some legislative proposal and not assigning it, as it is entirely within the recognized powers of the office, the president in each house is allowed to influence that legislation. The second juncture occurs when committee chairmen exercise their exclusive right to determine the calendar for the legislation assigned to them by the president. They can therefore kill a bill by never beginning debate on it. The third, which is limited to legislation following the ordinary procedure, is when legislation reported out of committee is placed by the president

---

34. Vittorio Mortara, *L'Analisi Quantitativa del Processo Legislativo* (Bologna: Il Mulino, 1970), pp. 237-238. Our sample also reveals that lateness of presentation is especially important for private legislation, which is the one that takes longer to be approved. Only one of the thirty-four private proposals in the sample presented in the last year of a legislature was finally approved.

on the floor calendar. It is at one or another of these three junctures that much legislation fails. This is clearly shown in Table 52, which lists the main causes of legislative mortality. Whether legislation is assigned to the ordinary or the decentralized procedure, almost all of it fails, as reported, before even coming to a vote in the house in which it was introduced.[35] Further, the majority of these failures result from the fact that the president or one of the committee chairmen never includes the legislation

TABLE 52. Failure, Approval, and Causes of Failure of Legislative Proposals, in Percentage[1]

	Nonapproved 53.75 (215)	Approved 46.25 (185)
1. Never assigned to a committee	18.1 (39)	—
2. Never included in the committee agenda	27.9 (60)	—
3. Parliament dissolved pending committee discussion	23.3 (50)	—
4. Reported out of committee, but never included in the floor agenda	9.3 (20)	—
5. Parliament dissolved pending floor discussion	6.0 (13)	—
Total failed before vote by first house	84.7 (182)	—
6. Parliament dissolved before vote by second house	1.9 (4)	—
7. Voted down by first house	8.8 (19)	—
8. Others (withdrawn, absorbed, no information)	4.7 (10)	—

[1] Since the sample is stratified by proponent, the figures do not reflect the universe of each class. However, since I found no substantial differences in the distribution of government and private proposals in the various classes (only exception: twice as many private proposals were not assigned to a committee as government proposals), comparisons between classes are possible. The drop in stages 4 and 5 is in good part due to the fact that most legislation, being assigned to the decentralized procedure, does not go to the floor.

35. The figure for the "Predieri-Mortara" sample (calculated from Mortara, ibid., p. 146, Table 1) is 75.6 percent. No further data, however, are available from this sample on the specific stages, before the first vote, at which failure occurs.

in the agenda. Fully 46 percent of proposed legislation never makes it beyond committee assignment and dies without ever being debated. And altogether only a minority dies while being debated on the floor or in the committees. Also, even in the case of failure during the debate, the presidents and committee chairmen may not be completely extraneous to the event. For one thing, once debate on a piece of legislation is initiated, the presidents or the chairmen, depending on the site of the debate, continue to influence the speed of that debate by the power they have to set the calendar for the next meeting.[36] They can therefore kill a bill by continuously adjourning its debate. For another thing, the president does not usually interfere with the obstructionism of the chairmen, as is shown by the fact that he makes limited use of his power to call out of the committees legislation whose reporting deadline is expired.

There is in turn evidence that, as with the assignment to the two approval procedures, the parliamentary leadership—wittingly or unwittingly—uses its powers to expedite or stall legislation in a selective fashion. For instance, government legislation is processed and placed on the agenda more quickly than private legislation (Table 53). This is one reason why government legislation takes less time to be approved. We know that most

TABLE 53. Days Spent by Approved Government and Private Proposals Waiting To Be Placed on the Agenda and in Discussion

	Government (149)	*Private (36)*
Waiting for discussion[1]	150	349
In discussion	31	130

Note: Numbers in parentheses are number of proposals.

[1] Waiting for assigment to a committee, to the committee agenda, and (if applicable) to the floor agenda in both houses. The differences between government and private proposals are not artifacts of different approval procedures. Although the ordinary procedure may require more waiting time because it involves three rather than two decisions (to assign to a committee, to the committee agenda, and to the floor), private proposals *that become laws* are not much more likely to have followed the procedure than their government counterparts.

36. In this connection, our sample shows that legislation that fails takes on the average longer than successful legislation in completing the stages before the one at which it is arrested. For example, a proposal that does not complete debate on the floor of the house where it was introduced typically spends more days being debated in committee than one that is later approved on the floor. The difference is by no means intuitive, but one reason may be lack of leadership interest in expediting the legislation that eventually fails.

proposals originate not from the government but from Parliament, and that many of them are of the most trivial kind. The agenda is one very important tool for slowing and, by extension, eliminating in the preliminary stages at least part of this legislation.

But the agenda is not used for this purpose only, since the quality of the legislation eliminated through it is highly diversified and includes important government legislation as well. Among government proposals that never became law, our sample contained sixteen of particular difficulty. They were national-sectional in scope and had depriving or mixed external effects. Three of them failed because they were never assigned to a committee. Of those remaining, five followed the decentralized procedure, but only one came up in the committee agenda. It eventually failed to make the agenda of the corresponding committee in the second house. Eight followed the ordinary procedure, but only three appeared in the committee agenda and, having passed the committee, reached the floor, where they died during debate before coming to a vote. The sample is too small to warrant precise conclusions and complex comparisons with the causes of failure of other types of legislation. There remains the fact that only four of those sixteen proposals—that is, one in four, compared with more than half of all government and private proposals that did not become law—ever saw debate.[37] It is a fact that fits well with another finding: Even when this type of government proposal succeeds in becoming law (there were nineteen such laws in our sample), it takes it longer than other government legislation even to come up for debate (Table 54). It spends an average of 211 days waiting for assignment to the committees and to the floor, compared to 141 days for other government legislation.[38] These findings support our contention that, not unlike what the president does with his power of assignment, the agenda is most probably used to table whichever major legislation lacks, in the leadership's opinion, a clear support basis. This behavior fits with the nonpartisan role requirements of presidents and committee chairmen.

37. Notice also from Table 50, that, although these proposals failed more frequently when assigned to the ordinary procedure, they also failed more frequently than other proposals, irrespective of procedure. The latter finding strengthens the point that, within each procedure, the agenda is used to eliminate more difficult legislation.

38. Notice also from the table that this legislation spends more time in discussion. This may seem intuitive, in view of its special importance. But it would seem equally intuitive that legislation of less importance should be slowed down by lack of interest and relevance.

TABLE 54. Days Spent by Approved Government Proposals Waiting To Be Placed on the Agenda and in Discussion, by Type of Proposal

	National/Sectional Mixed/Depriving (19)	Other (130)
Waiting for discussion[1]	211	141
In discussion	44	29

Note: Numbers in parentheses are number of proposals.

[1]Waiting for assignment to a committee, to the committee agenda, and (if applicable) to the floor agenda in both houses. The difference is only in part an artifact of more of the special government legislation following the ordinary procedure. Further analysis reveals that assignment takes significantly longer in each of three decisions involved (see footnote in Table 53). Also, variance around the mean for the smaller special legislation group is no greater than for the larger group.

The adjective *nonpartisan* may sound surprisingly when attached to committee chairmen. They are, after all, members of the coalition parties, must relinquish the chair if their party abandons the coalition, have a vote on committee legislation, and take in addition a crucial role in shaping and politically orienting the activities of their committees. They are less visible than presidents and in general better equipped than they to use the body they preside over to personal and partisan advantage, to foster government legislation or favorite projects. Let me recall the three discretionary powers they can exercise without committee interference: to convene the committee, to set the calendar, and to withhold legislation from the floor. Nevertheless, a chairman, not unlike a president and his assembly, must live with his committee, and the secrecy and informality of its operation suggest that conflict-avoiding strategies are often more appropriate in this regard than strictly partisan ones. A chairman confronted with a difficult piece of legislation on which his coalition cannot agree might be tempted to employ his special position, his skills, and his knowledge of the committee's ways to sell it. But there are some factors that make the strategy unlikely. For one thing, the chairman himself, as well as other members of the coalition, may have little desire to enact that legislation. For another, unlike his U.S. colleagues, he does not have the seniority and the other political and technical resources that place him in command of the committee and assist in negotiating skills. Also, he still operates in a partisan environment, which may not be so amenable to extensive manipulations; these may in fact revive old antagonisms. There are differences among chairmen, but in the view of the committee secretaries interviewed,[39] chairmen tend on such difficul occasions to take the path of least resistance. They find it advantageous to preserve credit by not pushing legislation. That is, in part, why the chairmen's use of their extensive powers is seldom seriously contested by other committee members. Not unlike the president, committee chairmen contribute to preserving the complex if unstable equilibrium of Parliament.

CONCLUSIONS

A careful reader may find much of the reasoning in the chapter, linking performance to practices and procedures, specious and questionable on the ground that parliamentary procedures and practices provide the context for, more than an incentive to, poor legislative performance. What if, for example, the decentralized procedure did not exist? Would legislation improve? Would greater room be made for more important legislation? Granted, most *leggine* are approved through the procedure; but does this make the procedure a cause of *leggine*? In the official Communist view, expressed in most of our interviews with Communist parliamentarians, the real cause is the lack of a clear political will in the government. Were the latter more determined in its action, it could easily use its political influence alone to impose a more comprehensive legislative program on the committees as well as on the floor. Hence, abolishing the procedure while the government remains indecisive would deprive the parties of a useful meeting ground, and the opposition of a valuable source of control over the government, without thereby strengthening legislative action.[40] Significant legislation would still be limited and would still be shunted aside in the parliamentary agenda, while *leggine* would maintain privileged treatment. Similarly, it can be objected, the importance of assembly presidents and committee chairmen in fixing the agenda and the use they make of the agenda are no a reflection of their legal powers but of the way

---

39. There is no Italian study of committee chairmen that I know of. Terzi, op. cit., pp. 55-56, in discussing who controls the agenda, argues that committee chairmen are the only parliamentary leaders that, thanks to the considerable formal powers they enjoy, insure in some way the realization of majority programs. But he also argues that lack of coordination among chairmen makes majority control of legislation partial and fragmentary.

40. Pietro Ingrao, "Intervento," in Istituto per la Documentazione e gli Studi Legislativi (a cura di), *Indagine sulla Funzionalità del Parlamento* (Milano: Giuffrè, 1969), Vol. 2, pp. 80-87.

their role has been defined by external political equilibria. A proof of this is the failure of the Conference of Presidents to develop into a means of legislative planning. It is not legal authority that has failed this body; it is the capacity of its members to find agreement on how to use it.

There is plenty to be said for these views. The importance of factors external to Parliament is a constant theme throughout this book. Also, procedural reforms do not guarantee that practices will change and more basic causes will be offset.[41] But the presence of more basic and very likely more strategic causes acting at a distance does not alter a simple fact: The practices and procedures we have examined in this chapter exist and operate. Whatever external factor sustains them, they have sealed an institutional reality that—awaiting change, however induced—feeds on and perpetuates itself. They have justified a routine that rewards displacement of energies and dispersion of resources and gives but the impression of activism.

Let me take, for example, the decentralized procedure. The simple fact that the procedure is available and its use is in no way jointly programmed and constrained shields and therefore encourages government irresponsibility.[42] The government can conveniently and safely count on the procedure's relative privacy and informality to practice what Piero Calamandrei, a prestigious intellectual and acute constitutionalist, called "majority obstructionism":[43] It can rely on its senators and deputies in the committees and on committee chairmen to delay and possibly arrest approval of legislation included only pro forma in the coalition program. The opposition, on the other hand, finds in the procedure an opportunity to exploit the fragmentation of government action and to achieve a limited modus vivendi. Convenient as all of this may be for survival, it still leaves the matter of mutual decisional roles unsettled; indeed, it further confuses them.

As to the effects of the procedure on individual members of

---

41. For an acute analysis of the internal causes of poor parliamentary performance and of problems of parliamentary reform, see Andrea Manzella, "L'Organizzazione dei Lavori Parlamentari in Italia," *Tempi Moderni*, Vol. 11, No. 32 (1968), pp. 1-33.

42. Manzella, ibid., places much emphasis on the lack of coordination and planning of parliamentary works, and argues that coordination is especially necessitated in view of the increasing investment in economic planning schemes since the beginning of the Center-Left.

43. Piero Calamandrei, "L'Ostruzionismo di Maggioranza," *Il Ponte*, 9 (1953), pp. 129-136.

Parliament, let me recall that its adoption, by attracting more legislation to Parliament, has increased rather than decreased the workload. Hence members of Parliament are overworked, their capacities overextended, and their span of attention overtaxed. As Giovanni Sartori observed twelve years ago, there are three extremely easy ways in which a member of Parliament can protect himself against this *surmenage*: by concentrating on easy issues, by reducing his span of attention, and by routinizing his behavior. Evidently, his responses perpetuate and aggravate the phenomenon. Hence today, just like twelve years ago, Parliament operates inertially by repeating itself.[44] Members of Parliament are perfectly aware of this plight. If they do not react, it is not simply because of ill-will, calculation, or insensitivity, but also because their energies are drained by immediate survival needs. They are the agents but also the victims of an institutional choice.

To prevent the committees from enacting legislation or to plan and restrain this power will not alone make government coalitions more cohesive, and will not significantly induce government and opposition to agree on respective decisional roles. It will not alone make legislative programs more incisive.[45] The crisis of Italian politics is now too generalized and advanced to be solved only by parliamentary reform. But insofar as the crisis stems from government inaction and from a long-standing inability of government and opposition to agree overtly on their respective decisional roles, Parliament, with the practices illustrated in this chapter, bears part of the original responsibility.

But let us turn finally to the external factors.

44. Sartori, op cit., pp. 365-369.
45. The reform of 1971 has introduced one restriction in the use of the decentralized procedure. It states that a project can be assigned to the procedure if it concerns "issues that have no special relevance of a general order." But since what constitutes legislation of special relevance is a matter of interpretation, it seems hardly the kind of reform that will make a difference. The other reforms introduced in 1971, some of which have been mentioned in the text, have much the same quality. They were not designed to alter behavior significantly, and they are very unlikely to do so. See an analysis of the new standing rules in Temistocle Martines, "Regolamenti Parlamentari e Attuazione della Costituzione," *Studi Parlamentari e di Politica Costituzionale*, Vol. 4, No. 13 (1971), pp. 5-16.

VI

Government and Party System: A "Sartorian" View

We saw in previous chapters that members of the Italian Parliament hold ambiguous views of their parliamentary role. While they see compromise as necessary in a politically diversified decisional body, and appreciate the dangers of excessive divisions, they also find compromise difficult to achieve, reveal mutual suspicions, and are strongly partisan in their relation to their parties and followers. Hence, Parliament possesses no clear decisional rule, no operational code well-rooted in the compatible orientations of its members. I also showed that these ambiguities reflect events in the evolution of the Italian party system since the war which have made the decisional rule, especially where it concerns the role of the opposition, the central issue in Italian politics. But my analysis remained at the level of convincing idiosyncratic interpretation and did not explicitly identify the features of the party system responsible for parliamentary attitudes and behavior. An explanation needs a model of the party system, capable of comparative extension beyond Italy.[1]

---

1. This chapter's theoretical framework follows closely Giovanni Sartori's analysis of the typology of party systems. After comparing Sartori's typology with other interpretations of the Italian party system by Giorgio Galli and other Italian colleagues, I came to the conclusion that Sartori's is the one that travels farthest and most explicitly places the Italian case in a comparative-explanatory dimension. My reelaboration refers to Sartori's extreme multiparty type, and I am obviously the only one responsible for weaknesses and misinterpretations. For a precise account of Sartori's typology and the methodological issues related to its construction and justification, see especially four works of his: "Modelli Spaziali di Competizione tra Partiti," *Rassegna Italiana di Sociologia* 6 (1965), pp. 7-29; "European Political Parties: The Case of Polarized Pluralism," in Joseph LaPalombara and Myron Weiner, eds., *Political Parties and Political Development* (Princeton: Princeton University Press, 1966), chapter 5; "The Typologies of Party Systems—Proposals for Improvement," in Stein Rokkan and Erik Allardt, eds., *Mass Politics* (New York: Free Press, 1970), chapter 12; "Rivisitando il 'Pluralismo Polarizzato'," in Fabio Luca Cavazza and

I will argue in this chapter that Italy's parliamentary performance is typical of extreme multiparty systems, in which many parties align themselves along the same ideological space. In such systems, the overcrowding of the space by numerous parties compels the parties to obtain electoral recognition by sharply contrasting their ideological images at the mass level and by further expanding, in effect, the already large ideological space, to the point where ideologically distant parties will question their reciprocal right to govern, and coalition parties will find it difficult to govern together. It is irrelevant for our purpose to discuss how such party systems originate, and to what extent they reflect extant conditions of social disaccord as well as electoral, institutional, and legal arrangements. Once such systems exist, it is their dynamic trait to maintain and spread ideological differentiation at the electoral level and in their external images, so as to allow for party survival. But these images are quite inappropriate as guides to decision-making. If nevertheless they are the only ones of importance to governing—either because they are made salient and imposed on government by circumstances external to politicians, or because politicians feel no strong commitment to the substantial preservation of the regime—the cumulation of divisive issues thus publicly entering the agenda of government should in the short run lead to major regime crises. Divisions at all levels cannot be afforded. Of special importance here is the fact that the *public* transformation of electoral images into decisional issues deprives political elites of the autonomy they need for governing together.[2] Weimar, the Fourth French Republic,

---

Stephen Graubard (a cura di), *Il Caso Italiano* (Milano: Garzanti, 1974), pp. 196-223. See also Sartori's forthcoming volume, *Parties and Party Systems: A Framework for Analysis* (New York: Cambridge University Press, 1976). On Giorgio Galli's interpretation, see his *Il Bipartitismo Imperfetto* (Bologna: Il Mulino, 1966), esp. chapter 2, and *Il Difficile Governo* (Bologna: Il Mulino, 1972), passim. Galli's view is essentially that the Italian is an imperfect two-party system, without alternance in government. The diagnosis suggests the treatment. Sartori's attention is more exclusively on the fragmentation and ideological polarization of parties, in the presence of which efforts to create alternance may spell disaster. For an interesting effort to demonstrate that Galli and Sartori have a lot in common, see Luciano Pellicani, "Verso Il Superamento del Pluralismo Polarizzato?" *Rivista Italiana di Scienza Politica* 4 (1974), pp. 645-674. My analysis of ideological polarization in this chapter differs substantially from the one I offered in my *Apathy and Participation* (New York: Free Press, 1970), chapter 5.

2. For the concept of elite autonomy and what prevents it, see William Kornhauser's discussion of elite accessibility in his *The Politics of Mass Society* (Glencoe: Free Press, 1959), esp. chapter 2.

the Second Spanish Republic, and the Allende government in Chile in the period immediately preceding their collapse seem appropriate cases in point.[3]

And even if electoral and party images do not directly instruct governing, thus permitting long-term survival, they yet reduce the realm of vital issues on which politicians can come together, especially since the electoral strategies underpinning such images tend progressively to expand the ideological space for which parties compete. Though politicians, as in the Italian case, may genuinely feel the need for compromise, the need is in tension with the electoral images they subscribe to, finds no logical or psychological justification in the latter, and hence does not significantly reform governing behavior, let alone the logic of electoral competition.[4] Between the need to govern together and the constraints of electoral images, it is the latter that provide the dynamics. Political elites can only throw in correctives which allow for survival; they cannot provide sustained agreement on the decisional rule.

I affirm that such agreement cannot be found and made operative until the electoral images of parties and party competition are changed so as to reduce ideological space. I affirm that political elites can help reduce such space only if they are willing to transform compromise from a surreptitious and nonlegitimized method for "governing-at-the-margins" into an explicit component of electoral and party appeals.[5]

THE NUMBER OF PARTIES: MANY PARTIES, TOO MANY PARTIES

Parties are strategic intermediate structures, straddling society and decisional institutions. To understand how they relate to society, whom they appeal to, how they couch their appeals, how they vie with each other for support, is to understand how

---

3. On the breakdown of democracy in these and other cases, see Juan Linz and Alfred Stepan, eds., *Breakdowns and Crises of Democratic Regimes* (forthcoming).

4. The reader should keep in mind, again, that this is especially so if Parliament and government, as seen in the previous chapter, offer no special institutional incentives to overcome the tension.

5. The urgency, and also the difficulties, of such transformation under the present Italian situation, and in the light of recent Communist successes, are examined in the second part of the next chapter.

politically homogeneous or fragmented society is. Indeed parties are the best indicators of the political society. To go one step further, they are what shapes and sets the tone of the political society; they are by and large what the political society is all about. But parties are also significant agenda setters for decisional institutions. They influence and control the flux of issues with which the latter deals and, by claiming representation of the political society, lend legitimacy to the agenda as what voters are concerned with. This second party role has particular importance for governing when representative institutions—as in the case of Italy—do not possess strong transformative resources of their own, allowing them to set their own agenda and shape their own solutions. In such a case, it falls upon the parties' transformative resources to exact agreement from party diversity. To understand how parties perform in this respect is to understand how governable a political society is.

It has been the main thrust of much early literature on parties that some party systems are capable of this transformation more than others and that, in this sense, they are more workable than others.[6] And the criterion of workability has seemed for a long time ready and simple: The fewer the parties competing for electoral support, the more workable the party system, on the simple ground that fewer parties means larger and more heterogeneous parties, competing at the center for the same electorate, and hence already aggregating and accommodating at the electoral level. Conversely, when many parties are present, what is fragmented at the electoral level cannot be easily reassembled, transformed, and made compatible for purposes of governing. In few words, as intervening structures parties cannot mediate in government what they cannot or will not mediate in the visible electoral arena.

Like all parsimonious models, however, the model of party number has not escaped criticisms and has more recently fallen in

---

6. See the classical statements in Sigmund Neumann, "Toward a Comparative Study of Political Parties," in Sigmund Neumann, ed., *Modern Political Parties* (Chicago: University of Chicago Press, 1956), esp. pp. 402-403; Maurice Duverger, *Political Parties* (London: Methuen, 1959), pp. 372-421; Gabriel Almond, "Comparative Political Systems," *Journal of Politics* 18 (1956), pp. 391-409; Gabriel Almond and G. Bingham Powell, Jr., *Comparative Politics* (Boston: Little, Brown, 1966), pp. 102-103; Ferdinand Hermens, *Democracy or Anarchy? A Study of Proportional Representation* (Notre Dame: University of Notre Dame, Review of Politics, 1941), esp. pp. 5-19.

some disrepute. If numbers are decisive, and if therefore a two-party system is the ideal of workability, the case of the First Austrian Republic, with a Socialist and Catholic party confronting each other and leading from the confrontation into a Catholic authoritarian regime, presents an interesting puzzle. Even if the puzzle were to remain a deviant case, in no way denying the central importance of party number, other authors point significantly to many cases of "working" multiparty systems—in the Scandinavian and Small Continental Democracies.[7] And since some of these democracies, such as Switzerland, the Netherlands, and Norway, seem on some counting to have no fewer parties than the classical cases of "nonworking" multiparty systems— Italy, the Third and Fourth French Republics, and Weimar Germany—this has induced some authors to reject the number of parties as a deceptively simplistic answer to the problem of governing. Gabriel Almond, for instance, has suggested that some multiparty systems work because they operate in a homogeneous political culture and some of their parties still perform a broadly aggregative function.[8] In other words, "many parties" is not synonymous with cultural fragmentation, and it is the latter that is the key factor. Arend Lijphart, on the other hand, points out in response to Almond that neither Switzerland nor the Low Countries are examples of homogeneous and secular political cultures, yet they work. He also points out that the feature that distinguishes these systems from the party systems of Italy (and implicitly of other nonworking systems) is not the number of parties, but the presence only in the latter of strong Communist parties.[9] Lijphart therefore shifts his attention from mass culture and the number of parties to elite beliefs and behavior, and seeks to explain why some multiparty systems work, despite cultural fragmentation, in terms of the particular culture of accommodation and consociationalism exemplified by the political elites of these systems.[10]

Yet it seems premature to discard party systems. We can in fact

7. Arend Lijphart, "Typologies of Democratic Systems," *Comparative Political Studies* 1 (1968), esp. pp. 14-17; Dankwart Rustow, "Scandinavia: Working Multiparty Systems," in Neumann, ed., op. cit., pp. 169-193.

8. Almond, op. cit., pp. 392-393. Almond, however, also argues for the fundamental usefulness of counting parties. See Almond and Powell, op. cit., pp. 102-103.

9. Lijphart, op. cit., pp. 17, 34.

10. Ibid., esp. pp. 17-22.

use the above analysis to rescue and revamp the counting criterion, provided that—as Sartori puts it—we know why and hence how we count. Lijphart is entirely and obviously correct when he says that Italy's failure is a failure of its political elites to bridge fragmentation. I have amply illustrated in this book Parliament's lack of institutional persuasion. But, in view of Lijphart's analysis, the failure is hardly surprising. If his distinction between consociational (e.g., the Netherlands) and centrifugal (e.g., Italy) democracies[11] hinges on the fact that only in the former do elites remedy party fragmentation, then party fragmentation is always a potential source of problems, and what needs explaining is not Italy but consociationalism. Why then is consociationalism easier in Lijphart's set of countries? Lijphart suggests that his countries have no large Communist party, in the presence of which neither government nor opposition would be capable of consociating. But Communism does not yet provide a comparative explanation. It is merely a label with limited extension, which points in turn to a more significant underlying difference.

Among consociational democracies, party fragmentation refers largely to ethnic, linguistic, or denominational differences; that is, to "preindustrial" or "communal" cleavages. Among centrifugal democracies it refers to a left-right spread, that is to "industrial" or secular cleavages.[12] Consociationalism, as an elite practice, is suited for the former democracies; it is not suited for the latter. It is suited for the former because their "communal" parties compete only in part with each other, hence their number need not be justified by separate ideological labels and creates no ideological spread likely to interfere with any predisposition the parties may show to govern together. These party systems are culturally segmented, in Val Lorwin's word, but they are not extreme and polarized.[13] It is not suited for the latter exactly because the opposite syndrome occurs. Here party systems are not segmented; they are, in Sartori's words, ideologically polar-

---

11. Ibid., pp. 30-31.
12. Sartori, "The Typology of Party Systems," op. cit., p. 336, and "Modelli Spaziali," op. cit., p. 14.
13. Val Lorwin, "Segmented Pluralism," *Comparative Politics* 3 (1971), pp. 141-176. For other references to patterns of accommodation in the Small European Democracies, see footnote 47, chapter I.

ized. The point of what precedes is not to say that societies divided along ethnic, linguistic, or religious lines have an easy time governing themselves. There is a rich literature testifying to the fact that preindustrial cleavages are very resistant to modernization, more difficult to handle than industrial cleavages—in that they involve all-or-nothing rather than incremental claims—and hence much more threatening for the fabric of politics. Few social scientists would argue squarely against this analysis. In fact, consociationalism, as a radical defense against the consequences of segmentation, is quite exceptional, and the countries illustrated by students of consociationalism are a minuscule minority compared to those that, in the West, East, or Third World, falter or crumble under the impact of segmentation.

The point is a different one. Very few segmented societies can yield political elites able and willing to bridge divisions, but if they do the very segmentation helps their efforts. Lijphart and other students of consociationalism argue that much. Rarely, on the other hand, will industrial cleavages alone lead to extreme polarization, but, if they do, polarization itself will hamper elite good-will.

Segmentation. Segmentation in its pure form means that each party has its natural and captive electorate, ascribed to it by reasons of linguistic, ethnic, or religious identity. This provides the leaders of each segment with a considerable leeway vis-à-vis their communities, the more so if, as various authors argue, the segments are kept separate and organizationally cohesive and are shielded from modernizing and equalizing experiences that may break boundaries between segments, increase conflict, and threaten established community leaders.[14] To go one step further, it takes little to realize that segmentation, thus described, resembles an international system in times of peace, in which separate units are preoccupied with maintaining mutually indifferent separate identities and with protecting themselves from external interference. Segmented systems can be governed by willing elites exactly because there is no competition among their parts

14. Lijphart, op. cit., pp. 25-27; Rodney Stiefbold, "Segmented Pluralism and Consociational Democracy in Austria: Problems of Political Stability and Change," in Martin O. Heisler, ed., *European Politics* (New York: McKay, 1974), pp. 117-177, esp. pp. 171-172; Eric Nordlinger, *Conflict Regulation in Divided Societies* (Cambridge, Mass.: Harvard University, Center for International Affairs, Occasional Papers in International Affairs, No. 29, January 1972), chapter 5 and pp. 104-116.

and no need to justify the existence of one at the expense of others, but rather there is extraneity of interests. In fact, the presence of many political parties, far from creating problems, helps the governing of a segmented system, in that a plurality of parties, none of which may safely dominate alone over the others, discourages a showdown and alleviates fears of repression.

Further, while segmented systems rarely appear in pure form, they limit the encroachment of industrial and ideological cleavages. As long as parties of the preindustrial variety remain active and successful, limited room is provided for secular parties, which need to compete with each other and with the older parties for electoral support.[15] In particular, little room is provided for extreme parties of the Left or Right, for the reason that these are typically parties with hegemonic and secular aspirations which can only be satisfied when segmentation breaks down. If the absence of such parties in countries like the Netherlands or Switzerland may not be telling, as these are also prosperous and pragmatic countries, it is enough to think of Third World countries. There is little room here for extreme secular parties—unless they are imposed forcefully from the top by modernizing elites—for they cannot peacefully break preindustrial cleavages.[16]

It follows that, reverting to our consociational democracies, no matter how many parties lay a significant claim to government, ideological crowding and extremism are avoided. Only a few nonextremist secular parties—such as the Socialists and Liberals in the Netherlands—will compete ideologically. The others, such as the three Dutch religious parties, tend to operate electorally on another plane. The electoral space is not unidimensional, long, and competitive; it is multidimensional, short, and semicompetitive. It follows that any number of large and composite governing coalitions is possible, including any type of party. Consociationalism, as I intended to demonstrate, not only cures but also rests on segmentation.

It follows finally that, when segmentation breaks, as seems to be

15. For the way in which industrial and preindustrial cleavages emerge and relate historically and thus affect the nature of the party system, see Seymour M. Lipset and Stein Rokkan, "Introduction," in Seymour M. Lipset and Stein Rokkan, eds., *Party Systems and Voter Alignments* (New York: Free Press, 1967), pp. 1-64.

16. Seymour M. Lipset, "Political Cleavages in 'Developed' and 'Emerging' Polities," in Erik Allardt and Yrjö Littunen, eds., *Cleavages, Ideologies and Party Systems* (Helsinki: Academic Bookstore, 1964), pp. 21-55.

happening in the Netherlands today, perhaps exactly because consociationalism has kept for too long the lid on secularization, consociationalism has difficulties operating, and unchecked party proliferation may promise excessive ideological crowding.

I have traveled a long way from Italy and its party system, but the case of segmentation is a most useful bench mark for appreciating the essence and the consequences of extreme and polarized party systems like ours.

Polarization. It should be clear by now that, in societies where secular cleavages dominate, electoral and mass politics is quite different from that in segmented societies. It is highly competitive, on the ground that ideally no party can count on a fixed electorate, assigned to it by ascriptive criteria. Hence, an increase in the number of competing parties has serious polarizing consequences for electoral politics and—as we shall illustrate more amply in the Italian case—for governing itself. As in all simple models, a few clarifications and disclaimers are necessary, to demonstrate that exceptions do not subtract from the model, and that the model can travel farther than others I can think of.

The model is employed to argue that government performance is a function of the ideological crowding at the mass level. But not all parties are relevant from this viewpoint and should be counted. Some parties, as Sartori notices, have no "coalition potential" in that—though government oriented—they are usually numerically and ideologically unnecessary for the formation of governing coalitions. Others have no "blackmail potential" in that—though permanent opposition—they are not strong and determinate enough to affect the electoral strategies of the other parties.[17] It follows that all these parties do now crowd the ideological space, as they are not significant electoral competitors and do not compel the other parties to adjust their ideological images. It follows also that they are irrelevant for government and that governments can discount them, as they affect in no way their policies and their capacity to perform. Usually, irrelevant parties are small parties, whether or not they have seats in Parliament. But size is not a definitive criterion.[18] Some very small parties, like the Republican party in Italy, can play important

17. Sartori, "The Typology of Party Systems," op. cit., pp. 324-325.
18. A discussion of how to operationalize criteria of relevance is contained in Sartori's *Parties and Party Systems,* op. cit.

government roles. In times of deep and continuing social conflict, as in Italy today, even parties that have no seats in Parliament and that in some cases put themselves outside the parliamentary game can affect the government and the established opposition itself.

The model cannot say what the threshold is where many parties become too many parties, for there is no single answer to the question. The threshold depends in part on how evenly or unevenly electoral support is distributed among the parties, on whether support is concentrated at the center or at the extremes, and on the ideological nature of the extremes. As we shall see, these are significant refinements in explaining differences between Italy, the Fourth French Republic, and Weimar Germany. The threshold also depends on underlying social tensions, which the presence of many parties exacerbates, but which in turn increase the ideological distance of the existing parties. The Scandinavian countries can afford many parties, without expanding the extremes; the major Continental countries during their democratic interludes could not. The model does not even say that many parties are always worse than the classical two parties, and that two parties are always capable of bridging differences. It does not say in other words that two-party systems are almost by definition devoid of ideological distinctiveness, dangerous enough for government. It only says that two-party systems can afford a lack of ideological distinctiveness more than multiparty systems. It says that the former systems punish ideological distinctiveness (or perish); the latter reward it.

In Anthony Downs' classical two-party model, and under the restriction that each party is of rather equal strength at its core, the parties engage in a straight-fight or winner-take-all competition for the control of government, along a reform-conservation dimension at times coinciding with a secular-religious one.[19] Since the stake is formally all-or-nothing, such competition requires particular tolerance and mutual restraint. Reasons for restraint, however, are offered by the very fact that only two parties compete for that extra vote that will decide the winner. After a substantial core of stable party supporters has been cornered, the incentive is to look for victory in the center, the halfway house

19. Anthony Downs, *An Economic Theory of Democracy* (New York: Harper and Row, 1957), chapter 8.

where most undecided voters are likely to be found, or in effect to raid each other's house. The growth of each party must occur at the expense of ideological purity and the social homogeneity of each party. The ideological space of the party system stays narrow, and government itself, while formally monopolized by one party, tends to be accommodative so as to ensure wide appeal at the next elections.

The model is so widely known that it hardly needs my simplistic restatement. What is rather important to emphasize, in view of the attacks to which it has been subjected, is that when a two-party system shows ideological polarization and does not work, this happens *despite* the incentives toward moderate competition at the center that the number obviously offers. Whether or not a moderate center of available voters exists, by reasons of social and cultural overlapping between parties, the logic of two-party competition tends to expand it. Hence, if the two parties, or perhaps only one of them, address their appeals toward their extremes and disregard the center, it is not because the center is not strategic in two-party competition, or even because abstention from the extremes represents a significant threat. The latter case is rare, as true believers, being politicized and probably active in the lower ranks of one or the other party, will likely turn out to vote for their party. A turn toward the extremes may rather be dictated by fear of new parties appearing there, in which case the two parties have failed their centripetal function and the system is only temporarily two-party. Another but rather distant possibility is that the parties function not as catchall parties, open in principle to all constituencies, but as encapsulating parties, each in command of two clear and homogeneous segments (I am using the term on purpose) into which society is divided. This is the case of the First Austrian Republic, in which Socialists and Catholics tightly controlled a radical-secular and a conservative-confessional *lager*. There is clearly no significant unattached center toward which the parties can converge, there is in fact no electoral competition to speak of. The parties belong not to the same ideological plane but to different ones, extraneous to each other. This however seems a rare occurrence in a secular society, where social diversity is clearly more likely than division into two social camps, and where therefore large parties tend to be heterogeneous parties.²⁰ That is why students of consociationalism—disregarding the fact that Austria had only one confessional party and no significant ethnic, regional, or linguistic parties—consider Austria a segmented society, in which the rule is that fewer parties make for more difficulties.

This much having been said, it should be intuitive now why, if two-party systems may indulge in ideological distinctiveness at their risk, extreme multiparty systems have exactly the opposite problem. Ideological distinctiveness is part and parcel of the dynamics of the latter. We can dispense with the demonstration of what happens as we keep adding parties to the original parties.²¹ We again discover, of course, that there are working multiparty systems which work because, even though coalitions may be needed to govern, such coalitions are contained within a narrow ideological spectrum, no significant party is in principle prevented from governing, and governments rotate in principle as they do under two-party systems. When however the number of parties passes a threshold,²² working multipartism becomes extremely unlikely. The reason is that the nature of party competition is at this point substantially altered.

In the first place and as the reader already knows, the ideological space begins to get too small for the number of parties that intend to occupy it. Parties cannot easily justify their number and have increasing difficulties advertising themselves as distinctively different "products." Voters, on the other hand, have difficulties in recognizing parties. All of this favors in various ways increasing ideological distinctivenesses in mass appeals. The parties cannot compete with each other by acting as catchall parties, because marginal voters are few and such techniques would threaten the survival of some parties, perhaps exactly those that resort to them. Catchall parties are appropriate only where few

---

20. Robert Dahl, "Introduction," in Robert Dahl, ed., *Regimes and Oppositions* (New Haven: Yale University Press, 1973), pp. 4-10.

21. See the demonstration in Sartori's "Modelli Spaziali di Competizione tra Partiti," op. cit., pp. 21-27.

22. Sartori's threshold is five, but the demonstration of a fixed threshold in terms of spatial models of party competition is, in my view, questionable. Sartori's argument, if I understand it correctly, hinges on the fact that five (significant) parties engender a center, occupied by one or more parties, with centrifugal effects on party competition. But I doubt that the existence of a center is necessarily triggered, despite the spatial metaphor, by an uneven number of parties. Sartori, ibid., pp. 28-29, "The Typology of Party Systems," op. cit., pp. 336-337, and esp. *Parties and Party Systems*, op. cit., chapter 10.

parties exist and where the aim is not to eliminate parties but to attract marginal voters. Most of the parties cannot hope to become majority parties, nor do they have a definite incentive to grow, for—unlike the case with parties in two-party systems—they can govern in coalition, and their strength may not be as decisive in this regard as their location along the party spectrum.[23] Hence parties are left with the only strategy that seems to guarantee their survival: the adoption of clearly distinguishable party images. This in effect increases the distance even between parties occupying adjoining positions in the ideological space. If the number of parties is to remain stable, the ideological space must be expanded, and the number of parties alone contributes to this expansion.

Voters, on the other hand, far from punishing such behavior, are very likely to contribute to it, for, in their search for meaning, they will tend to order and stretch the space. While in two-party systems, as Donald Stokes has indicated in his critique of Downs' model,[24] voters can perceive parties as located along different spaces—depending on the issue areas—in extreme multiparty systems they will help the simplification of party images by locating parties along the same Left-Right continuum, irrespective of issue areas. The best evidence that this is likely to occur has been given recently in a paper by Samuel Barnes on spatial models of competition in Italian politics.[25] Not only are Italian voters perfectly capable of locating their parties along the same Left-Right dimension on a variety of issues. Also, each party is perceived as falling approximately in the same relative place on most issues, and such simplified mass images of the party space correspond to how the parties themselves perceive their position. There is little doubt that Italian parties have been quite successful in transmitting their simplified ideological images to the voters, and that the voters have been equally successful in ordering them. The presence of a major Catholic party—apparently active on a different religious dimension—is no serious obstacle to the

23. Giuseppe Di Palma, "The Study of Conflict in Western Society: A Critique of the End of Ideology" (Morristown, N.J.: General Learning Press, 1973; a Module in the Political Science Series), pp. 8-9.
24. Donald Stokes, "Spatial Models of Party Competition," in Angus Campbell et al., *Elections and the Political Order* (New York: Wiley, 1966), chapter 9.
25. Samuel Barnes, "Left, Right, and the Italian Voter," *Comparative Political Studies* 4 (1971), pp. 157-176.

ordering, as the party places itself and is perceived at the center on most issues, including in part even the religious one, where the extreme Right presents itself as "more clerical than the pope."

A second facet of the increase in the number of significant parties is that, as the ideological space increases, the extremes of the span are going to be occupied by parties ideologically removed from the center. More precisely, in a Western and especially European context, the extremes are extreme not only by relative location; they are also most likely extremist or antisystem—they present themselves electorally in substantial disagreement with the existing regime and are perceived as antisystem by the voters. That is, once a numerical threshold is surpassed, we exhaust the range of parties—labor, liberal-radical, christian democratic, agrarian, conservative—that traditionally occupy the area of government. We are faced next with those twentieth-century staples of antisystem politics—the marxist, fascist, or right-wing authoritarian parties induced by their historical commitments to place themselves at the margins of the political spectrum. This is not to say that these parties will not abide by the rules, or even that their leadership may not in some cases have a genuine interest in reforming their images and their dispositions. It is simply to say that antisystem parties, crowded out toward the extremes by tradition and by the competition of many other parties, have a hard time reforming their images—even if they want to—as the very difficult history of the Italian Communist party since World War II suggests. The coincidence of number with the existence of antisystem parties, being simply detected, does not explain why antisystem parties appear and succeed. But the explanation is not necessary for our purposes. What needs understanding is the coincidence itself. And we can buttress our case by recollecting something stated above: It is unlikely that antisystem parties will be found when only two or few significant parties operate. On one side, the incentive to compete for the middle electorate discourages antisystem parties. On the other, if these nevertheless appear, the system is most unlikely to endure.

As a consequence of these two features in the proliferation of parties—the crowding of the ideological space and the appearance of antisystem parties—electoral competition is no longer centripetal, as in other party systems. I should restate what centripetal competition exactly means, as the notion is of great importance in understanding how governing is affected by electoral politics. Competition is centripetal not simply when parties compete for the votes of the center, but when they do this by shading ideologically into each other and by becoming catchall parties. Such convergence of images is encouraged when the center is available, discouraged when—as it happens in Italy— one or more parties already control it.[26] That is, though electoral victory is not as important as in other party systems, the parties to the right and left still desire the votes of the center. But they cannot easily obtain them by moving toward the center; they must move the center toward them. It is not the wings that travel ideologically "in" toward the center; it is the center that is moved ideologically "out." The reason is not simply that the wing parties (especially the extreme ones) have a strong intellectual and organizational investment in their ideology, or that, in a crowded ideological space, parties need ideological distinctiveness, or that the risks of being outflanked from the rear are serious. The reason lies more precisely in the fact that the center is occupied and the other parties cannot easily outbid the center party on its own ground; they cannot occupy its space, they can only empty it. Again, the behavior of the PCI, though in part atypical, is symptomatic. The Communist party knows perfectly well that, just as its chances to accede legitimately to government rest on its capacity to narrow ideological space and to dispel its antisystem stigma, so they also rest on its capacity to achieve an understanding with the center. In short, the recipe requires nothing less than breaking the logic of the multiparty system! This predicament helps explain the ambivalent electoral strategies of the party. On one side it opens toward the center by advocating a Catholic-Marxist alliance to save the country; on the other it tries to empty the center by attacking it politically, by holding it responsible for all the defects of the present regime, and by in effect advocating a new political regime. The point now is not whether the PCI is right or wrong in its attacks on the center; the point is that the attacks are made necessary by the fact that the center parties monopolize a vital sector of the electorate.

The center has an obvious advantage over its competitors. It is

---

26. Sartori, "The Typology of Party Systems," op. cit., p. 328.

the pivot on which the system of competition revolves and, as is obvious by now, it is usually the government. Its electoral attractiveness rests on the fact that, in an ideologically fragmented environment, it provides the rallying point, the *juste milieu*, for a silent majority of bewildered voters. Its success is almost guaranteed at the outset of any new multiparty experience (if not for any other reason than that otherwise there would be no democratic experience to talk about). The parties of the center controlled a substantial majority of the votes at the outset of the Weimar Republic and the Fourth French Republic, and Italian Christian Democracy alone obtained its largest success ever (48.5 percent of the votes) in 1948, when it faced the Communist party frontally. Further, the very fact of being the government provides the center with important political and electoral resources promising some continuing success. It would seem then that the existence of a center provides a balance against centrifugal incentives. All the center has to do is to exist, to be itself. It may in fact need no elaborate and distinctive ideology, beyond presenting itself as the "defense of the republic." I shall return later to some of these points, when discussing how an extreme multiparty system can endure.

However, the fact of being the "defense of the republic" also has negative consequences for the center, for voters will evaluate its performance exactly on these grounds. And since, as we shall also see, such defense can usually be conducted only at the price of government stagnation and immobility, the electoral success of the center is in doubt. This is especially so since the parties of the center, operating as they do in the presence of significant antisystem parties, do not enjoy universal legitimacy. In fact, many of their very supporters do not belong to them. They flock to them in a wait-and-see, law-and-order attitude, and are not necessarily immunized from authoritarian solutions if these promise tranquillity. Hence initial successes may wither away. Even if the center manages to save the republic in the initial stages, and politics becomes less heated (without necessarily losing its ideological connotations), it will not necessarily be rewarded. The passing of the danger and increasing attention to the immobility of the system may rob the center of some of its support. Both Christian Democracy and its allies lost substantial ground after 1948, never to regain it. If the future, on the other hand, remains much in doubt, and political conflict gives no sign of abating, the center may again lose ground for failing the expectations of its silent majority. The republic cannot be saved twice. The center parties lost substantial ground, both in Weimar and in the Fouth Republic, in the space of very few years or months after the reestablishment of democracy.[27]

How successful and predominant centrifugal competition is, how much it helps the wings of the party system, and how fast it moves voters out of the center depend on circumstances extraneous to the number of parties. The staying power of the center depends first on whether or not it is dominated by one party and on how the center plays the competitive game; second, on other national and international circumstances not susceptible of a *reductio ad unum* which in the case of France and Weimar lead to collapse. What is important at this point is to stress that this process has its origin in the party system, and that it creates problems for the center. The latter is compelled to correct and supplement its electoral strategies of containment, which alone do not pay. To react to the centrifugal pulls of the opposition, it must itself become "centrifugal" by moving left or right, depending on where the electorate is moving. In the case of Italy, where the republic has been defended and preserved, and the electorate goes mainly toward the Left and extreme Left, Christian Democracy has an electoral problem. It also has a legitimizing one: it must justify its permanent rule and the permanent isolation of the Communists as formal opposition. In response, it tries to capture voters to the left and refurbishes its credentials by allying itself with the Socialist party. But the centrifugation of the party has serious consequences for its internal unity. The party does not break but develops, after the first few years of relative "defense of the system" unity, intense and organized factionalism which replicates the external spectrum of parties and protects the party from serious losses to the Right.

In the case of France and especially Germany, where the dangers to the system continued and the center was not dominated by a single large party, the center parties moved progressively apart. The German Social Democratic party—the founder of the republic—was actually rarely part of the Weimar government

27. On the deterioration of the coalition in the initial stages of the Weimar Republic, see Karl Dietrich Bracher, *The German Dictatorship* (New York: Praeger, 1970), pp. 67-79.

after 1920, preoccupied as it was with recapturing part of its Marxist image tarnished by the events of 1919-1920. And the Catholic Zentrum party had its share of responsibility in the success of Hitler, whom it tried to ensnare exactly by moving right. In effect the impulses of centrifugation in the last years of Weimar became so strong that they shrank the center—partially by robbing its electorate, partially by pulling its parties toward their natural extremes—and created a Left-Right confrontation which, imposed on *that* party system, provoked a democratic breakdown.

In conclusion, the center, especially if it is itself divided, is not always in the best position to stem centrifugal appeals. It gains no votes—in fact it most likely loses them—as it loses cohesiveness. Hence, we recognize centrifugation by looking not only at whether the extremes gain, but also at whether the center parties develop organized factions (Christian Democracy in Italy), and whether they have difficulties staying together. It naturally makes a great difference whether the center holds, though divided or uncohesive, or whether the extremes outbid it. But the difference is not under scrutiny at this point.

If I can adopt and paraphrase Giovanni Sartori's terminology, we can summarize the above characteristics of extreme multiparty systems in secular societies as follows: Extreme multiparty systems are:

1. *Multipolar;* that is, the system of electoral competition is based on more than two poles (two parties or sets of parties). It has right, left, and center parties, and the latter are the pivot of the system. Bipolar systems have no center parties but competition between Left and Right.

2. *Polarized;* that is, the ideological distance between poles is considerable, involving the absence of basic consensus.

3. *Centrifugal;* that is, because of the existence of a center, party competition is away from the center.

Before discussing how these characteristics affect governing in Italy, I shall spend a few final words to show that electoral competition in Italy has the above characteristics. The analysis in the next section applies to the Italian situation until the local elections of June 1975. I shall discuss at the end of the next chapter if and how the impressive electoral victory of the Communist party makes our model obsolete.

THE ITALIAN CASE

That the Italian party system is multipolar is the simplest thing to show and has amply been shown by others. Any set of electoral returns bears out the case. The Italian Parliament has been dominated for most of its postwar history by eight "significant" parties (in the sense given above), which have now been reduced to seven since the merger of the MSI (Neo-Fascist) and Monarchist parties before the 1972 elections. Not all these parties have always been present and always carried the same labels. Other parties have also successfully run for periods of time. Table 55, reporting parliamentary elections since the war, shows that the eight parties are—in the conventional left-to-right sequence known to any informed

TABLE 55. Election results, Chamber of Deputies, 1946-1972, in Percentage

	1946[1]	1948	1953	1958	1963	1968	1972
PCI	18.9	31.0[2]	22.6	22.7	25.3	26.9	27.2
PSI	20.7[3]		12.7	14.2	13.8	14.5[4]	9.6
PSDI		7.1	4.5	4.5	6.1		5.1
PRI	4.4	2.5	1.6	1.4	1.4	2.0	2.9
DC	35.2	48.5	40.1	42.4	38.3	39.1	38.8
PLI	6.8	3.8	3.0	3.5	7.0	5.8	3.9
Monarchists	2.8	2.8	6.9	4.8	1.8	1.3	8.7[5]
MSI	—	2.0	5.8	4.8	5.1	4.5	
Others	11.2[6]	2.4	2.8	1.7	1.2	5.9[7]	3.8

[1] Elections for the Constituent Assembly.
[2] Communists and Socialists allied in the Fronte Democratico Popolare.
[3] Socialists and Social Democrats still unified.
[4] Socialists and Social Democrats reunited in the Partito Socialista Unificato (PSU).
[5] Monarchists and Neo-Fascists unified in the MSI-Destra Nazionale.
[6] 5.2 percent to the Uomo Qualunque, a right-wing party whose electorate was in part later absorbed by the MSI.
[7] 4.5 percent to the Partito Socialista Italiano di Unita Proletaria, a left-wing socialist party that split from the Socialists after the formation of the PSU in 1966 and dissolved after the elections of 1972.

voter—the Communists (PCI), the Socialists (PSI), the Social Democrats (PSDI), the Republicans (PRI), the Christian Democrats (DC), the Liberals (PLI), the Monarchists, the Neo-Fascists (MSI). The table also shows that the system has a center, occupied by the DC, the largest party since the war.

The table further implies that the system is polarized, especially to the extreme Left. The PCI became the second largest party immediately after the war,[28] and the Neo-Fascists vie today for third place with the Socialists. The point of polarization, however, is not conclusively proved by electoral results. Insofar as it refers to ideological distance between poles and to how ideological distinctiveness is used for electoral purposes to disqualify the opponents, it could only be proved by an analysis of mass strategies and electoral appeals which, as far as I know, has not been systematically conducted by anybody. This analysis could easily reveal that the smaller Neo-Fascist party is much more delegitimizing in its appeals than the PCI. If, in other words, the relative size of parties indicates a polarization to the left, the ideological style of the Neo-Fascists indicates a right-wing polarization which, despite more limited electoral successes, has in the last few years threatened peaceful coexistence much more seriously. Insofar as polarization refers especially to how the voters receive the ideological messages of the parties and how they evaluate parties other than theirs, the exhaustive study is also still to be conducted. However, a survey study by Giacomo Sani, conducted in 1972, bears out very clearly at least one point of the process of polarization: after years of delegitimizing messages from its opponents, the Italian Communist party is perceived by many to most voters (depending on the aspect of the party on which they are questioned) as an illegitimate party.[29] As his data show, only Socialist voters, and then only

---

28. Though it is impossible to distinguish Communist from Socialist votes in the election of 1948, given the electoral alliance of the two parties in the Fronte Democratico Popolare, preferential voting gave the Communists 133 seats in the Chamber of Deputies, the Socialists only 50. Resignations by Communist deputies partially redressed the balance.

29. Giacomo Sani, "Mass Perceptions of 'Anti-System' Parties: The Case of Italy" (paper delivered at the American Political Science Association meetings, Chicago, September 1974). Sani's data reveal also that voters perceive considerable ideological distance between their own and other parties, and show limited sympathy for parties progressively removed from theirs. Voters are also as suspicious of the extreme Right as they are of the extreme Left. They hold the parties of the Right responsible for political violence; they do not favor their entry in the government and consider them a threat to democracy. In most cases, voters hold the same attitudes toward both extremes. Another recent research by Sani

less than half of them, would favor as of 1972 a government alliance between the Communists and the Christian Democrats. Some half of the voters for the center parties (and more substantial majorities of right-wing voters) perceive "parties of the extreme Left" as a threat to democracy and hold "Communists" responsible for political violence. This occurs after years and years of efforts by the Communist party to sell the alliance with Christian Democracy as the only remedy to the country's problems and to dispel its antisystem image.

The last characteristic, centrifugation, is just as difficult to clinch. Strictly speaking, the electoral successes of the extremes are not conclusive proof, unless accompanied by evidence of the nature of the extremes' appeal for the center. Centrifugation is also checked by the fact that the center in Italy is dominated by the Catholics. With the above proviso, I can suggest the following indicators:[30]

1. The PCI has steadily, if slowly, grown from 18.9 percent after the war to 27.2 percent in 1972, with no indication that the growth will stop. Though Communist appeals, especially in the last years, contain elements of moderation and convergence, outbidding and ideological posturing also remain strong. Combined, the appeals take some voters away from the center; they confirm others in their centrist choice.

2. The extreme Right, after going through various ups and downs, shows no signs of significantly losing ground. It seems premature to predict that the recent crisis will help its growth, but it is even more premature to bury it.

3. The DC, as indicated, is divided internally by strong centrifugal tendencies generated by organized factionalism. The reasons for factionalism are various, but one that cannot be discounted is the logic of centrifugation imposed on the party by the rest of the party system. (Factionalism will be briefly analyzed in the next chapter.)

---

indicates that anticommunism among voters has four components: the perceived antireligious nature of the party, its identification with the Soviet Union, its assumed lack of commitment to the rules of the game, its alleged responsibility for the political violence of the late sixties and early seventies. Giacomo Sani, "La Strategia del PCI e l'Elettorato Italiano," *Rivista Italiana di Scienza Politica* 3 (1973), pp. 531-579. See the last part of the next chapter for more recent data reported by Sani and bearing on a thawing of anticommunism.

30. Sartori, "Rivisitando il 'Pluralismo Polarizzato'," op. cit., pp. 203-205; Galli, *Il Difficile Governo*, op. cit., pp. 253-254.

Let me finally clear the ground of two types of objections to the evidence above. The first is that centrifugation is contradicted by the fact that since the war the three poles of the system have maintained essentially the same strength. The Marxist Left (PCI and PSI) had 39.6 per cent of the votes in 1946, it had 38.7 in 1972,[31] and it has always hovered just below 40 per cent. The center (PSDI, PRI, DC) had 39.6 in 1946 (when the PSDI was still with the Socialists) and 46.8 in 1972. The Right (PLI, Monarchists, MSI) had 14.8; it now has 12.6. However, the important point is that—as Table 55 shows—in each of the two wings it is now the extreme party that dominates: The PCI, not the Socialists; the Neo-Fascists, not the Liberals. One point of centrifugation is that the *mezze ali*, the "half-wings" as Italians call them, never gain or tend to lose.

The other objection is that, for all the centrifugation, the Socialist party has abandoned its alliance with the Communists and moved into the government. Aside from the fact that after years of Center-Left government the Socialists feel more than ever ill-at-ease in the role, their new role does not refer to electoral competition but to government coalitions and deserves later treatment when the so-called "social-democratization" of the Communist party will also be considered. As to the electoral strategies of the PSI since entering government, though the Socialists have made efforts to differentiate themselves electorally from the PCI, it can be said that they have made even greater efforts to keep themselves apart from the Catholics. Were one to go only by the Socialists' public declarations in regard to the DC, one would hardly guess their partnership. And the point is that, in the presence of continuing electoral polarization, the partnership does not improve coalition performance. Equally interesting, since joining the coalition the PSI has become extremely sensitive to centrifugation and has developed extreme factionalism resembling that of their uneasy allies. From this viewpoint, the case of the PSI since the Center-Left belongs under point 3 above.

THE PARTIES AND GOVERNING

We have now, I am confident, come full circle. The analysis above does more than suggest the importance of mass party politics for

---

31. If we add the votes of the PSIUP (1.9 percent), soon to be reabsorbed by PSI and PCI.

government. It brings new circumstantial evidence via the analysis of party systems to the point made throughout the book. Italian political elites cannot agree on the decisional rule: who shall govern with whom, who shall be the "majority."

In this regard, the most important information to emerge from the study of extreme multiparty systems is that their wide ideological spread and their centrifugation allow only center governments. The logic of competition and alternance in government between a Left and a Right, appropriate for more moderate party systems, would here break the polity by imposing a one-sided decisional rule that could thwart if not terminate the competitive game. More precisely, alternance is politically inconceivable in Italy; it is politically conceivable—although not always attained— and it informs party competition in more moderate party systems.[32] Only once, with the ill-born and short-lived 1960 cabinet of Prime Minister Tambroni, did a sector of Christian Democracy break, overtly and defiantly, the center formula. But Tambroni's alliance with the extreme right provoked the most serious political crisis and mass confrontation since the election crusade of 1948. The center formula is the only possible formula, which is equivalent to saying that it exists *faute de mieux*. This information alone takes us a long way toward understanding how mass party politics makes governing Italy well-nigh an improbable task.

For the sake of emphasis, I shall begin by eliminating one palpably incorrect explanation of why governing is improbable; that is, that Italian governments are almost always either formal coalitions or Christian Democratic governments with the external support of other parties, so that decisions in the cabinet and in Parliament always require agreement among different parties. I recognize that, if more than one party governs, parties cannot decide together without compromising their respective demands, interests, and programs, and that achieving and maintaining compromise is not always easy. But coalition politics is not exclusive to extreme multiparty systems, there is nothing inherently impossible in it, and it doesn't seem to create excessive problems elsewhere. Even if we were to find persuasive evidence that government by one party can "get things done" more expeditiously than coalitions, it would still prove only the generic differ-

---

32. Galli, *Il Bipartitismo Imperfetto*, op. cit., chapter 2, and *Il Difficile Governo*, op. cit., pp. 258-259; Pellicani, op. cit., pp. 652-653.

ence.[33] Nor is the problem in the fact that coalitions do not have enough votes to support themselves in Parliament. Such a view is incorrect in its empirical premise and its theoretical consequence.

Italian coalitions almost always have a substantial numerical majority on paper, and the opposition, even if the extremes are pooled, rarely has alone the capacity to overthrow governments. The coalitions die because they are internally uncohesive, and not at the hands of a parliamentary vote of nonconfidence but by mutual cabinet agreement. They die because partners cannot stay together. On this point Lawrence Dodd has persuasively shown that the coalitions that cannot stay together for long are not coalitions of minimum winning status but, quite on the contrary, oversized ones—containing more partners than are strictly necessary to control Parliament.[34] Examples of such coalitions are most of the cabinets during the Third and Fourth French Republics. The reason for their instability, Dodd argues, is that, since one or more of the partners are unnecessary, and since the partners are motivated above all by the desire to control ministries and spoils, the coalition will tend to be reshuffled to secure a larger share of the spoils for fewer partners. This however does not explain a *string* of oversized cabinets. I would argue that the reason for instability is in the very factors that make the coalition oversized. Here Dodd's shrewd quantitative analysis tries to demonstrate that coalitions are oversized when, in party systems highly fractionalized as to number and strength, relatively many parties are in principle available to bargain for a position in the coalition (no constraints), but their reliability once in the coalition is uncertain (imperfect information). Large-size coalitions are possible and compensate for uncertainty, but the unreliability of the partners still makes them fall. To put it somewhat differently but more to the point, and having the Italian case in mind, I would say that oversized coalitions are born to save the republic and to expand

---

33. Richard Rose has strongly argued that government by one party is not sufficient to establish strong "party government." British government, for instance, is not that model of responsible and programmatic party government that it is made to be. See Richard Rose, "The Variability of Party Government: A Theoretical and Empirical Critique," *Political Studies* 17 (1969), pp. 413-445.

34. Lawrence Dodd, "Party Coalitions in Multiparty Parliaments: A Game-Theoretic Analysis," *American Political Science Review* 68 (1974), pp. 1093-1117.

the area of legitimacy. Many parties of the center are available, but not all are reliable, because as size increases ideological spread increases. In other words, unreliability is more a consequence than a cause of coalition size, and it leads to instability.[35]

That Italian cabinets are mostly oversized is clearly demonstrated by Robert Axelrod and by Adriano Pappalardo.[36] Italian cabinets are not minimum winning coalitions, as one should expect from some leading coalition theories; they are long and connected coalitions that often include all adjacent partners and thus end up by having more votes and partners than are strictly required (Table 56). For example, an alliance between Christian Democrats and Socialists over the head of Republicans and Social Democrats, though advocated by some Socialists and Christian Democrats, is politically unthinkable. But so also is one that would leave the Socialists out, though not for numerical reasons. The purpose of these strategies of broad alliance is clear: to absorb within the area of the center as many parties as possible so as to build its legitimacy, to show responsiveness to electoral trends, and to stave off antisystem parties. This was the strategy asserted by De Gasperi even as his party alone, after the victory of 1948, controlled a majority in the Chamber of Deputies, and it remains the strategy of the DC party today. But its price is also clear: the more government majorities expand, the greater their ideological spread, and the less they can govern.[37]

---

35. Dodd's analysis seems at first to conflict in important points with mine. For instance, he classifies France before 1956 as a case of "depolarized hyperpluralism" and France from 1956 to 1958 as well as Weimar as one of "polarized hyperpluralism." In Dodd's case, however, depolarization seems to refer to parliamentary politics, not to mass politics and party images. He is talking, in other words, of *trasformismo* in Parliament, which can give way to parliamentary polarization under external precipitating circumstances. In this sense, his argument does not differ from mine, except on nominalistic grounds.

36. Adriano Pappalardo, "L'Analisi delle Coalizioni," *Rivista Italiana di Scienza Politica* 4 (1974), pp. 197-230; Robert Axelrod, *Conflict of Interest* (Chicago: Markham, 1970), pp. 175-185.

37. Majorities can also be expanded not by increasing the number of partners, but by reforming proportional representation so as to give a premium to larger parties or to electoral coalitions of winning parties. It is questionable, however, whether such reforms can have beneficial effects. If the number of partners in government remains the same, ideological disparity remains, and the fact that each party has more parliamentary seats makes little difference. If the reform allows fewer parties to govern, coalitions may last longer, but the parties left outside may still create problems for the coalition, as this is still a

TABLE 56. Government Coalitions in Italy, 1947-1976[1]

	PSI	PSDI	PRI	DC	PLI	Monarchists	MSI
De Gasperi IV (5-47)				X	Y	Y	
De Gasperi V (5-48)		X	X	X	X		
De Gasperi VI (1-50)		X	X	X	Z		
De Gasperi VII (7-51)		Y	X	X	Y		
De Gasperi VIII (7-53)		Z	Y	X	Z		
Pella (8-53)		Z	Y	X	Y	Y	Z
Fanfani I (1-54)		Z	Z	X			
Scelba (2-54)		X	Y	X	X		
Segni I (7-55)		X	Y	X	X		
Zoli (5-57)			Z	X	Z	Y	Y
Fanfani II (7-58)	X	Y	X				
Segni II (2-59)				X	Z	Z	Z
Tambroni (3-60)				X	Z	Z	Z
Fanfani III (7-60)	Z	Y	Y	X			
Fanfani IV (2-62)	Z	X	X	X			
Leone I (6-63)	Z	Z	Z	X		Z	
Moro I (12-63)	X	X	X	X			
Moro II (7-64)	X	X	X	X			
Moro III (2-66)	X	X	X	X			
Leone II (6-68) [2]	Y	Y	Y	X			
Rumor I (12-68)	X	X	X	X			
Rumor II (8-69)	Y	Y	Z	X			
Rumor III (3-70)	X	X	X	X			
Colombo (8-70)	X	X	X	X			
Andreotti I (2-72)		Y	Y	X	Y		
Andreotti II (6-72)		X	Y	X	X		
Rumor IV (7-73)	X	X	X	X			
Rumor V (3-74)	X	X	Y	X			
Moro IV (12-74)	Y	Y		X	X	Z	
Moro V (2-76)	Z	Y	Z	X	Z		

Note: X indicates participation in the cabinet.
    Y indicates support without participation in the cabinet.
    Z indicates abstention in the vote of confidence for a new cabinet.
[1] Beginning with the first coalitions without the PCI.
[2] Socialists and Social Democrats reunited in the Partito Socialista Unificato (PSU)

Again, the problem of ideological differences among partners in Italian governments is not the generic problem of ideological differences among any set of partners in any coalition. To be sure, we can readily recognize that the political issues with which Italy has been faced and with which government partners have to compete are very serious indeed and have been at the core of Italian politics since the end of the war. They concern foreign policy and the place of Italy in the West, an issue which, while now less dominant, is still of importance. They concern the place of the Church and Catholicism in Italian life. They concern civil rights and the growth of a more open and free society from the ashes of Fascism, provincialism, and traditions. They concern the model of growth of the economy and society, social reforms, and the expansion of political and economic equality. They concern the place of the working class, susceptible to the attraction of Communism, in a plural political order. These issues of distribution, secularization, and legitimacy[38] encompass very basic and conflicting conceptions held by government partners about what should be done. On their solution rests basically the future of the country in a continent subject to ever-increasing transformation. It is understandable that to achieve agreement on solutions can be very difficult. There is in fact no clear agreement on the distribution issue between the present partners—especially between the Socialists on one side and the Republicans, Social Democrats, and Christian Democrats on the other. The secular issues, with one confessional and three secular parties in the coalition, splits the coalition in half. And especially today, with a governing Socialist party seriously concerned with the role of its old Communist allies, the legitimacy issue, the one that goes most to the core of the country's problem, is far from finding agreement.

But to focus on the ideological spread in this fashion is in part to commit a tautology, in part to suggest difficulties extraneous to the

---

center coalition. These reforms have a purpose only if they can permanently and successfully eliminate parties and produce in the long run a basic realignment that also undercuts polarization. But this chain of events is rather unlikely.

France used a "majority-premium" electoral law in 1951 and 1956, but the old government coalitions continued and French politics showed no special improvement. De Gasperi had a similar reform passed in 1953, but the premium clause failed to operate and the law was soon repealed. See chapter III.

38. Sartori, "European Political Parties," op. cit., pp. 161-163.

party system.[39] I suggest that the weight of external difficulties is more readily recognizable in the case of Weimar and of France before de Gaulle, less in the case of Italy, which is a purer case of what a party system can do to government. I shall conclude the analysis of party-system impact by showing and in part recollecting that the party system has four main effects on Italian government. It produces (1) Coalitions of Ideologues; (2) Negative Coalitions; (3) Beleaguered Coalitions; (4) Irresponsible Coalitions.

Coalitions of Ideologues. Let me recall here the opening paragraphs of this chapter. When the ideological space of the party system becomes overcrowded, parties can find space only by insisting on clear ideological distinction and by artificially increasing the space. It is this property of the party system and of electoral competition, more than obviously divisive historical events, and more perhaps than the ingrained cultural traits of Italian politicians, that explains why distinctive ideological appeals characterize mass politics, even in an era where the content of such appeals would seem obsolete. Let me recall also that elite politics, even within the coalitions, cannot be insensitive to the ideological style of mass politics. Two equally successful, equally legitimate, but contrasting styles of doing politics—one for elections and party organization, another for government—cannot easily exist in secular and mobilized societies. They may more easily exist in segmented societies.

Our analysis has reported in previous chapters the attitudes toward interparty relations at government and mass level held by Italian members of Parliament. They indicate strong attachment to an image of the parliamentarian as strictly a party delegate, strong populist views of one's relation with the party electorate, and concomitantly great uncertainties about the possibility of compromise and reciprocity in parliamentary politics. More important, the analysis also indicates something at first surprising: there is no clear difference in these attitudes among members of Parliament, national party leaders, and local party leaders. I had expected that, by reason of their tasks, the latter would insist more heavily on the partisan role of members of Parliament, and would

---

39. Notice also that the legitimacy issue is not akin to the others and does not prove the point. It does not refer to disagreement on decision content; it refers to disagreement on decision rule.

see compromise in government as less possible and more condemnable. I observed no such differences in any of the parties.

Confronted with such apparently puzzling results, and confronted with the fact that even Christian Democratic parliamentarians (supposedly the least partisan of all) show strong partisan attitudes, I cannot but conclude that the party system builds coalitions of incompatible ideologues.

Negative Coalitions. Such ideologues have little capacity to find agreement because government coalitions are thrown together, as Roy Macridis puts it in discussing the French case, by negative reasons.[40] They are negative, no-alternative, containment coalitions, oppositions to the opposition, in sum center coalitions designed to resist antisystem parties and imposed by necessity. It follows that they do not come together on any precise program, except a constitutional one. They do not necessarily have and they are not required to have an economic, foreign-policy, or secular platform. They are not required to have one because, especially in the beginning stages of such party systems, preserving the system is sufficient. Later they do not have it because, as cohesiveness decreases, common platforms are more difficult to find. In point of fact, center coalitions are more likely to have programs when they are not strictly necessary for holding partners together: in the beginning stages. By common acknowledgment of most politicians, even from the opposition, the most productive governments in Italy were those of the De Gasperi period, when the cohesiveness of the coalitions thrown together by the urgency of the constitutional issue also allowed for a higher degree of policy activism. Whatever their merits, the accomplishments of those governments involved at least two important choices for the future of the country: the entry into the Western system of alliances, and the liberalization of the economy, important premises for the rapid growth of the country in years to come.

After that period, and until a temporary resurgence of activism in the first few years of the Center-Left, coalitions lived meager lives. The constitutional issue still drew them together, but the lesser urgency of the issue allowed a progressive ideological

---

40. Roy Macridis, "Oppositions in France: An Interpretation," *Government and Opposition* 7 (1972), pp. 166-185.

differentiation among government partners and thus made agreement more difficult. I have indicated in Chapter II the considerably shorter life of the coalitions after 1953. It is a period when each partner becomes more and more concerned with its survival and its own party politics, and when smaller parties often exit from coalitions to establish some electoral credit before elections, to reunite the party, or to bargain for a stronger government voice. All such strategies help the solidity of coalitions little; they can serve only the electoral fortunes of each party. And even when the composition of the coalition formula is substantially altered, the reform does not give the coalition new effectiveness. The Center-Left was inaugurated in Italy in 1963. In similar fashion, the Socialists moved into the French government immediately before World War II and during the Fourth Republic, and the Social Democrats were replaced by the German People's party in the Weimar coalitions. But these changes did not increase the vitality of the formulas. They did not increase cohesiveness; they in fact decreased it. That is because these reshufflings did not anticipate change but followed it. They altered the coalitions in response to a process of electoral centrifugation. They are nevertheless important alterations. Though they don't build coalition strength, they buy something which is, as the next chapter will show, in its way extremely valuable. They buy time, a chance to endure.

Beleaguered Coalitions. To speak of negative coalitions is to speak next of beleaguered coalitions, of *democrazia assediata*. It naturally makes a lot of difference who the besieger is and where the major threat comes from. It makes a lot of difference to know that in Italy the major contender is the *Italian* Communist party, in Weimar Germany it was eventually Nazism, in France it was Gaullism. But the ideological content of the extreme parties is now beside the point; so are (until the next chapter) disquisitions on how serious the Communist threat is, and on whether the Italian Communists have a revolutionary or social-democratic vocation. Beyond the ideological labels, the means, and the intents of the oppositions, the climate of a siege is created by the very logic of extreme multipartism, which sustains itself by sustaining such climate. Elections are not called to decide whether to change personnel and policies, but as if to decide whether the regime shall be preserved. Mass politics is infused by parties with a spirit of ultimateness and is perceived accordingly by the voters. I shall recognize that the center has an interest in maintaining such spirit, thus justifying its continuing reign. But this behavior brings forth a self-fulfilling paradox: center governments falter. They now falter not simply because their partners come from disparate ideological families and because ideological compatibility is not a strict requirement, but because their legitimacy remains in question.

We are again faced with the core problem of Italian governments: absence of a fixed decisional rule. It will be sufficient to recall what I said in Chapter I. When governments feel beleaguered, their actions become indecisive and their internal unity is threatened. Democratic governments, and more precisely center governments, by their nature cannot and are unwilling to impose themselves over basic opposition, and are compelled to tread water carefully. Even if the government had resources and unity allowing it to impose its choices over the opposition, its equity and therefore the democratic authenticity of the system would be in question. It is in the nature of democratic governments to recognize and protect the free expression of competing interests, even those of the extreme opposition, and to rest its action on the free agreement of these interests. Their authenticity depends on it. Hence, when opposition is basic and consent cannot be obtained, viable government becomes a rarity and the most likely consequence is inaction.

Let me clarify. The problem with center governments is not that they are illiberal. Even during the period of containment before 1953, it is questionable that Italian governments acted illiberally. To recognize instances of illiberal behavior is something different from qualifying the regime as illiberal. And whether democratic governments should actually act illiberally to save themselves is beside the point. The fact is that they usually do not. Center governments have helped maintain the specter of Italian Communism alive; they have done little to curtail its freedoms. This is because democracies have, vis-à-vis basic opposition, exactly the opposite problem that authoritarian regimes have. The latter not only are not required by their very nature to liberalize, but they cannot afford to liberalize. Any opposition is by definition dangerous, and any toleration is also dangerous because, as Robert Dahl puts it, if authoritarian regimes should tolerate some opposition, they might no longer be able to enforce any limits to toleration.[41] The danger begins exactly when liberalization begins. Democracies, on the other hand, are not only required to liberalize, they cannot afford not to, especially when the opposition is numerically consistent. If communism were repressed—many Italian democrats and coalition members feared—where would the curtailment of freedom stop? And wouldn't the opposition repay democracy in kind?

Let me clarify further. The problem with Italian governments is not that they are moderate. Moderatism *is* a choice; it *is* a way of doing politics. It differs from reformism and from conservatism in what it aggregates. It aggregates center opinions and, so to say, toward the center. In terms of its capacity to respond to various demands it is in principle not inferior to the other two alternatives. It may be more difficult to classify, and therefore may displease social scientists or voters in search of clarity. It may involve aggregation of a different type, requiring more the balancing of different policies than the formulation of univocal ones. Still, it is policy-making, involving agreement among partners. But moderatism is most likely—if I may be excused the pun—among moderate party systems, especially two-party systems of the American variety, where the electoral convergence of the two wings toward the center finds a ready analogue in government, and parties can afford to dissatisfy their extremes somewhat. It is most unlikely in the Italian party system, where the initiative must move from the center but cannot hope to reach and aggregate the extremes. In sum, because moderatism is a choice it always ends up by dissatisfying some groups. Center governments cannot afford this. Thus, typically, the Christian Democratic party, a diversified party par excellence in terms of its composition and the variety of interests it incorporates, cannot be a moderate party. Differently stated, the problem of Christian Democracy is not its make-up but its location. Though the party numerically dominates the coalitions, some minority members of the coalitions have correctly lamented that the party never really essays to mediate conflicts between partners, let alone impose its program on the others. It may bear marginally on the point, but it is worth noticing that Fanfani, the only "strong" man in the

---

41. Dahl, *Regimes and Oppositions*, op. cit., pp. 12-13 and 16-18.

majority party, chose during the present crisis to head the party, with whose fortunes he is mainly preoccupied, rather than the coalition.

I have already anticipated that the *immobilisme* described here has a "function"; it buys time, if not credit, for the center. But, to reassert what is essential at this point, the paradox of center politics is that time is bought at the price of inactivity and ineffectiveness.

Irresponsible Coalitions. Though the roots of ineffectiveness are in ideological disagreement and in the uncertainty of the decisional rule, there is more to ineffectiveness, once center governments set in, than a question of disagreement. It would be naive to portray politicians of the center as only weak-kneed democrats, new to the political game and paralyzed by the fear of stepping on delicate toes. The fact is that, in another paradox, center governments, for all the attacks and vituperation to which they are exposed, are never called to electoral accountability and do not have to do anything about it. That is, the fact that the center is a no-alternance formula gives its politicians irresponsible power and allows them the luxury of instability, disagreement, *immobilisme*. Since each partner of the center coalition knows that it will continue to stay in government (provided it does not try to "govern"), there is very little need to maintain cohesion in the coalition so as to prevent the opposition from taking over. As long as the voters are not likely to hold the center parties accountable and to turn them out, the parties are not required to follow a program of government and to build a record on which to seek victory in the competitive bidding against the opposition.

This irresponsible behavior is typical of the smaller parties of the coalition, since they know that all they need to stay in government is to count on a small, stable, and homogeneous electorate. They also know that, though limited, their bargaining power vis-à-vis the major party is greater than their strength (they are needed); and they know that they can always blame the major party for their inaction. But this behavior is just as typical of the major party which, because of its strength, can always blackmail the electorate by presenting itself as the only defense of the republic, and can reflect the blame for inaction on the unruly and unreasonable minor parties. The voter remains confused, loses interest, and registers the internal bickering, but continues to vote. And when center coalitions are unlikely to be thrown out, they have an incentive to devote their energies to the simplest things governments can do—sit tight, occupy power, and use power to their own advantage, so as to perpetuate it and to reward friends and supporters. Politics thus becomes a pure game of power, mostly concerned with *sottogoverno,* logrolling, minute compromises, reciprocal noninterference. It is more difficult and not necessary to govern; it is easier and sufficient to sit in government.

I have now reintroduced one facet of ineffectiveness presented in my analysis of legislative performance. Disagreement on the rule does not mean that no decisions are taken; it means that only highly disaggregated ones are. There is a double or circular way of looking at the phenomenon, as I pointed out when discussing *leggine.* To some extent we may say that, since center governments cannot find agreement, they displace their monopoly resources toward occupying and parceling out power. To some extent we may also say the reverse: the habit of monopolizing power diverts the center parties from coping with disagreement among themselves, distracts them from the business of conflict resolution, impedes the integration of the coalition.

Italian politics presents therefore a strange and at first contradictory scenario. Parties and factions, whether in government or opposition, outbid each other ideologically; the language of politics is heavily charged with symbols, dogmas, and principles. Issues and events that in other countries hardly stir a ripple become *causes célèbres,* call for party pronouncements, are dissected and analyzed by the mass media, are scrutinized for causes, meanings, and *cui prodest.* Foreign events (the end of the Greek junta, the post-Franco period in Spain, the crisis of the new Portuguese regime) are debated by parties and in Parliament as historical lessons of import to Italy, and serve usually to fix and validate competing ideologies. But everyday government is mostly kept busy with something else. Both government and individual members of Parliament are busy perpetuating the old politics of *trasformismo.* Both phenomena are facets of the same coin.

CONCLUSIONS

The reader looking for symmetry in the chapters will find no conclusions here, only a heading. As the book closes, my conclusions constitute the last chapter.

VII

Centrism, Its Uses and Its Present Crisis: Which Way Italy?

This chapter intends to do two things: to explain how centrist politics has survived for thirty years, and to discuss its recent crisis, especially in the light of Communist successes in the elections of June 15, 1975.

The model illustrated in the last chapter may leave a lingering doubt. In view of everything said there, how did Italian democracy endure for so long? The answer is as follows: the model only says that extreme multiparty systems produce polarized politics and highly ineffective and immobile regimes; it does not say that, hence, regimes collapse of their own accord. It does not even say that they are always in such danger. Their capacity for survival lies in the fact that they are centrist regimes. Reflecting on the paradoxes of centrist regimes, I have discovered that they have functions and that they are not entirely defenseless. They have a way of providing for their maintenance, and even a way of dealing with challenges, especially those having to do with socio-economic growth and economic crisis. In a way, as I have repeatedly indicated throughout the analysis of legislative behavior, it is the very decisional ineffectiveness of the Italian regime that has constituted its saving grace. Also, centrist regimes have a way of buying support, despite polarization. They do it, as exemplified in Chapters II and V, by fragmenting interests and by coopting them politically through the distribution of benefits narrow enough to avoid conflict. Though multiparty systems cannot afford, because of polarization, the competition of broadly aggregated interests, they can, through centrism, avoid to some extent competition and turn to the advantage of the regime the individualized treatment of interests. Thus the parliamentary politics of *trasformismo* and clientelism has been political cement of a sort, for both politicians and strategic supporting groups, and has offered a buffer against the dangers of economic growth and crisis. But Parliament is not the only place where the cooptation of interests has operated. A politics of cooptation is a politics of corporate interests, also conducted through corporate bodies. And the decisional limitations of traditional representative instituitions have led to some reallocation of decisional powers to other institutions—mainly public corporations closely linked to top party politicians—which have also offered political and economic buttressing.

Is centrism coming, however, to an end as a consequence of the recent political and economic crisis and of the electoral successes of the PCI? Is indeed not only centrism but Italian democracy in imminent danger? Nobody can tell for sure. It is easier to account—as I have tried to do in the core of the book—for what institutions do to men. It is less easy to account for men and events, and what men can invent to turn events and save themselves. Scientific ignorance advises restraint.[1] I do, however, have my views, as guarded as they are, on two points. First, the nature of present societal and political change in Italy is such that, even if centrism as a cabinet formula survives, the parliamentary and corporate politics of hidden and marginal accommodations may no longer suffice as cement against polarization. Hence, my remarks on how centrism buys support and shows stability apply to the past, not necessarily to the future. If they are formulated in the present tense, it is most often for esthetic reasons. Second, contrary to some views, I do not see the crisis of centrism, the victory of the PCI, and the cultural and political ferments of the country with an entirely positive eye. That is, there are those who read in these events an end to polarization, an end to thirty years of stultifying Catholic rule, and the beginning of a more modern, open, and civic society. There are, in fact, those who read them as evidence that polarization has not existed in Italy for a long time. Without by any means suggesting imminent collapse, I will on the other hand argue that these events, though

---

1. This is a theme on which the most acute among the contributors to *Il Caso Italiano* insist. See Fabio Luca Cavazza and Stephen Graubard (a cura di), *Il Caso Italiano* (Milano: Garzanti, 1974).

promising in many ways, confirm and, if inappropriately handled, increase polarization.

MAINTAINING THE SYSTEM: LA RÉPUBLIQUE DES CAMARADES

An interesting historical parallel, bearing on the longevity of the two, can be drawn between the Italian Republic and the Third French Republic. Writers like Michel Crozier, Maurice Duverger, Stanley Hoffmann, and Roy Macridis have remarked that since the last century French political culture—elite and mass—has been characterized by a deep-seated suspicion of authority and therefore of strong governments in a country yet open to the temptations of both.[2] The sources of such suspicion are obviously historical and cultural and can be traced back to the abuses and arbitrariness of the Ancien Régime, the traumas of Jacobin terror, and the reassertion of *étatisme* under the First and Second Empires. Suspicion was a reaction to the conflicts and turmoil of these periods, as regimes replaced each other, legitimist and republican legality were questioned, and regime formulas divided and cut across classes, parties, and the corporate bodies of the state. It was also a way of protecting traditional France against the dangers of rapid modernization and secularization.

It was the genius of the Third Republic and its center parties that they managed to curb authority and alleviate fears. It was their genius that, while the republic was never immune from authoritarian solicitations, these rarely held the day. The reason for the French success was in the fact that the republican regimes managed to engineer an armistice between hostile forces, a state of coexistence based on strong restraints upon governments and on a deep distrust of the active state. The fact that hostile forces always surrounded the republic and sought to take over made republican governments wary of strong action, lest it evoke retaliation in kind. Hence, the state had to be limited. The best

---

2. Michel Crozier, *The Bureaucratic Phenomenon* (Chicago: University of Chicago Press, 1964), Part IV; Stanley Hoffmann, "Paradoxes of the French Political Community," in Stanley Hoffmann et al., *In Search of France* (Cambridge, Mass.: Harvard University Press, 1963), esp. pp. 3-21; Maurice Duverger, "The Eternal Morass: French Centrism," in Mattei Dogan and Richard Rose, eds., *European Politics* (Boston: Little, Brown, 1971), pp. 237-246; Roy Macridis, "Oppositions in France: An Interpretation," *Government and Opposition* 7 (1972), pp. 166-185.

protection for all—in government or outside—was a diffident attitude toward government on the part of every individual and party.

In this way, the center parties managed to create the only arrangement within which the system could survive and to attract the only forces that could stay together. This arrangement—negative though it was—served not only to stave off the extremes, but to make living together at least bearable and to create a spirit of limited and guarded tolerance.

As Duverger puts it, "the center alliance permitted the two halves of France to live together. It provided a democratic framework for that existence."[3] It is the measure of the success of this strategy that it allowed the Third Republic to last almost seventy years, and it allowed the center parties to buy time.

In Italy too, the emergence of limited government after World War II can be partially read as a reaction to historical events: the trauma of over twenty years of Fascist dictatorship. In Italy too, the weakness of the postwar regime has been, in a way, one of its assets, providing the system with its rubber-ball quality: Men and formulas fall, but bounce back, at the slightest impact. This is not to exaggerate the similarity between the two countries. It was probably easier for French governments to buy time, especially in the earlier period of the republic. Party politics did not interfere as heavily with the business of government because organized mass politics had not quite formed, and ideological spacing has not become essential for party competition. In the same vein, the endurance of the center formula in Italy before World War I is better understood if we keep in mind the limited suffrage and the limited party development of the period. On these dimensions, Parliament and government in contemporary Italy have been less shielded than their predecessors.

Nevertheless, the French example brings home a point. Beleaguered governments can survive exactly because they maintain themselves inert. If, despite thirty years of confrontation, Communists and Christian Democrats have been able to sit together in Parliament and tolerate each other, it is exactly because they have left the big issues out of Parliament. To be more precise, the big issues may well be the object of lengthy floor

---

3. Duverger, op. cit., p. 242.

debates, since Parliament is a most appropriate arena for the parties' ideological games, but they have rarely been objects of decision and have rarely entered the committee rooms, where the legislative process is initiated. In this sense, Stanley Hoffmann's characterization of Parliament in the classical age of the Third Republic, the age of the republican compromise, is still suggestive:

> Parliament was supreme but immobile.... In such a way, the risks for the social and political stability of France which many had seen in universal suffrage and in the representation of all opinions were minimized, since the scope of what Parliament could do was restricted, and the sharp edges of political opinions could be worn out in the "camaraderie" of Parliamentarism.[4]

MAINTAINING THE SYSTEM: THE POLITICS OF CLIENTELISM

The Italian Parliament offers incentives to sustain the "good behavior" of majority and opposition. We know them—they go by the name of *leggine*. The fact that *leggine* number in the thousands, that they are often approved concurrently, and that the Communists are not ready to give them up for the uncertain pleasures of responsible opposition, tells us plenty. In a renewed version of Giolittian *trasformismo*, the cooptation of the Communist party in everyday legislative transactions smooths the edges of confrontation, "transforms" the adversary, and buys time for the system. On the other side, such cooptation, without giving the Communists any significant share of the action, rewards communist prudence and buys them precious political credit.

Beyond making life together tolerable, *trasformismo* has another raison d'être. The reciprocal back-scratching of the parties, especially the major ones, helps them build political support among middling social groups which are essential to each party. The importance of these groups is electoral and numerical, as they make up a good part of the constituency of each party, especially of the Christian Democratic party, and are a potential reserve of new and untapped votes, especially for the Communist

---

4. Hoffmann, op. cit., p. 15. For an analysis of the functions of Italian centrism bearing on points similar to Hoffmann's, see Nicola Matteucci, "La Grande Coalizione," *Il Mulino* 20 (1971), pp. 3-24.

party. Their importance lies also, and more to the point, in the fact that they have a key stabilizing role for the system as a whole, and a legitimizing one for the parties that can attract them. These groups include the old middle and lower-middle classes: small and middle peasants, artisans, shopkeepers, small businessmen, retail distributors, clerks, and bureaucrats in the traditional state and local bureaucracy. They are the product of a social and economic structure which is not completely modernized and rationalized and which still preserves overlayers of marginal producers, distributors, middlemen, and suppliers of conspicuous and personalized services. But the groups also include members of the new service, scientific, and technico-administrative sectors that have emerged with the greater rationalization of production and distribution, with the expansion of education, and with the growth of the welfare state. In Italy, members of the welfare bureaucracies are quite numerous in view of the traditional large size of the Italian civil service.

As difficult as it is to classify these heterogeneous social categories, so it is to pin them down and define them politically.[5] They belong conventionally to the political center, but they also lack political unity and stability and are traditionally available for a variety of political appeals and for adventures of an authoritarian type. They are an important hunting ground for the Christian Democratic party and its allies, and their close control is essential to legitimize the continuing hegemony of the center and to prevent dangerous political destabilization at the mass level. But, as indicated in the previous chapter, ideological appeals are not sufficient to keep them in place—especially after the first few years of center rule—and do not easily unify them. Hence, support must be bought by the center parties through policies favoring middling groups. Similarly, the Communist party has all the interest in preventing these groups from slipping to the right. It has, in fact, an interest in making them part of its constituency so as to expand its political reach, compete with the government on its own ground, and acquire legitimacy. Here too, where ideological appeals cannot succeed, then service-rendered may.

And the important point is that because of the fragmentation

---

5. On both points and on the ambiguous effects of modernization on the class and occupational structure of Italy and other countries, see the excellent study by Paolo Sylos Labini, *Saggio sulle Classi Sociali* (Bari: Laterza, 1974).

and heterogeneity of middling groups, the services expected do not require aggregative reforms and long-range policies, but more simply the preservation of old status, the protection of newly acquired positions, and the rendering of small favors. This is how middling groups become political clienteles; this is how *trasformismo* has its uses for clienteles, for the government, and for the opposition. *Trasformismo* becomes closely connected to clientelism, where by clientelism I mean a form of exchange in which parties distribute selectively goods specially designed for narrow groups in anticipation of limited but crucial support (votes or, more simply, abstention from opposition and benevolent tolerance).[6] *Leggine* are a most appropriate vehicle of clientelism. Their low level of aggregation, the fact that their effects are circumscribed to the immediate beneficiaries and designed to preserve and marginally improve their acquired positions, and the fact that these beneficiaries are always narrow categories make *leggine* a central tool of consensus-building among the middling groups and make Parliament the latter's important patron.[7]

To prove that clientelism buys time for the system is probably impossible, and the case must rest on its persuasiveness. To prove that it buys support for the Christian Democratic party and its allies presents difficulties, since the support has always been there. But I shall bring assistance to the argument later on, in discussing party factionalism. To buttress my claim that the PCI

---

6. In the extreme, the client may be one person, in which case the good he receives need not be shared by others. On selective incentives as a spur to organizational participation and support, see Mancur Olson's classical analysis in his *The Logic of Collective Action* (Cambridge, Mass.: Harvard University Press, 1965), esp. pp. 60-65. Clientelism in contemporary Italy differs substantially from prefascist clientelism in that today the patrons are parties and party factions rather than notables, clients are categories rather than individuals, and the favors clients obtain are narrow policies (*leggine*) rather than individual benefits. The point is made by François Bourricaud "Partitocrazia: Consolidamento o Rottura?" in Cavazza and Graubard, op. cit., p. 104. An important analysis of political clientelism in Southern Italy is found in Luigi Graziano, "Patron-Client Relationships in Southern Italy," *European Journal of Political Research* 1 (1973), pp. 3-34. A recent analysis and review of theories about clientelism can be found in René Lemarchand and Keith Legg, "Political Clientelism and Development," *Comparative Politics* 4 (1972), pp. 149-178.

7. Incidentally, by constituting itself a patron, Parliament robs the bureaucracy of much of its influence vis-à-vis its clienteles. The politicization of much regulatory activity, which falls in other countries within the bureaucratic domain, may paradoxically alienate a bureaucracy that is also an essential component of the consensus groups.

gains something from its voting and sponsorship of *leggine*, I ask the reader to look at Table 57. It does not demonstrate that *leggine* buy support for the PCI, but it shows that the PCI has been successful in its efforts to diversify its membership and to recruit among the middle classes and the professionals (as well as among economically and politically marginal groups such as pensioners).[8] The attention which the Communists, especially in parliamentary committees, have always paid to these categories probably helps this success. As a prominent Communist deputy, commenting on *leggine*, expressed himself:

> ... but *leggine* also have their uses. When they are well designed they are a very important means, if not to overturn the prevailing power relations between the middle ranks and capital, at least to protect the exploited middle ranks. We must not isolate ourselves from this reality. (PCI 44)[9]

Aside from the interesting ideological justification of the Communists' legislative behavior, the quotation confirms the great

TABLE 57. Occupational Composition of PCI Membership, 1960 and 1973[1]

	1960	*1973*
Industrial workers	37.4	41.05
Agricultural laborers	15.5	6.25
Peasants[2]	18.0	7.0
Artisans, shopkeepers, small businessmen	5.9	8.4
Clerks and technicians	1.9	4.2
Professionals, intellectuals, teachers	0.6	1.4
Students	0.3	1.6
Homemakers	14.1	12.3
Pensioners	6.3	16.75
Others		1.03

[1] From official Communist data
[2] Mezzadri, Coloni, Fittavoli, Coltivatori Diretti

8. The decrease in peasant membership is strictly tied to the dramatic decrease in the number of peasants in the gainfully employed population.
9. The word used by the respondent is middle *ceti*, rather than *classi*. It can probably be best translated as "ranks" or "categories." Middle "class" would not justify a Marxist alliance with these groups as readily middle "ranks."

importance that parties attribute to middling groups for their own party fortunes. It also indicates a legislative convergence among parties that can make for system survival.

Greater appreciation of the importance middle groups have for center governments and for system stability is obtained if we consider the crucial role of some of these groups in a dual economy—one combining tradition and inefficiency with modernization and rationalization. I am here especially referring to middle groups active in traditional sectors of the economy—small businessmen, artisans, shopkeepers, small distributors, small landowners, sharecroppers—which are in principle in competitive disadvantage vis-à-vis the modern, large-size, and capital-intensive sector. A number of students have amply demonstrated that insofar as Italy is still largely a dual economy—both in the South and in the North—it still reserves large space to these economic sectors.[10] In fact, with the exception of small landowners and sharecroppers, there is little indication that these traditional sectors tend to disappear and be absorbed by the advanced sector.[11] More important, the same students have also demonstrated that their survival is not just the consequence of objective lag and retarded or uneven growth, but an event willed by the Italian political class.

One reason is simply at hand: Since the traditional sector, despite the small size of its productive units, employs a disproportionate share of the labor force, it can function as a buffer against the uncertainties and dislocations of economic growth and rationalization, as well as against the obvious dangers of economic recessions and unemployment. During periods of economic expansion and labor mobility, it can offer cheap if pre-

---

10. Evidence on the points that follow can be found in M. Paci, *Mercato del Lavoro e Classi Sociali in Italia*, (Bologna: Il Mulino, 1974); G. Bonazzi, A. Bagnasco, S. Casillo, *Industria e Potere Politico in una Provincia Meridionale* (Torino: L'Impresa Edizioni, 1972); Suzanne Berger, "Uso Politico e Sopravvivenza dei Ceti in Declino," in Cavazza and Graubard, op. cit., pp. 292-314. Also on the same points and in the same volume, see Giorgio Galli, "L'Intersecazione delle Classi Sociali nei Partiti," pp. 183-195, and Alessandro Pizzorno, "I Ceti Medi nei Meccanismi del Consenso," pp. 315-338. A general statement on the survival of traditional sectors and their function in an advanced economy is Michael Piore, "On the Technological Foundations of Economic Dualism" (Cambridge, Mass.: MIT, Department of Economics, Working Paper No. 110, May 1973).

11. Evidence in Francesco Forte, "L'Impresa: Grande Piccola Pubblica Privata," in Cavazza and Graubard, op. cit., pp. 339-340.

carious employment for surplus labor, which lacks the necessary qualifications, or which the advanced sector cannot absorb without further and uneconomic expansion. It thus assuages the frustrations of rising expectations. In times of recession and falling exports, it can absorb industrial unemployment at least temporarily, because in an inefficient, paternalistic, and labor-intensive sector, especially if geared for internal consumption and service, labor contraction is less immediately affected by the economic cycle. Thus the personal miseries of falling opportunities can be alleviated. In both cases, the traditional sector is used to dump on, and to pay for, the crises and the limited absorbing capacities of the advanced sector.

But to play this role, and thus protect economic and political stability, the traditional sector itself needs protection and political recognition. This is what successive governments have consistently granted, with the frequent support of the opposition, through a variety of measures addressed often to specific components of the sector. The measures concern privileged credit, restricted licensing of potential and especially larger competitors, the absorption by the state of social security payments for workers employed by small business, pensioning plans for small owners and entrepreneurs, the contractual and fiscal protection of small farming units, and public-works expenditures. It is clear that, irrespective of their real electoral force, their power to affect electoral changes, and their actual pressure, the traditional groups thus weigh considerably on the policies of the government. It is clear that traditional groups also foist more than a tinge of popular conservatism on the conventional working-class ideology of the Communist party. But it is also clear that the political parties have an interest in maintaining a privileged alliance with these groups.

A more sustained process of economic rationalization could sharpen and simplify social structures, class alignments, and political issues beyond what political parties and the country are ready to bear. In a way, it is the very inefficiency of the economic system, the overlaying of social groups, and their protection by political parties that provide the country with "niches" against economic dislocation. An apparently stronger, more rationalized structure could not take it as much in stride.

MAINTAINING THE SYSTEM:
THE POLITICS OF CORPORATE INTERESTS

I have depicted clientelism as a maintenance strategy controlled by and large by Parliament and the traditional structures of representation. But the control is not exclusive, and a particularly important role in the preservation of the system is also played by a large network of corporate public bodies created especially after the war, often escaping parliamentary and cabinet control, and organized outside the ministerial bureaucracy. Among the most important are public economic corporations entrusted with far-reaching productive, investment, and financing functions in many vital sectors of the economy. Of these, some—like IRI (Institute for Industrial Reconstruction), probably the largest holding company in Europe—are an inheritance from Fascism.[12] Of similar political importance, because of their number and the financial resources they administer and control, are the many national welfare agencies entrusted with the administration of health, welfare, and pension plans for nearly all public and private wage and salary earners, for significant sectors of the self-employed, and for their families.

I shall dispense with the intricacies of these bodies' formal powers and legal relations to Parliament, and come to the essential point I intend to make about them: that these bodies, because of the powers they have acquired, because of the partisan criteria for staffing, and because of the intricate network of corporate relations they have created, also contribute to the perpetuation of the centrist regime and act as buffers against both collapse of the regime and its democratic rationalization. To be sure, their very existence and their policies have become, and often rightly so, the ready symbol of the distortions of continuing

---

12. Among the English studies of Italian public corporations, see Michael Posner and Stuart Woolf, ed., *Italian Public Enterprise* (London: Duckworth, 1967); Stuart Holland, ed., *The State as Entrepreneur* (London: Weidenfeld and Nicolson, 1972); Kevin Allen and Andrew Stevenson, *An Introduction to the Italian Economy* (New York: Harper and Row, 1975), chapter 7; Andrew Shonfield, *Modern Capitalism* (Oxford: Oxford University Press, 1965), Part I, chapter 9. In Italian, see Giuliano Amato (a cura di), *Il Governo dell'Industria in Italia* (Bologna: Il Mulino, 1972); Giuseppe Petrilli, *Lo Stato Imprenditore* (Bologna: Cappelli, 1967); Romano Prodi, *Sistema Industriale e Sviluppo Politico in Italia* (Bologna: Il Mulino, 1973); Giorgio Ruffolo, *L'Impresa Pubblica* (Torino: Einaudi, 1968); Centro di Ricerca e Documentazione "Luigi Einaudi" (a cura di), *Le Baronie di Stato* (Firenze: Sansoni, 1968).

centrist rule. Corruption, inefficiency, waste of public money, particularism, spoils, incompetence, politicking, secrecy, irresponsibility, empire-building, self-perpetuation, and everything else that is disaffective about rule by the center have been imputed to these bodies. Hence, they are certain testimony to the perpetual crisis of the regime. But their capacity to endure and to buy time for the regime is something else.

It is probably already intuitive in the reader that these corporate bodies play an important part in the politics of clientelism. They expand and institutionalize its network and, by so doing, tend to consolidate and expand the area of strategic consensus and support around the regime.[13] If these corporate bodies, to use David Easton's distinction, do not enjoy and in fact erode "diffuse" support, they can nevertheless accrue "specific" support by the incentives and benefits they distribute to their clienteles. And, even aside from this support function, they provide the major government parties with enough seats to root their power. Indeed, more than parliamentary clientelism, in which the opposition is allowed a share, the politics of what in Italian are called *enti pubblici* is an essential preserve of government parties, in fact of the major party, its major factions, and their top leaders.

In connection with this law of increasing concentration, it may be worth extensively paraphrasing Gianni Baget Bozzo, himself an active figure in the Catholic movement.[14] According to him, the electoral retrenchment of Christian Democracy in 1953 induced the party to adopt a double government strategy: on one side, the devaluation of Parliament as a center of decision; on the other, the multiplication of politically controlled *enti pubblici* escaping public scrutiny. Parliament was allowed to lose, after 1953, those connotations typical of a parliamentary regime and based on the confrontation between government and opposition. It became an assembly "with its lobbies, its internal structures, both secret and visible: an American Congress without the presidency."[15] But Christian Democracy regained by the creation

---

13. An acute and compact analysis of the clientelistic role of public corporations is contained in Giuseppe Are, "Sistema Imprenditoriale e Classe Politica," *Il Mulino* 23 (1974), pp. 256-289.

14. Gianni Baget Bozzo, "Dibattito sulla Grande Coalizione," *Il Mulino* 20 (1971), pp. 720-724.

15. Ibid., p. 723.

of the *enti* what it lost in Parliament. Beginning with De Gasperi, the party created its real power outside the formal structure of the state. That explains the Communists' unrelenting diffidence toward the *enti*. Little does it matter that their policies, especially among economic corporations, are often leftist and reformist. What counts is that the Communists have little or no voice and the regime all the voice in running them. "L'ente crea l'esistente," Palmiro Togliatti philosophized in an untranslatable Hegelian pun.[16]

How public corporations build support and maintain the regime is quickly, if superficially, told. At the top they are usually staffed by political appointees, chosen often for their partisan more than for their professional merits. Throughout the ranks, especially in the lowest, spoils and clientelism are an important component in the choice of personnel. Thus, starting with their recruitment policies, corporations operate as important party agents. Their funds escape public and parliamentary scrutiny either because their budgets are not part of the state budget, or because their budgets are more debated than analyzed, or because they have opportunities for self-financing.[17] Hence, many of their choices are not guided by economic or institutional criteria, and expenditures can be channeled to benefit groups and constituencies that are judged important for party and factional support. In fact, public corporations can coopt in the process of distribution of their resources a host of other agencies (banks, cooperatives, chambers of commerce, and local governments) which expand the network of party alliances and create a class of public and private mediators closely tied to the central government. In this way, corporations act as patrons in behalf of the government and as subcontractors of patronage at lower levels. In exchange they obtain political support and the institutionalization of party rule.

16. *Ente* means both "agency" and "being," especially "supreme being." The position of the PCI on state enterprises is illustrated in Istituto Antonio Gramsci (a cura di), *La Riforma dello Stato* (Roma: Editori Riuniti, 1968). See especially contributions by Edoardo Perna (pp. 21-50), Silvio Leonardi (pp. 153-166), Salvatore D'Albergo (pp. 243-256 and 375-379), and Giuliano Amato (pp. 351-355).

17. On legal and political relations with Parliament and government, see Carol Johnson, "Relations with Government and Parliament," in Holland, ed., op. cit., pp. 202-218; Franco Rizzo, *Il Controllo del Parlamento sugli Enti Pubblici* (Milano: Giuffrè, 1969).

But this is not the only way in which corporations act as the grand electors of the government. They can also raise clientele money to support government parties and factions, and they can divert their own funds to this task. If they are welfare agencies, hidden financial investments of welfare payments can provide them with the needed money. And the fact that, as agencies with a public service function, they are normally allowed to run huge deficits regularly redeemed by the state helps defray these hidden partisan costs and dump them on the classical taxpayer. If they are economic corporations, run often according to strict cost-benefit criteria, their economic success and their ability to refinance themselves are also an important source of funds for party financing. It all seems like an unorthodox way of buttressing government, but recently a Christian Democratic minister publicly asserted the explicit duty of state corporations to finance government parties.[18]

I shall conclude by briefly pointing out that some economists insist on a fundamental distinction between public corporations. Most agencies, especially welfare agencies, are incarnations of the inefficiencies and irrationalities of a dual economy; their effect is at most to expand clientelistic networks and to buttress the dual economy and its governing class against excessive shocks. Others, especially public economic enterprises operating on the profit motive, have been established and have grown to operate outside the dual economy. More importantly, and to secure their swift intervention, they exist outside the legal strictures of the central bureaucracy, artfully kept cumbersome by politicians interested in the preservation of political clientelism.[19] Their separation from the ministerial bureaucracy, and the privileged financing policies they enjoy, allow public economic enterprises rapid economic action and rationalization in times of expansion, in competition with and as stimulus for the advanced private

---

18. On party finances and whether the state should finance parties, see Roberto Crespi, *Lo Stato Deve Pagare i Partiti?* (Firenze: Sansoni, 1971). Against state financing as recently introduced in Italy is Gianfranco Pasquino, "Contro il Finanziamento di Questi Partiti," *Il Mulino* 23 (1974), pp. 233-255. On how in turn public corporations get financed, see Stuart Holland, "The Financial Formula," in Holland, ed., op. cit., chapter 8.

19. Are, op. cit., pp. 275-276, argues that bureaucratic inefficiency is the result of political choices, and that holding the bureaucracy responsible for it is strategically beside the point.

sector.[20] They also allow them survival and maneuverability in periods of retrenchment so as to protect the economy from slump and excessive unemployment. Here too, then, as in the preservation of the traditional sector, government parties find a way, by shifting power outside of Parliament, to shield the system from collapse. Here, too, the "colonization" of the sector by the majority strengthens center rule.

It should be clear, however, that this is colonization of a special sort. The public enterprises escape not only the central bureaucracy and Parliament, but also the scrutiny of the majority parties. These have no likely control on the economic policies of public enterprises. Rather, an alliance of political convenience operates, involving factions or leading politicians of the majority parties. It short-circuits coalition cabinets as well as party apparatus, it centers on selected camarillas of top corporate managers and party leaders,[21] and it leaves corporate interests essentially in control of their institutional goals. The result is not only colonization but also—to use a similar geopolitical metaphor—balkanization of both the government parties and the public corporations. The similarity to the effects of parliamentary clientelism is obvious.

MAINTAINING THE SYSTEM: PARTY FACTIONALISM

Leaving the geopolitical metaphor, clientelistic and corporate politics have the same effect on the majority parties: they trigger and institutionalize extreme party factionalism, an important structure through which the center maintains itself in power. In turn factionalism sustains clientelism. The best evidence of the length to which parties can go in this process of institutionalization comes, for good reasons, from the two leading parties of the majority: the Catholic and the Socialist.

To be sure, factionalism is not entirely supported by the incentives and requirements of clientelism; it also has an ideological component. In another of its paradoxes, center rule tends to

---

20. The point is especially argued by Andrew Shonfield, "L'Impresa Pubblica: Modello Internazionale o Specialità Locale?," in Cavazza and Graubard, op. cit., pp. 270-291. See also Shonfield, op. cit. For a diverging view, see Prodi, op. cit.; Forte, op. cit., pp. 339-368.

21. A recent "exposé" of such camarillas is contained in Eugenio Scalfari and Giuseppe Turani, *Razza Padrona* (Milano: Feltrinelli, 1974).

reproduce within itself the ideological divisions of the parties it leaves out of government. An organized center, a left, and a right are easily recognizable and have always existed both in the DC and the governing PSI. Each faction has tended to emphasize different government alliances, different equilibria, or different "strategies of attention" toward the oppositions. Each has tended to carve for itself a place in the left-right, conservation-reform continuum so as to locate itself ideally close to other parties, even outside the coalition. The result is often, as we have seen, centrifugation of the coalition: the left of Christian Democracy can, for instance, move further left than the right of the Socialist party. But the puzzle of many ideological parties further divided in organized ideological factions is readily explained. For one thing, center coalitions are negative and beleaguered coalitions, whose partners do not firmly agree on the decisional rule and are sensitive to pressures from the opposition. Ideological factionalism is therefore to be expected. Factionalism increased and intensified in the Socialist party after it joined the coalition. And ideological divisions are understandable in a party like the Christian Democratic, whose cadres are held together by a religious bond cutting across left and right, by the need to defend the republic, and by the attraction of timeless power.

But ideology is not all there is to factionalism. Factionalism, one is tempted to argue, is also a way of escaping the excessive strictures of ideology, which freeze political action and isolate each party from the next. It is a way, cumbersome perhaps, of unscrambling party politics and getting it moving. Factionalism, I would argue more precisely, is also an institutional device through which governing parties—unable otherwise to govern—divide, entrench, and consolidate their power. A simple fact bearing on the point is that Christian Democracy and the Socialist party don't just have two or three factions, which is all that would be needed to allow ideological diversification, some capacity to talk to other parties, and some internal democracy to boot. They have, altogether, around fifteen factions,[22] many more than are

22. Around nine in the DC, four to seven in the PSI. See Gianfranco Pasquino, "Le Radici del Frazionismo e il Voto di Preferenza," in Giovanni Sartori (a cura di), *Correnti Frazioni e Fazioni nei Partiti Politici Italiani* (Bologna: Il Mulino, 1973), pp. 75-91. The volume, a collection of essays previously published in the *Rivista Italiana di Scienza Politica*, is the best recent contribution to the study of factionalism in Italian political parties. See also Michele Sernini, *Le Correnti nel Partito* (Milano: Istituto Editoriale Cisalpino, 1966);

ideologically needed in an already extreme multiparty system, but certainly not that many when the stake is control of rich government spoils and neither party is restraining factional competition for control.²³

I have said above that the increasing factionalism of the PSI, following its entry into government, indicates ideological factionalism. But it just as well indicates what Sartori calls "interest" or "convenience" factionalism,²⁴ in that, upon joining the government, the Socialists have been easily conquered by the logic of clientelism. The fact that factions are organized, stable, well-financed, with their own recognizable leaders and often their mass media, could prove their ideological nature. But it may just as well prove their "convenience" nature, as organized and stable factions are favored by the vertical and centralized organization of these parties and are in a better position to compete for the positions of leadership that give them access to spoils. Even the fact that they all justify themselves ideologically does not disprove their clientelistic functions: how else could they justify their existence? And evidence submitted by Alberto Spreafico and Franco Cazzola, to the effect that Socialist factions do not differ from each other in the social and economic composition of their supporters, at least suggests that factionalism cannot be easily linked to socioeconomic differences and broad left-right aggregations.²⁵ Indeed, the strength of most factions is not evenly

---

Luigi D'Amato, *Correnti di Partito e Partito di Correnti* (Milano: Giuffrè, 1965). For early contributions by an American scholar to the study of Italian factionalism, see by Raphael Zariski, "Party Factions and Competitive Politics: Some Preliminary Observations," *Midwest Journal of Political Science* 4 (1960), pp. 27-51; "The Italian Socialist Party: A Case Study in Factional Conflict," *American Political Science Review* 56 (1962), pp. 372-390; "Intra-Party Conflict in a Dominant Party: The Experience of Italian Christian Democracy," *Journal of Politics* 27 (1965), pp. 1-32. More recent English-language contributions are Alan Stern et al., "Factions and Opinion Groups in European Mass Parties: Some Evidence from a Study of Italian Socialist Activists," *Comparative Politics* 3 (1971), pp. 529-559; Raphael Zariski and Susan Welch, "The Correlates of Intraparty Depolarizing Tendencies in Italy." *Comparative Politics* 7 (1975), pp. 407-433.

23. Sartori's view is that factions are allowed to proliferate by the fact that Christian Democracy and the Socialist Party usually adopt proportionality in the elections of their national councils. Under the rule, even a small faction has an incentive to run and to claim an adequate share of the spoils. Giovanni Sartori, "Proporzionalismo, Frazionismo, e Crisi dei Partiti," in Sartori, op. cit., pp. 9-36.

24. Ibid., p. 20.

25. Alberto Spreafico and Franco Cazzola, "Correnti di Partito e Processi di Identificazione," *Il Politico* 35 (1970), pp. 695-715. To be sure, Spreafico and Cazzola point neverthe-

distributed across the country, nor is it linked to socioeconomic characteristics of the various areas; it is concentrated locally in the areas from which their leaders come and in which their clientelism more successfully operates.[26]

From our viewpoint, the most important aspect of factionalism is this: it transforms and displaces the problem of governing from one of negotiating and aggregating conflicting opinions into a more tractable one of allocating seats of power.[27] It is a scheme of government with considerable attraction for a former opposition like the PSI not used to governing together with other parties, and a scheme that, again, can buy time for the system.

I have discussed how the weaknesses of center politics can also be its points of strength. I shall conclude the first part of this chapter by recalling a number of other factors not easily classifiable, and some exogenous to the system, that explain the endurance of the system. In discussing them, I shall point out future dangers.

MAINTAINING THE SYSTEM: THE BALANCE OF FORCES

A widely observed and important difference between Italy on one side and Weimar and the Fourth French Republic on the other is the fact that the Italian center is occupied by a single large party dominating all coalitions. The difference is by now too obvious for the reader to need further belaboring. I shall simply point out four facts. First, the size of the Christian Democratic party provides an element of continuity in government which the other countries did not have and, without providing sustained leadership, it limits (especially before the

---

less to the importance of ideology in the factionalism of the PSI, and explain the failure of Socialist unification in terms of conflicting ideologies. But Felice Rizzi brilliantly shows that the explanation is not sufficient, and that personal ambitions and factionalism centered on the control of spoils played a crucial role in ending unification: Felice Rizzi, "Dall'Unificazione alla Scissione Socialista (1966-1969)," *Rivista Italiana di Scienza Politica* 3 (1973), pp. 407-424.

26. Franco Cazzola, "Partiti, Correnti e Voto di Preferenza," *Rivista Italiana di Scienza Politica* 2 (1972), pp. 569-588.

27. Alessandro Pizzorno, "Elementi di uno Schema Teorico," in Giordano Sivini (a cura di), *Partiti e Partecipazione Politica in Italia* (Milano: Giuffrè, 1969), pp. 5-40. In essence, a rule of proportionality as described in Chapter III operates among the parties in government. But proportionality is limited to the allocation of offices and does not extend to the aggregation of policies.

entry of the PSI) the centrifugal pull of the other partners. Second, the Christian Democratic party, given its size, has alone created a network of clientelistic and corporate interests and pervaded the state and local apparatus to an extent very likely unmatched in the other two countries. Third, the party is alone much more of a deterrent to opposition parties than the weaker coalition partners of Weimar and France. Fourth, the party is a Catholic party active in a Catholic country, with a capacity for cultural penetration and organizational encapsulation via the Church and supporting movements that neither the German Zentrum nor the French MRP could even approach. On all these counts, Christian Democracy might rule for thirty years by the simple fact of its existence; the governing parties of Germany and France could not.

A related difference, especially vis-à-vis France, is the impressive electoral stability of Christian Democracy until most recently. No flash parties in Italy have been able to steal Catholic votes for more than short periods of time. But in France flash parties were rampant, and Poujadism and Gaullism—two antisystem movements—progressively drained the MRP and other center parties of their original strength. What accounts for this difference in stability and loyalty is somewhat unclear. Philip Converse and Georges Dupeux, in a classical paper comparing French with American party loyalties, point to features of imperfect socialization and imperfect transmission of party loyalties in the French family, leading to generalized party instability.[28] The same imperfect socialization seems true of the Italian family.[29] Nevertheless, stability in Italy is much greater. Very likely, it is the organizational and cultural encapsulation cited above that explains Catholic success and staves off flash parties.[30] If we couple this success with the fact that the opposition is monopolized more

---

28. Philip Converse and Georges Dupeux, "Politicization of the Electorate in France and the United States," *Public Opinion Quarterly* 26 (1962), pp. 1-24.

29. Samuel Barnes, *Representation in Italy: Institutionalized Traditions and Electoral Choice* (unpublished manuscript, dated June 1975), Table VI-1. Barnes reports that knowledge of father's party preference is just as low in Italy as it was in France when Converse and Dupeux collected their data. He also reports that knowledge of father's preference has little impact on the transmission of partisanship.

30. See footnote 30 in Chapter III for the relevant literature. See also most recently Giacomo Sani, "Political Traditions as Contextual Variables: Partisanship in Italy" (paper delivered at the Annual Meeting of the Midwest Political Science Association, Chicago, May 1-3, 1975); Barnes, op. cit., chapters 5, 6, and 7.

than in France by an equally successful and pervasive Communist party, we have in Italy not only extreme multipartism but also the elements of Giorgio Galli's "imperfect bipartism." Contrary to Weimar and France, where the center was surrounded on both sides, the party system is mainly polarized to the left, and, *as long as the two major parties can afford a degree of tolerance*, this corrects the strains of extreme multipartism and helps the regime endure.

Tolerance between government and opposition depends on whether or not the system is confronted with special crises, even if these are not manufactured by the system. I have indicated that it is difficult to catalogue and weigh the consequences of such crises. It is equally difficult to escape the fallacy of making them necessary causes after the fact: when their occurrence is followed by the collapse of the system. It is nevertheless more than an educated guess to say that what has given Italy thirty years of leeway is also the fact that the country has never been faced with external issues as objectively intractable as those that Weimar and the Fourth Republic had to face.

Its minor international status and aspirations, the loss of its colonies, the fact that its membership in the Western alliance was also imposed by geopolitical circumstances, and its rapid Allied-supported reconstruction—in sum, Italy's position as a second-rate power treated with benign neglect by the major powers—spared Italy the agonies and lacerations of France and Weimar. It robbed opposition on the right and left of an opportunity to attack and erode the performance of the regime by effectively eliminating a host of potentially troublesome issues from the political agenda: they were no longer issues. It allowed the regime to resist the opposition from a safer haven and to address its energies to the consolidation of its power. Perhaps more important, it gave the opposition, especially the Communist party, good reasons to shelve any aspirations to immediate power, however obtainable, and persuaded it to a long truce with the regime. That is, the elimination of major crises made the opposition more restrained toward government and supplied the latter with some legitamacy. The trauma of French decolonization, and the cumulation of inflation, depression, and foreign-policy issues under Weimar, had the opposite effects and precipitated collapse. Otherwise said, regimes like the Italian can survive at low levels of performance, and even accrue some credit, as long as conditions are normal and steady, but can lose original credit and even collapse if a major crisis, which oppositions can exploit to change the game, invests them.[31]

But, one could object, tolerance is not simply a function of the level of crisis but also and above all of the types of opposition. Indeed, one does not need to point to Italy's lack of crises to understand the adjustment of its Communist party, since the party was from its beginning nonrevolutionary and "Italian" and had in fact opted even before the end of the war for a long-term strategy of alliance with the Catholics. It is enough to know this to know the relative stability of the present system. It is enough to know who the Nazis were, and who the German Communists, to know that neither party was ever at any point willing to give an inch to the system, and that each party was committed to precipitating crises and fostering divisions wherever they could find or fabricate them. Similarly, one does not need to show lack of crises to explain the extreme longevity of the Third French Republic. The fact is that neither the Socialists nor the legitimists and right-wing forces (nor, later on, the relatively small Communist party) ever had the political clout, the will, or the ideological cohesiveness to effectively exploit or fabricate crises and change the game. And in Italy before World War I, Giolitti's failure to absorb the Socialists and move them toward the area of government preceded the war crisis and was the result of the ideological barrier between socialists imbued with a sense of destiny and liberals too busy with the power they held. In sum, on the strength of these historical examples, it can be argued that what has kept Communists and Catholics under the same Italian roof for so long is the former's original sin, their early "social-democratization."

I have formulated this last explanation of the endurance of the system in very strong terms not because I strongly believe in it (as I will show in the next section), but to induce some doubt in the reader, which I shall use to restate and conclude my case. The doubt is that perhaps the Italian system has never been seriously polarized, and polarization has at any rate substantially de-

31. An interesting analysis of the impact of international factors on the performance of polarized systems is contained in Gianfranco Pasquino, "Pesi Internazionali e Contrappesi Nazionali," in Cavazza and Graubard, op. cit., pp. 163-182.

creased.³² For one thing, governments in Italy have shown a remarkable capacity to absorb the Communists in the parliamentary game; for another, the Communists impress more and more observers as a responsible party concerned with closing ideological differences and committed to a gradual and peaceful march toward government. Where, then, does the system really stand, and where is it going?

TOWARD DEPOLARIZATION?

My answer to the objection that the Communists have been absorbed in the parliamentary game is rather straightforward. I need only recall the theme of the book: the parliamentary game is what it is—a game with limited stakes.³³ It alters in no way the fact that the decisional rule is still unresolved, as shown by our parliamentary interviews, and that therefore crucial issues do not make the decisional agenda. The existence of a game of sorts does not prove depolarization; it proves a stalemate without which the system would no longer be here. What deserves emphasis is not only that the system has endured, but also that the stalemate has endured.

To be sure, it is important to know that the Communist party willingly plays the parliamentary game. It is also important to know that the party presents itself as the staunchest defender of parliamentary powers and prerogatives. But what do these attitudes conclusively prove? Only the fact that the party plays and defends "the only game in town."³⁴ We may add that playing the

---

32. One of the latest statements to this effect is in Luciano Pellicani, "Verso il Superamento del Pluralismo Polarizzato," *Rivista Italiana di Scienza Politica* 4 (1974), pp. 645-674. See Sartori's answer in the same issue: Giovanni Sartori, "Il Caso Italiano: Salvare il Pluralismo e Superare la Polarizzazione," *Rivista Italiana di Scienza Politica* 4 (1974), pp. 675-687.

33. These are essentially the conclusions Cazzola draws from his analysis of legislative behavior and outputs: Franco Cazzola, "Consenso e Opposizione nel Parlamento Italiano. Il Ruolo del PCI dalla I alla IV Legislatura," *Rivista Italiana di Scienza Politica* 2 (1972), pp. 71-96.

34. From this viewpoint, Putnam's survey evidence that PCI leaders, though radical in economic matters, comfortably accept the rules of the pluralistic game is somewhat beside the point. Contrary to Putnam's stated claim, the evidence does not speak to whether the party is antisystem. See Robert Putnam, "The Italian Communist Politician," in Donald Blackmer and Sidney Tarrow, eds., *Communism in Italy and France* (Princeton: Princeton University Press, 1975), pp. 173-217.

game, no matter how limited, gives the party a chance to show its democratic credentials and its governing vocation and to essay breaking its isolation. But does it amount to the social-democratization of the party, and can it break the isolation?

The trouble with speaking of social-democratization is that the term has no clear connotation and no clear bearing on depolarization. If it simply means that a party forsakes revolutionary strategies, then the PCI has been a social-democratic party at least since the end of the war. But no Leninist doctrine advocates such strategies as the only avenue to power. And a nonrevolutionary party can still advocate or be perceived as advocating a different regime. If then social-democratization means that upon accession to power the party remains committed to a plural system of party competition and constitutional freedoms, the trouble is that this notion can only be proved after the fact, and the historical evidence is, to say the least, limited and uncertain. The Communists have governed (not alone) in Finland, but the special role of the Soviet Union in the case indicates disturbingly that the decision to preserve democracy was not made in Helsinki alone. The Allende presidency and its Communist allies promised the preservation of a plural system in Chile, but the partial failure to do so, owing also to the intolerance of the regime's enemies, indicates again that the choice is neither one-sided nor irrevocable.[35] And popular front experiences even, as in France, during relatively peaceful times have been short-lived, atypical, and at least not relevant to our point.[36] The fact therefore that Italian Communists have been committed for years to a democratic method says little about the preservation of that method later on, especially if, despite the social-democratic label we wish to pin on it, the party professes itself Marxist and Leninist. The point is not that the Communists are insincere, but that their future choices depend on existing situations and opportunities. I have been reminded in this regard[37] of Schumpeter's pointed observations

---

35. Arturo Valenzuela, "The Breakdown of Democracy in Chile," in Juan Linz and Alfred Stepan, eds., *Breakdowns and Crises of Democratic Regimes* (forthcoming).

36. Neither in France nor in 1936 Spain did the Communists actually join the popular front government. Also, the very fact that Communist parties dropped the term *popular front* after the war indicates that popular fronts appeared before the war as stepping-stones to Communist takeover.

37. By Juan Linz.

on the democratic commitment of the German and other European socialists before the war. They deserve quoting at length:

> ... those socialist groups that have consistently upheld the democratic faith never had either a chance or a motive for proposing any other. They lived in environments that would have strongly resented undemocratic talk and practice.... In some cases they had every reason to espouse democratic principles that sheltered them and their activity.... In Germany where ... the avenue to political responsibility seemed to be blocked, socialists, facing a strong and hostile state ... were still less free to deviate from the democratic creed, since by doing so they would only have played into the hands of their enemies.
>
> ... It is true in a sense that in 1918 the Social Democratic party of Germany had a choice, that it decided for democracy.... But the party split on the issue.... Many ... though submitting to party discipline, disapproved. And many of those that approved did so merely on the ground that, from the summer of 1919 at least, chances of succeeding in more radical (i.e., in this case, antidemocratic) courses had become negligible....
>
> I am not going to blame German Social Democrats for the sense of responsibility they displayed or even for the complacency with which they settled down in the comfortable armchairs of officialdom.... But it takes some optimism to cite them as witnesses to the unswerving allegiance of socialists to democratic procedure.[38]

There are points of similarity between the PCI and the German Socialists under the Empire. Aside from the large size of the two parties and their prominence in Parliament, the similarity concerns especially their organizational skills, the cultural encapsulation of their membership, the constant devotion of their cadres and leaders, their seriousness, and their rejection of adventures. But if "seriousness" is the third meaning of social-democratization, then, as the German example suggests, this character is also a response to the isolation in which the party has found itself and to the lack of reasonable alternatives. More important, the choice has not yet broken the isolation of the party. The same "negative integration" that held together the German socialist culture but kept it outside the system has also plagued the Italian Communists.[39]

---

38. Joseph Schumpeter, *Capitalism, Socialism and Democracy* (New York: Harper Torchbook Edition, 1962), pp. 238-239.

39. On the "negative integration" of German Socialism, see Guenther Roth, *The Social Democrats in Imperial Germany* (Totowa, N.J.: Bedminster Press, 1963). The similarity

The key to the isolation of the Communists is still in the nature of the party system and the way mass politics is conducted. That the Communist party devotes increasing energies to the task of breaking its isolation and moving toward an understanding with the center parties, and with the Catholics in particular, is unquestionable. It is equally unquestionable that governing elites are increasingly concerned with the plight of the country and realize that the problem is, above all, a political one: the excessive polarization of the system and the isolation of the opposition. But depolarization is not signified (nor can it be achieved) by marginal parliamentary convergences. These provide important continuity; they do not change the game. Polarization exists in the party system and can only be lessened by substantially altering the ideological images with which parties compete. And this is a task of considerable difficulty, as parties are also victims of the images they have built. In the case of the Communist party, the electoral images remain Marxist and internationalist, and altering them involves incalculable risks for the party. It would mean endangering the unity of a subculture of activists and local cadres which has been held together exactly by such identities. That is why every effort by the party to reform its image (for example, by criticizing illiberalism in the Soviet Union, by accepting the European Community or Italy's membership in the NATO alliance) is counterbalanced by a reassertion of its internationalism, its friendship with the Soviet Union, and its membership in the Socialist camp.[40] These are not mere slogans; they go to the core of the identity the party must protect to preserve its organization in a country where it does not rule. But as long as the identity remains, non-Communist opinion stays suspicious; other parties have an obvious reason to maintain polarization, and the Communist party responds in kind. No matter how responsibly and restrainedly the party behaves, it appears in the eyes of many an antisystem party. No matter how genuinely the parties worry

---

between Italian Communists and German Socialists is one on which many Italian analysts draw in the running debate on the vocation and the future of the PCI. For a critical analysis of Weimar as a crisis model relevant for Italy, see Gian Enrico Rusconi, "Weimar— Un Modello di Crisi per l'Italia degli Anni Settanta?" *Quaderni di Sociologia* 24 (1975), pp. 5-54.

40. An acute analysis of these points is in Giorgio Galli, "Il PCI Rivisitato," *Il Mulino* 20 (1971), pp. 3-24.

about the impasse, they remain poles apart. Are there ways out of the impasse? Are there ways of reforming the party system?

One way out has been advocated for years by several political analysts. It is the development of a system of alternance in government that would do away with irresponsible center governments, give the Communists a chance to govern together with parties close to them, and thus break the stalemate and centrifugation of centrist politics. It should be clear by now, however, that this is no cure at all, as the root of the problem is not centrism but polarization. To cure the symptom is not to cure the disease. To put it more mildly, whether alternance can work at all depends on the circumstances leading to it. One thing is a system of alternance following a genuine and smooth process of depolarization among parties, in which parties reform their images and ideological space is narrowed. Depolarization would in effect create a new and more workable party system. And the importance of this development would be not so much whether alternance between Left and Right becomes a consistent practice. In many workable party systems one party or coalition has controlled government for long stretches of time. The importance would lie in the fact that the idea of alternance would become politically and culturally acceptable.

Another and much less manageable approach, on the other hand, would be a system of alternance coming on the heels of a major and sudden electoral realignment, a major loss of votes by the Christian Democratic party, and a gain by the Left that would make a leftist government comprising the PCI numerically possible. Nobody, least of all the PCI, can fail to realize the dangers involved in a major realignment and the risks of increasing rather than decreasing polarization, especially if the realignment were in fact to usher in, very quickly, a government of the Left. Yet it is exactly a major realignment that occurred in the local elections of June 1975. The Communist party obtained approximately 33 percent of the votes, the Christian Democrats fell off to approximately 35 percent, the lowest percentage since 1946.[41] Since the Socialist party also scored good gains, Com-

41. Separate elections were held for regional, provincial, and city councils. They took place in almost all of Italy but did not always cover the same territory. In parentheses are the results of the parliamentary elections of 1972 in the areas where local elections also took place in 1975. Regional elections: PCI, 33.4 (28.3); DC, 35.3 (38.4); PSI, 12.0 (9.8).

munists and Socialists, together with smaller Marxist groupings, can now count on an unprecedented 46 to 47 percent of the votes. Though the elections were local, parliamentary elections will take place at the latest in the spring of 1977. Will the Left continue its growth and reach the 50 percent mark? Will the PCI become the strongest party in the country?

Research by Giacomo Sani conducted after the elections and based on electoral and public-opinion extrapolations indicates that the chances of a leftist victory cannot be discounted.[42] Approximately half of the new votes gained by the Left come from switchers, and switching to the Left (at least to the PCI) has been a constant feature of the party system, not likely to stop. The other half comes from changes in the composition of the electorate: older and more conservative voters dying and being replaced by new and more radical voters. The effects of replacement have been made more dramatic by the fact that, owing to electoral reform, young people of 18 to 21 have been allowed to vote for the first time in 1975, and have voted overwhelmingly for the Left.

Further, the preferences of the young seem to have generational roots and are therefore unlikely to become more conservative with advancing age. They best exemplify a gathering crisis of Catholic culture, which does not allow Christian Democracy to hold onto its electorate as easily as in the past.[43] Signs of its coming have been detected especially more recently in the serious defeat of the DC in the 1974 divorce referendum, in the party's strained relations with Catholic labor unions and with supporting Catholic organizations, in the progressively more detached attitude of the Church toward the party, and in an accelerated and unprecedented process of secularization of society and expansion of civil liberties checked in the past by traditional and religious concerns. Beyond this, realignments are also triggered

---

Provincial elections: PCI, 32.7 (27.2); DC, 34.8 (39.4); PSI, 12.7 (9.9). City elections (more than 5,000 inhabitants): PCI, 32.2 (28.8); DC, 34.7 (36.5); PSI, 13.3 (9.6).

42. Giacomo Sani, "Secular Trends and Party Realignments in Italy: The 1975 Elections" (paper delivered at the American Political Science Association meeting, San Francisco, September 1975).

43. Arturo Parisi, "La Matrice Socio-Religiosa del Dissenso Cattolico in Italia," *Il Mulino* 20 (1971), pp. 637-657. See also, on the "Questione Democristiana" and the crisis of Catholic culture, the debate in *Il Mulino*, beginning with the issue of November-December 1974.

by a crisis in the clientelistic structures of government and by a fall in the benefits it has distributed for the last thirty years.

Here is exactly the danger. The crisis of Catholic culture and government and the ensuing realignments do not signify at all a depolarization of society, at least not yet. Quite on the contrary, the crisis, if inappropriately handled, may increase polarization in the short but decisive range. One disturbing element of uncertainty is in the fact that the parties of the Left are not always able to control the secularization, expansion of civil liberties, and increasing community participation which, as just mentioned, accompany the growth of the Left. That is, the electorate of the Left, which is most active in these developments, often outruns its parties. It creates, for instance, serious problems for the PCI, which, on issues such as abortion, divorce, the revision of the Concordat with the Vatican, the unionization of the military, and the curbing of police and judicial powers, intends to move cautiously so as not to alienate established interests.

Were the Left to form a government under these conditions—assuming that Communists and Socialists can agree to govern together—the loss of power and resources after decades of comfortable hegemony could split Christian Democracy and move the party or at any rate its conservative factions toward the Right and precipitate a confrontation. The confrontation would be the more likely as electoral trends, being generational, would otherwise confine Christian Democracy to the opposition for years to come, and the new government could try to consolidate its support by using the same corporate-clientelistic structures so aptly created and exploited by the DC in the past. For all the moderation of the Communist party, suspicion of and resistance to a Communist-controlled government would in turn motivate a self-fulfilling prophecy. Polarized party systems can muddle through as long as center governments last, but cannot tolerate and are not easily reformed by the logic of Left-Right confrontation.[44]

---

44. This explains the risks of an electoral reform (which no party is seriously advocating) replacing proportionality with a single-ballot plurality system. Though it would reduce the number of parties, its imposition on an extreme multiparty system, before party images are changed, could throw Christian Democracy to the right and create a dangerous vacuum of power in the center. The apparent success of a similar strategy with the introduction of presidentialism and electoral reform in France does not conclu-

Good evidence of the dangers involved in a system of alternance under the present conditions comes from the fact that the Communist party always rejected what it calls the "fifty-one percent formula" and, after the June 1975 elections, rejected it more than ever. Communist statements that the party does not intend to govern alone or in alliance with only the Socialists, even if it were entitled to do so by electoral returns, may have been dictated in the past by the recognition that Communist chances of becoming a majority in the immediate future were poor. But they were also dictated, as they still are, by the fear that such a development could split the country and endanger the party. As a minimum, Communist rejection of the formula serves to relieve fears among the other parties and to exorcise the specters of Allende's Chile and of the Second Spanish Republic.[45] True, Sani's research just cited shows that among non-Communist voters perceptions of the PCI as antireligious and antidemocratic have considerably declined since the early seventies, as have fears of a Communist-run government. But suspicion toward the party still remains widespread. Much more important, polarization, especially in times of potential transition, is not a matter of where the majority stands, but of how strongly opinions are held by each side. The Communists have little desire to test their sudden popularity through a government of the Left.

In a country which, despite rapid secularization, remains heavily Catholic and in which a Catholic and Socialist culture confront each other, the alternative envisioned by the Communists is a *compromesso storico,* an alliance between the two camps

---

sively disprove my point. The special circumstances under which de Gaulle's experiment succeeded do not alter the fact that regime manipulations, as in France itself, are almost always aleatory.

45. Interpretations of the Chilean and Spanish cases as instances of polarization following alternance are offered by Valenzuela, op. cit., and by Juan Linz, "From Great Hopes to Civil War: The Breakdown of Democracy in Spain," in Linz and Stepan, op. cit. Enrico Berlinguer's anaysis of the collapse of Chilean democracy leaves no doubt that the Communists are well aware of the risks of polarization, were they to accede to power on a strictly working-class, strictly fifty-one percent formula. See Enrico Berlinguer, "Riflessioni sull'Italia dopo i Fatti del Cile" (a series of articles first published in *Rinascita,* September 28, October 5, and October 12, 1973, and reprinted in *Biblioteca della Libertà,* XI, No. 51 [July-August 1974], pp. 125-138). Useful material on the position of the PCI toward strategies of access to power is contained in Arrigo Levi, *PCI la Lunga Marcia verso il Potere* (Milano: Etas Kompass, 1971).

and their parties that would break the stalemate.[46] The caution and tolerance with which the PCI, after its electoral victory, is acting toward the present lame government, in effect helping its survival, is designed to close the gap and make the *compromesso* more palatable. So is the international campaign in which the party has been engaged recently to take its distance from the Soviet Union, to condemn the strategies of the Portuguese Communists, and to advertise publicly the adoption with their French and Spanish comrades of joint platforms extolling political pluralism. But the *compromesso* is a very old formula, which non-Communist public opinion has still to buy. To be sure, Sani's research reveals also that opposition to the *compromesso* has considerably declined. Still, only one-fourth of the voters of the center accept it. Also, both the DC and the secular parties oppose it, and the PCI itself sees it at times as a distant solution to be prepared with care and without excessive precipitation.

As to Christian Democracy, the party—despite the deep crisis, the loss of direction, and the fragmentation of initiatives from which it suffers after the elections—seems firm on one point: the party and its chances to govern cannot be rescued at the price of governing with the Communists. Though Christian Democrats are not ready to abandon power, and frantically seek new formulas to rescue themselves, the *compromesso* is not one of them. The *compromesso* is also a disturbing formula for the secular parties which, always distrustful of Catholic and Communist questing for power, see in it the ominous convergence of two authoritarian cultures and the further clientelization of Italian politics. The Socialists, though considering the old Center-Left dead, do not advocate replacing it with the *compromesso*, whether or not the latter would include them. They show greater interest in an alternative of the Left. They are attracted by the example of the Communist-Socialist alliance in France and impressed by the success of their French comrades and the key role they play in the

---

46. The entire issue of the cited *Biblioteca della Libertà* is dedicated to *Il Compromesso Storico* and contains analyses and debates by politicians and political analysts. See also similar earlier analyses under the title *La Grande Coalizione* in *Il Mulino* 20 (1971), pp. 3-24, 391-424, 694-740, 993-997, and Domenico Fisichella, "L'Alternativa Rischiosa: Considerazioni sul 'Difficile Governo'," *Rivista Italiana di Scienza Politica* 2 (1972), pp. 589-613.

alliance. Yet they also fear the dominance of the PCI and, with the exception of the party's own left wing, do not consider the alternative an immediate strategy. They therefore work in the shorter run to achieve a more equal government partnership with a renovated DC, which would give them the key mediating role between the government and the Communists.

What lies, at any rate, underneath such intricate strategies and conflicting calculations is a simple fact: resilient party images complicate the solution of the governing issue. And the solution has not been made easier by electoral realignment. To restate, at the root of the problem of governing Italy is not so much the monopoly of the center but ideological polarization.[47] Just as lingering polarization makes a system of alternance dispensing with the center extremely dangerous, so it makes the type of grand coalition advocated by the PCI still unpalatable. There are those who count on precipitation of the present economic crisis to solve the issue of governing for the parties by, in effect, forcing the Communist party into a government of national salvation. Such a prospect would be the bleakest for the Communists and for the country. Nobody can guarantee how the PCI would behave when compelled to deal in first person, and from a position of increasing prominence in the coalition, with what would turn out to be an escalating crisis and an unmanageable transition. The Communists would be all too happy if they could spare themselves this.

Yet time and events are not working in favor of the Italian parties. The solution of the governing issue cannot be postponed much longer, perhaps not beyond the end of the decade. Can the parties change their ways and reform their public images between now and then? Can they essay new forms of governing which, without immediately opening national government to the Communists, prepare for the transition? The progressive entry of the Communists into significant positions of local government—already secured, with the last elections, in more than half of all regional and local administrations—could buy them respectability and could prepare for the transition. So could a politics of more open, over-the-counter accommodations between government and opposition on the issues that matter.

---

47. Sartori, "Il Caso Italiano: Salvare il Pluralismo e Superare la Polarizzazione," op. cit.

But how likely are these evolutions? And is there enough time? Nobody can tell for sure. I have accounted for the institutions; I cannot account for men and events. The system, I have indicated, has resources to mend itself. But the resources have now been strained by years of improvident government, by an international economic crisis that in part escapes national control, and by a rapid process of secularization that parties find difficult to direct. The marginal and surreptitious parliamentary accommodations that brought thirty years of uncertain coexistence under steadier conditions are no longer sufficient.

Postscript

June 20, 1976: the Communist party wins an unprecedented 34 percent in new parliamentary elections. But, thanks to fears of Communism, Christian Democracy, with 39 percent, regains entirely its original strength. The emptying of the center has occurred, in full strength, at the expenses of the minor parties, including the Socialists. Coalitions of the center are no longer politically possible. An era of Italian politics has come to an end. The predicament is clear: all governing formulas that made possible thirty years of muddling through have been exhausted. Christian Democrats and Communists confront each other without the buffer of the minor parties. And the small parliamentary accommodations that eased the Communists' long march toward power have lost their function. Yet neither Christian Democrats nor Communists can govern alone.

Having failed to arrest the Communists and having lost their allies along the way, the Christian Democrats have been compelled to form an emergency minority government that relies, for the first time since the war, on the abstension of the Communists and all other constitutional parties. Equally important and unprecedented, the Chamber of Deputies and several parliamentary standing committees are now chaired by Communist parliamentarians. These negotiated developments should, in the mind of all parties, defuse the difficult transition by establishing a new partnership between Parliament and government. At the same time, in Christian Democratic eyes, they should also rescue

Christian Democracy from the prospect of forming governments together with the Communists. But I suspect that realignments are too far gone for the Communists to be relegated to the role, however prominent and publicly exalted, of parliamentary partners. The withering away of the minor parties makes any intermediate and holding solution extremely fragile. And a government that, abandoned by its old partners, lives at the pleasure of the Communists, cannot exorcise them by fine constitutional hairsplitting. Before Parliament can put its new leadership to the test, and no matter how unpalatable this may be to many, Italy may be compelled from uncertain compromise to historical compromise. What historical compromise means for Italian democracy is a somewhat different story.[48]

48. See Giuseppe Di Palma, "Eurocommunism?" *Comparative Politics* 9 (1977), forthcoming.

APPENDIX

Classifying Legislative Proposals

Eleven judges were used to classify legislative proposals in the sample drawn for the study. The following is an account of the instructions and procedures for classification. Most of the instructions were discreet and nonexhaustive, owing to the inherently subjective nature of the classifications. Neither the subjects impacted by legislation, nor the effects and level of aggregation of the legislation can be ascertained by objective and unambiguous criteria. The instructions were developed by the author after an analysis of the proposals and an ad hoc listing of the most likely difficulties which *these* proposals might have created for the judges. In this sense, they would have little value if applied to another body of legislation in another country. What counts, however, is that the classification "works"; that is, as shown in Chapter V, it relates as expected to differences in legislative processes and behavior. Its success is most likely due to two facts. First, despite the difficulties in principle, most of the proposals reveal in fact and at first inspection intuitive qualities of disaggregation and low impact that cannot escape a reasonably sensitive judge. Second, the instructions were drafted so as to ease the identification of nonmodal legislation (aggregative legislation, with external and depriving effects).

DIRECT AND EXTERNAL EFFECTS

Before asking the judges to classify the proposals for the quality of their direct and external impact, and so as to facilitate this task, they were asked to recognize and distinguish the "direct subjects" of each proposal, as well as their "external subjects." Judges were given the following instructions:
  1. Direct subjects are subjects whose behavior or whose status

(legal, financial, symbolic) a proposal intends to regulate/benefit or change directly.

External subjects are not directly regulated by the proposal, but are *likely* to be indirectly affected by it by reason of their institutional, interest, or symbolic relation with direct subjects or with the proposed legislations.

2. Whenever a law regulates an organized unit (civil service, local government, interest groups, professional associations, or the like), it is the unit that is the direct subject, not the individuals or other organized units whose behavior or status the former unit may in turn affect—unless these are themselves expressly required to perform a given behavior by the proposal.

3. Whenever a law regulates more than one organized unit, for instance by transferring competences from one to the other, direct subjects are all the organized units.

Examples of 2 and 3 (examples are fictitious):
  a. If the Internal Revenue Service is provided with new criteria and new resources for assessing taxable income, direct subject is the Service, not taxpayers.
  b. If the right to calculate and reimburse medical expenses under compulsory medical insurance is transferred from the central to the local offices of a particular welfare agency, direct subjects are both the local and national offices.
  c. If a new unit of local government, for example a new province, is created, direct subjects are the new province and the ones from which it has been carved.

4. Whenever an organized unit is regulated, indirect subjects are *minimally all* the subjects having an institutional or interest relation with it—that is, their "clientele"—within the geographical boundaries of the unit.

Examples:
  a. In the examples (3a, b, c) above indirect subjects are taxpayers, the public served by the welfare agency, the inhabitants of the provinces affected.
  b. If a proposal regulates the legal status of Chambers of Commerce, its indirect subjects are merchants in the national territory.
  c. If a proposal extends privileged agricultural credit to cooperative banks in Sicily, its indirect subjects are Sicilian farmers.

d. If the proposal above on the assessment of taxable income concerns only income from independent work, indirect subjects are nevertheless all taxpayers.
e. If universities are given the exclusive authority to hire and fire faculty, indirect subjects are all university constituencies (professors, students, etc.).

5. Whenever a proposal does not regulate a recognizable organized unit, but rather regulates any and all subjects likely to manifest a given behavior, or to possess/acquire certain characteristics, or to belong to a given category, those subjects are the direct subjects of the proposal.

Examples:
a. If a freeway speed limit is introduced, motorists are the direct subjects.
b. If a proposal provides that property of newly constructed private housing shall be tax-exempt, buyers of such housing are the direct subjects.
c. If protective restrictions are imposed on the working hours of private household servants, servants are the direct subjects.

6. Whenever no organized unit is regulated, external subjects of the legislation shall be recognized as follows:
a. If the legislation is addressed to the whole national community, and a distinction between direct and external subjects is impossible, the same subjects shall be classified as both.

Example:
If a new tax on added value is introduced, all consumers are to be classified as direct and external subjects.

b. In other cases, and to avoid the pitfall that everything has consequences for everybody, only those groups shall be considered external subjects which, without being directly regulated by the law, are potentially affected by the law because of recognizable interests, beliefs, or culture.

Examples:
If new housing is tax-exempt, building contractors are external subjects.
If servants' working hours are protected, people employing their services are external subjects.
If legislation concerning birth control education is liberal-

ized, Catholic and other groups with a vested interest in it are external subjects.

7. If all the above criteria for identifying external subjects fail, classify the law as having no external subjects.

Agreement by eight of the eleven judges, each independently scoring all proposals, was required for a classification to stand. The judges had little difficulty in classifying proposals whose direct subject was an organized unit but, because of the looser criteria supplied and the greater complexity of the matter, had greater difficulty recognizing and distinguishing immediate and external subjects in the other cases. Thus, 22 percent of the proposals failed to achieve minimum agreement. In order not to lose cases, these proposals were rediscussed by the whole panel, with the participation of the author, and a consensus on all of them was eventually reached. Average agreement on the proposals not resubmitted to the panel was 8.4.

CLASSIFYING THE EFFECTS: BENEFICIAL AND DEPRIVING

All proposals were subsequently labeled to indicate their direct and, if any, their external subjects, and were resubmitted to the judges. Each judge was asked to indicate whether each of the proposals had beneficial, mixed, or depriving effects on its direct subjects. He was also asked to say whether the proposals had in fact effects on the external subjects and, if so, whether these too were beneficial, mixed, or depriving. The classification of effects turned out to be relatively easy, very likely because the most difficult hurdle had been the identification and classification of subjects. Once this was done, the judges had rather precise boundaries within which to contain their assessment of effects. In fact, as I had hoped, most of the subjects turned out to be rather well defined, internally homogeneous, and even narrow organized units. Hence the judges had limited difficulties in recognizing what the specified subjects stood to gain or lose. I asked the judges to classify a subsample of forty proposals on a pretesting basis and supplied them with limited instructions as to how to recognize the nature of their effects. Since agreement was immediately high, I extended the procedure to the whole sample, with the same instructions, which were as follows:

1. In classifying effects consider what the subjects perceive to be the effects, not what you perceive them to be, *and whether they resent, appreciate, or remain indifferent to them.*

2. In classifying effects disregard whether or not the proposal is of easy application. Always assume that the proposal will be properly applied and will do what it says.

3. Effects can be symbolic, ideological, cultural, as well as economic. All should be considered.

4. There are no external effects when either there are no external subjects or, in your opinion, the proposal makes no difference whatever in the minds of external subjects for their behavior or for their symbolic or economic status.

5. Effects on direct or external subjects are mixed when, if the subject is only one, the effects are more than one, and some depriving, some beneficial. Effects are also mixed when the subjects—individuals or groups—are more than one, or the subject is internally diversified (for example, a broad sector of the civil service), and in your opinion some of the subjects tend to lose, others to gain.

Effects are mixed only if the balance is rather even, either in terms of the relative size of the affected groups, or in terms of the relative losses or gains as perceived by the subjects. Otherwise, classify the effects as mainly beneficial or depriving, depending on the balance. Mixed effects do not require that what one subject gains is taken away from the loser. A loss can occur even without actually depriving a subject, if the other subject nevertheless gains status, *and if in your opinion the former will resent the new balance.*

6. Effects should be classified as beneficial (or depriving) even if in your opinion they are rather marginal or transitory. As indicated under point 4, only if you are convinced that effects are totally absent, and only in the case of external effects, should you classify proposals as having no effects.

Fifteen percent of the proposals remained unclassified, because the judges could not reach the minimum agreement on all classifications as to effects. Only those proposals were preserved for which at least eight judges agreed on their direct effects, eight on *whether or not* they had external effects and, assuming that a proposal was judged to have external effects, at least seven of the judges so agreeing also agreed on *the nature* of the external effects. The fact that only 15 percent of the proposals failed to get classification can be considered a remarkable success, given the number and strictness of the tests. Most of the proposals failed on the presence and nature of external effects. When unclassified proposals are not counted, average agreement was 8.9 on the classification of direct effects, 9.4 on whether or not proposals had external effects, and 7.3 on the nature of external effects.

CLASSIFYING EFFECTS: NATIONAL, SECTIONAL, MICROSECTIONAL

After having finished with the first two classifications, the judges were asked to classify the direct subjects of each proposal according to whether they were the national community or a unit serving it; a composite and large sector of it, organized around broad but recognizable activities and institutions; or smaller and more homogeneous groups, involved in unique and specialized activities and institutions. They were expressly instructed to disregard the importance of the legislation for the subjects affected; for example, a proposal introducing a new national holiday and closing all business for the day is national in scope, though it is of limited importance. The following criteria for recognizing scope were given:

National Legislation: All legislation is national that regulates all citizens likely to engage in a given behavior or to possess/acquire certain characteristics. All legislation is national that regulates an organized unit, if the unit serves the national community—that is, if it serves all citizens likely to engage in a given behavior or to possess/acquire certain characteristics. Legislation having to do with housing, transportation, economic planning, taxation, banking, educational reform, civil and penal legislation, and the like, is likely to belong to this class, provided it fits the requirements above.

Examples:
1. If the Internal Revenue Service is provided with new criteria

for assessing taxable income, or if a tax on added value is introduced, legislation is national.
2. If endowment funds for the Bank of Naples are increased, legislation is national, since anybody can use the bank's services.
3. If a freeway speed limit is introduced, legislation is national, since anybody using a car is affected.
4. If prison reform, even minimal, is proposed, legislation is national, since anybody may end in jail.
5. If tax exemption for newly constructed housing is introduced, the legislation is national, since any citizen may buy a new house.
6. If legislation concerning birth control education is liberalized, the legislation is national, since all citizens may resort to birth control methods.

Sectional Legislation: All legislation is sectional that regulates citizens belonging to a specific and recognized social category—occupational group, interest association, and the like—provided the category is large, rather diversified, and active in an area of significant import for society. All legislation is sectional that regulates organized units serving these social categories. Legislation may fall here that has to do with the main sectors of the economy—agriculture, industry, commerce—with broad social categories such as metalworkers, elementary teachers, or sharecroppers, or with large sectors of the civil service, even if only within regions of the country. All legislation is sectional that is addressed to specific regions of the country.

Examples:
1. If a law regulates reimbursement of medical expenses for local government employees, the law is sectional.
2. If a law regulates the legal status of Chambers of Commerce, the law is sectional.
3. If a law extends privileged agricultural credit to Sicilian farmers, the law is sectional.
4. If a law implements a program of cooperative housing for members of the armed forces, the law is sectional.

Microsectional Legislation: All legislation is microsectional that regulates citizens belonging to social categories narrower and more homogeneous than the ones above, and of more limited and specialized scope in their activities. All legislation is microsectional that regulates organized units serving these social categories. All legislation is microsectional that is addressed to smaller territorial areas of the country.

Examples:
1. If a law regulates reimbursement of medical expenses for private household workers, the law is microsectional.
2. If a law regulates the legal status of fine arts academies, the law is microsectional.
3. If a law extends privileged agricultural credit to farmers in the province of X whose crops have been destroyed by recent floods, the law is microsectional.
4. If a law implements a program of cooperative housing for personnel of the Air Force, the law is microsectional.
5. If a law establishes a new province, the law is microsectional.
6. If a law increases government contributions for the production of olive oil, the law is microsectional.
7. If a law authorizes the Ministry of Public Participations to buy stock in the Ferrari automobile manufacturing company, the law is microsectional.

Minimum agreement for a classification to stand was again set at eight judges. Thirteen percent of the proposals failed the test, and in almost all of the cases disagreement had to do with whether proposals were sectional or microsectional. In order not to lose further cases, these proposals were rediscussed by the whole panel, with the participation of the author, and agreement in all cases was eventually reached. Since one criterion used in reaching agreement was to compare the unclassified proposals with those that had already been agreed upon, this tended to flatten out the distribution. Indeed, the whole process of classification tended to involve comparisons between proposals, and therefore to produce a flattened continuum. I tried to avoid this effect by offering only three categories and by presenting them as much as possible as distinct rather than placed on an ideal continuum. Average agreement on the proposals not resubmitted to the panel was 8.3.

Index

Almond, Gabriel, 8, 223
American politics, 35, 66, 196, 215, 265
Axelrod, Robert, 243

Barnes, Samuel, 231
Bentley, Arthur, 210
Blondel, Jean, 68
Bureaucracy, 10, 11, 25, 43, 106, 190, 191, 193, 198, 259; clientelism and, 5, 77, 199, 265; reforms and, 77, 78; legislation and, 80, 85ff, 152; redistributive policies and, 87; corruption and, 264f. *See also* Clientelism; Christian Democratic Party; Public Sector

Cabinet, 53, 191, 193, 255; control over Parliament, 132; attitudes of former members, 151. *See also* Coalitions; Legislation; Parliament
Calamandrei, Piero, 217
Catholicism, 104, 106, 108, 117, 121, 162, 173, 231, 245, 255, 265, 268, 272, 274, 278, 280f, 282
Cazzola, Franco, 37, 54, 56, 59, 270
Centrism, 116, 118, 124, 128, 233ff, 241ff, 249ff, 256, Chap. VII passim. *See also* Coalitions; De Gasperi; Moderatism; Party Systems; *trasformismo*
Chamber of Deputies. *See* Parliament
Chile, 221, 276, 282
Christian Democratic Party, xi, 5, 28, 37, 49, 56, 65, 91, 106, 132, 135, 137, 177, 179-182 passim, 205, 234, 238, 239, 241, 243, 245, 247, 250, Chap. VII passim; governmental performance of, xiv f; legislative success of, 49, 53, 54; amending initiative of, 60; parliamentary reform and, 76, 77f; postwar history of, 105-131; postwar growth and support of, 118; on reciprocity and compromise, 139 f, 142, 143; attitude toward concurrence, 147 ff, 154 f; attitude on *delegificazione*, 152; majority relations with PCI, 155; attitudes on elite autonomy, 160, 162, 168 f; and electorate, 167, 168 f, 171; and conception of party, 173; party competition and, 233 f, 235, 236; strength of, 239 f. *See also* Bureaucracy; Centrism; Clientelism; Coalitions; Political Parties; *trasformismo*
Church. *See* Catholicism
Civil Service. *See* Bureaucracy
Cleavages. *See* Political Culture
Clientelism, 5 f, 88, 90, 107, 117, 123, 125, 143, 191, 193, 199, 255, 258-270 passim, 272, 281, 283. *See also* Bureaucracy; Christian Democratic Party
Coalitions, 28, 114-116, 241 ff; Center-Left, xiv, 37, 53, 122-130, 191, 240, 247, 248, 283; in postwar, 115-130; and instability, 243; of ideologues, 246 f; negative, 247 f; beleaguered, 248 ff; irresponsible, 251 f; factions in, 268-271. *See also* Italian government; Parliament
Committees, 42, 46, 55, 61 ff, 186 f, 193-218 passim; resources of, 196, 197, 211, 258; compared to American, 196, 215; turnover in, 197; power of, 197; chairmen of, 196 f, 211-215 passim. *See also* Legislation; Parliament
Compromesso Storico. *See* Historical Compromise
Conciliar pact, 130
Concurrent majority, 20, 66, 67, 95-105, 129, 146-155. *See also* Decisional effectiveness; Decisional rules
Conference of Presidents, 208, 217
Consociationalism, 223, 224 f, 226
Constituent Assembly (1946-1948), 106, 109
Constitution, 82, 87, 194, 199; Parliament and, 40 ff; synchronic interpretation of, 109 ff, 129; postwar drafting of, 105-114
Constitutional Court, 110, 111, 113
Converse, Philip, 272

295

Cost-benefit analysis. *See* Political performance
Cotta, Maurizio, 185
Council of the Judiciary, 110, 111, 113
Crozier, Michel, 256
Cultural fragmentation. *See* Consociationalism; Political culture

Dahl, Robert, 249
Decisional effectiveness, 14, 74, 93 f, 254; equity and, 19 f; decisional rules and, 20-24, 130; definition of, 22, 74; democracy and, 23; political parties and, 27 f, Chap. VI passim; political culture and, 29-33, 155; funnel of causality and, 33, 35; institutional persuasion and, 33, 36; Parliament and, Chap. II passim; legislative behavior and, 64-70. *See also* Decisional norms; Decisional rules; Political performance
Decisional Norms: "negotial" conceptions and, 133-146, 182, 184; and right/duty to govern, 145 ff; and restrained partisanship, 156, 168, 182. *See also* Concurrent majority; Decisional effectiveness; Decisional rules; Rule of reciprocity; Proportionality
Decisional rules, 19-24, 66, 94, 95-105, 185-190; disagreement on, 21, 128, 143, 144, 155, 219, 221, 241, 275; party attitudes toward, 100-105; postwar compromise on, 105-114; electoral stalemate and, 114-131, 143. *See also* Concurrent majority; Decisional effectiveness; Decisional Norms; Proportionality; Rule of reciprocity; Political performance
De Gasperi Alcide, 105, 116, 117, 124, 126, 150, 243, 247, 266. *See also* Centrism; Christian Democratic Party
Delegificazione, 151; attitudes toward, 152; Parliamentary prerogative and, 152; concurrence and, 153 ff. *See also* Legislation; Parliament
Democracy, 32, 66, 171, 183, 249 f; and decisional rules, 18-24; authenticity of, 23; decisional effectiveness and, 23
Di Palma, Giuseppe, 37
Dodd, Lawrence, 242, 243
Downs, Anthony (Downsian model), 172, 228, 228n
Dupeux, Georges, 272
Duverger, Maurice, 256, 257

Easton, David, 8
Eckstein, Harry, 16
Economic Miracle. *See* Italian economy

Education: student unrest, xii; reforms and, 90
Elections, 248; 1974 local, xi; postwar, 106; of 1948, 113, 280; of 1953, 118; electoral stalemate and, 113, 114, 282. *See also* Electoral system; Party systems; Political parties
Electoral System, 40n, 107 f, 184; 1953 electoral law and, 115 f
Electorate: relation of elites to, 157, 159, 161, 171, 174; centrality of party to, 163, 170; as political families, 163 ff, 174; and party competition, 222; composition of, 280, 281; realignment of, 279 ff, 284. *See also* Party systems; Political parties
Elites, 121, 130, 161, 278; decisional rules and, 22, 94, 96, 98, 102, 145, 221; and Italian political culture, 29, 30, 32, 33; institutions and, 35 f; decline of prewar, 105 f; restrained partisanship and, 152, 171, 182; autonomy of, 157, 168, 169, 171, 182, 220; and responsibility toward electorate, 163 ff, 174, 182, 246; socialization of, 175-181; and party system, 223; consociationalism and, 224, 226; cleavages and, 225, 227; economy and, 262. *See also* Politicians; Political culture; Political parties
England, 188; majority rule in, 20, 35, 71, 94
European Economic Community, xi, xiv, 278

Fanfani, Amintore, 118, 119, 123, 250. *See also* Centrism; Christian Democratic Party
Farneti, Paolo, 114
Fascism, 32, 105, 108, 179, 180, 181, 245, 257, 264
Finland, 276
Fourth French Republic. *See* France
France, 9, 71, 98, 235, 246, 247, 256, 273, 274, 276, 283; Fifth Republic of, 6, 64, 68; oppositions in, 68; Fourth Republic of, 105 f, 107, 220, 223, 228, 234, 242, 248, 271, 272; Third Republic of, 223, 242

Galli, Giorgio, 273
Germany, 98, 274; legislative initiative in 47-49; Weimar, 220, 223, 228, 234, 235 f, 243n, 246, 248, 271, 272, 273, 277
Giolitti, Giovanni, 274
Gramsci, Antonio, 172, 173
Grand coalition, 49, 54. *See also* Coalitions

INDEX

Historical Compromise, 129, 282 f
Hoffmann, Stanley, 256, 258

Ideology, 7, 78, 165, 170, 172, 173, 198; party competition and, 220-240. *See also* Downs; Party systems; Political culture; Political parties
Immobilisme. See Centrism
Incivisme, 29, 32, 34. *See also* Political culture
Institute for Industrial Reconstruction, 264
Institutions: decisional effectiveness of, 14, 35, 217 f; institutional persuasion and, 35, 36, 107, 114, 224; postwar development of, 105-131 passim. *See also* Decisional effectiveness; Parliament; Political performance
Interest groups, 11, 74, 87 f, 123, 255, 259, 263; legislation and, 79 ff
Italian Communist Party, xi, xv, xvi, 28, 29, 32, 37, 49-65, 54, 75, 98, 99, 132, 137, 178, 182, 192, 195, 198, 200, 207 n, 208 f, 216, 221 n, 233, 236, 248, 249, 254, Chap. VII passim; electoral gains of, xv, 238, 280; as anti-system party, 28; legislative success of, 49, 53, 64; legislative behavior of, 54, 55, 56 ff, 77 f, 91; in committees, 63, 261; amendment behavior compared to other Communist parties, 63 f, 68 f; attitude toward decisional rules, 100-105 passim; postwar history of, 106-131 passim; Popular Front and, 113; postwar growth and composition of, 118; impact of Hungary on, 119; attitude toward reciprocity, 139 ff, 142, 143; attitude toward concurrence, 147 ff; attitude toward *delegificazione,* 152; attitude toward elite autonomy, 160 f, 168; and electorate, 165, 168, 169; self-image of, 173, 174; strength of, 239 f; socialdemocratization of, 240, 274 ff. *See also* Party systems; Political parties
Italian economy: current conditions, xiii; inflation and, xiii f, 4, 13; Southern Italy and, xiv, 2 f, 12, 29, 120, 262; economic miracle and, 2-5 passim, 120 ff; Northern Italy and, 2, 29, 120, 262; imbalance of, 3; labor costs and, 3 f, 4 n, 262; services and, 4; legislation and, 71; dual nature of, 262 f
Italian Government, 25; ineffectiveness of, 5, 214, 218; illegitimate decisional rules and, 22, 218; party system and, 27; postwar history of, 105-131 passim; coalition formation in postwar, 115-130 passim; right/duty to govern and, 145 ff; decentralized legislation and, 194-207; irresponsibility of, 217 f, 218; ideological differences in, 245. *See also* Decisional norms; Decisional rules; Institutions; Parliament; Parliamentary prerogative; Political performance
Italian Socialist Party, xiv, xv, 28, 37, 49, 53, 137, 143, 178, 238, 240, 243, 245, 248, 268-271 passim, 274, 279 f, 281, 282; legislative success of, 49, 53; reform and, 76, 77; attitude toward decisional rules, 100-105 passim; postwar history of, 106-131 passim; Popular Front and, 113; attitude toward reciprocity, 139; attitude toward *delegificazione,* 152 f; attitude toward elite autonomy, 160; attitude toward electorate, 166; attitude toward representative mandate, 168; conception of party role, 173; attitude toward parliamentary procedure, 199 f; party competition and, 235. *See also* Coalitions; Party systems; Political parties

Labor unions, 3 f, 4, 5, 123, 280; lost working days and, xi n; strikes and, xii. *See also* Interest groups; Italian economy
Lateran Pacts (1929), 106
Leggine, 75, 201, 216, 252, 258, 260, 261; reform and, 75-78 passim. *See also* Legislation; Political performance
Legislation, 8, 26; Italian evaluation of, 11-13; methodological focus on, 26 f; output of, 41-43, 65 f, 123, Chap. V passim; budgetary laws and, 42, 85; government and private bills compared, 43-63 passim, 66 f, 81 f, 83 f, 89, 90, 117, 190, 194, 202, 210 f, 213, 214; coalitions and, 49, 191, 192, 218; dissolution and failure of, 58, 210; amending powers and, 59, 194; success of amendments and, 61 ff, 68; decisional effectiveness and, 66 f; amendments and influence on, 67-70; criteria of evaluating, 68; resources and quality of, 70 ff, 123, 203 f; incrementalism and, 72 ff; impact of, 79-90 passim, 93 f; level of aggregation of, 79-94 passim, 123; concurrent majority and, 146-155 passim; emergency legislation, 192; decree laws and, 192, 192 n; procedures and, 194-218 passim. *See also* Bureaucracy; Decisional effectiveness; Decisional rules;

Leggine; Parliament; Parliamentary agenda; Political performance
Liberal Party, 53, 122, 238, 240
Lijphart, Arend, 96, 223, 224
Lorwin, Val, 224

Macridis, Roy, 247
Majority rule, 20 f, 66, 95-105, 114, 130, 132, 217. *See also* Decisional effectiveness; Decisional rules
Manley, John, 156
Moderatism, 250. *See also* Centrism
Monarchist Party, 237, 238, 240, 274
Mortara, Vittorio, 37, 58, 88, 211
Movimento Sociale Italiano, xv, 33, 237, 238, 240, 274

National Council for Economy and Labor, 110, 111, 113
NATO, 278
Nordlinger, Eric, 96

Pappalardo, Adriano, 243
Parliament, xv, 6, 7, 10, 11, 15, 24-27, 33, 34, 35, 36, 98, 100, 101 ff, 132, 161, 162, 170, 173, 227 f, 257 f, 275 ff; control over government by, 25, 155; constitutional features of, 40 ff; activity of, 41-94 passim; compared with other European legislatures, 41 f, 47-49, 63, 65, 68; resources of, 42 f, 196; committees in, 42, 46, 55, 61 ff, 186 f, 193-207 passim; alliances in, 54, 55n, 109, 115, 130, 242, 246-252, 268-271; decisional effectiveness and, 79, 87, 93, 134; public sector and, 79-89 passim, 264, 268; postwar history of, 105-131 passim, 237; role of opposition in, 110 f, 114, 116; government, majority, and opposition in, 133; effect of parties on, 133; weakness of, 133; "negotial" attitudes in, 133-146 passim, 182, 183, 184; government's right/duty to govern and, 145 ff; concurrence in, 146-155 passim; prerogative of, 146 f, 150 ff; restrained partisanship and, 156, 182; populism in, 157 n, 159; and socialization, 175-184 passim; organizational and procedural dimensions in, 185-190 passim, 217 f; legislative procedure in, 190-218 passim; President of the Assembly in, 205 ff, 216. *See also* Coalitions; Committees; Decisional effectiveness; Decisional norms; Decisional rules; Institutions; Parliamentary agenda; Political parties; Political performance

Parliamentary agenda, 193, 220, 275; power over, 207 ff; Conference of Presidents and, 208 f; legislative influence and, 209 f, 211; parties and, 221 f. *See also* Parliament
Parliamentary prerogative, 146 f, 150 ff, 153, 155; *delegificazione* and, 151 f
Partisanship. *See* Elites; Politicians; Parliament
Party Systems, 27; Sartori's typology of, 219 n, 220, 227 f, 236; workability of, 222; number of parties and, 220-236 passim, 248, 273; culture and, 223; Communist party and, 223, 224; consociationalism and, 223, 224, 226; polarization in, 224, 227, 238, 255 f, 275-285 passim; coalitions and, 227; two-party system and, 28, 228 ff; anti-system party and, 232 f, 278; Italian, 237-240, 250, Chap. IV passim, Chap. VII passim; French, German, Italian compared, 271-275 passim. *See also* Coalitions; Electoral system; Parliament; Political parties
Pasquino, Gianfranco, 99
Political Apathy, 29
Political Class. *See* Elites
Political Culture, 7; as explanation of governmental ineffectiveness, 29, 31 ff; characteristics of Italian, 29-31; characteristics of Anglo-Saxon, 30; small democracies and, 34, 223, 224, 226; politicians and, Chap. IV passim; party system and, 223, 225 ff, 246; pre-industrial cleavages (segmentation) and, 224 f, 226, 230; industrial cleavages and, 224 f; secularization of, 245, 280 ff, 285. *See also* Decisional Norms; Parliament; Party systems; Political performance
Political Parties, 11, 91, 100, 137, 159, 172, 173, 183, 186, 197, 215, 221, 237-238; factions and, 6, 220, 268-271; and role in shaping demands, 17, 166, 169, 170, 172; as causes of governmental ineffectiveness, 27 f, 36; ideological cleavages and, 27 ff, 137, 220, 252; success of small, 53 f; legislative amendments and, 60; and attitudes toward decisional rules, 100-105 passim, 221; postwar history of, 105-131 passim, 257; irresponsible behavior of, 133, 190, 251; attitudes toward reciprocity, 137, 143, 221; attitudes toward concurrence, 147-151, 153-155; elite autonomy and, 157 f, 161, 170, 220; legitimating function in Parliament, 160, 222; elitist model of, 170 ff;

organizational model of, 170 ff; objective model of, 170 ff; and competition, Chap. VI passim, 276; and agenda, 221; segmentation and, 225 ff; catch-all, 229, 230 f; encapsulating, 229, 272; antisystem, 232 f, 278; flash parties, 272. *See also* Decisional norms; Parliament; Party systems; Political culture; Political performance; Politicians

Political performance: criteria of evaluation, 7-37 passim; output and, 7 f, 64-70; rule-making focus of, 8, 9, 27; parliament and, 10, 24-27; normative theories of, 10; cost-benefit analysis and, 10-14; programming and, 13; demand satisfaction and, 15-19 passim; decisional rules and, 19-24 passim; Italian Parliament and, 24-27 passim. *See also* Decisional effectiveness; Decisional norms; Decisional rules; Elites; Parliament; Political culture; Politicians

Politicians, 12, 13; political culture of Italian, Chap. IV passim; comparing British and Italian, 136, 176; elite autonomy and, 157-184 passim; as party delegates, 163, 169; and responsibility toward electorate, 163 ff, 171; and partisan concept of representative mandate, 166 ff; political socialization and, 175-184 passim; attitudes toward parliamentary procedures, 200. *See also* Elites; Political culture; Political parties; Political performance

Polsby, Nelson, 17, 187
Populism, 157 n, 159, 171, 182, 183, 246
Post-industrialism, 2
Predieri, Alberto, 37, 42, 58, 109, 211
Proportionality, 95-105, 107, 108, 109, 129, 130
Public Sector, 25, 87; clientelism in, 5 f, 6 n, 264-268. *See also* Clientelism; Christian Democratic Party
Putnam, Robert, 136, 176

Redistributive policies. *See* Legislation (impact of)
Reforms, 75, 76, 82, 88 f, 90, 111, 112, 113, 123, 124, 125, 126, 141, 175, 208, 218, 245, 278
Representation. *See* Electorate: Elites; Parliament; Politicians
Republican Party, xiv, 124, 227, 238, 240, 243, 245

Rule of reciprocity, 135-146 passim, 155 f; prisoner's dilemma and, 135; government's right/duty to govern and, 145; *régime d'assemblé* and, 145; restrained partisanship and, 156, 168, 182. *See also* Concurrent Majority; Parliament; Political Culture
Rule-making. *See* Political performance
Rules of the game. *See* Decisional rules
Rumor, Mariano, xi

Salisbury, Robert, 71
Salvati, Michele, 120 n, 124
Sani, Giacomo, 238, 280, 282, 283
Sartori, Giovanni, 6 n, 27, 218, 224, 227, 236, 270
Schumpeter, Joseph, 277
Secularization. *See* Political culture
Senate of the Republic. *See* Parliament
Small democracies, 21 n, 34, 36, 42, 133, 223, 224, 226 f, 228, 229 f
Social demands. *See* Political Performance
Social Democratic Party, xiv, 119, 124, 128, 238, 240, 243, 245
Socialization, 8; under fascism, 32; anticipatory, 81, 91, 177; generational theory of, 175 f, 176-181 passim; institutional, 176 f, 180; Italian and French compared, 272; and electorate, 280, 281
Southern Italy. *See* Italian economy
Soviet Union, 119, 276, 278
Spain, 221, 252, 282, 283
Spreafico, Alberto, 270
Steiner, Jürg, 95, 96, 108, 109
Stokes, Donald: critique of Downsian model, 231
Syndrome of malaise, 1-7 passim, 15, 79, 121; in Italy, xi-xvi

Tamburrano, Giuseppe, 123
Third French Republic. *See* France
Togliatti, Palmiro, 106, 266
Trasformismo, 31, 99, 255, 258, 260

Verzuiling, 34
Violence, xii-xiii
Voting, 171; stability of Italian vote, 32; in legislature, 54-63; amendments and, 63 f

Weimar. *See* Germany